INTERNATIONAL POLITICAL ECONOMY SERIES

General Editor: Timothy M. Shaw, Professor of Political Science and International Development Studies, and Director of the Centre for Foreign Policy Studies, Dalhousie University, Halifax, Nova Scotia, Canada

Recent titles include:

Pradeep Agrawal, Subir V. Gokarn, Veena Mishra, Kirit S. Parikh and Kunal Sen
ECONOMIC RESTRUCTURING IN EAST ASIA AND INDIA: Perspectives on Policy Reform

Gavin Cawthra
SECURING SOUTH AFRICA'S DEMOCRACY: Defence, Development and Security in Transition

Steve Chan (*editor*)
FOREIGN DIRECT INVESTMENT IN A CHANGING GLOBAL POLITICAL ECONOMY

Jennifer Clapp
ADJUSTMENT AND AGRICULTURE IN AFRICA: Farmers, the State and the World Bank in Guinea

Seamus Cleary
THE ROLE OF NGOs UNDER AUTHORITARIAN POLITICAL SYSTEMS

Robert W. Cox (*editor*)
THE NEW REALISM: Perspectives on Multilateralism and World Order

Diane Ethier
ECONOMIC ADJUSTMENT IN NEW DEMOCRACIES: Lessons from Southern Europe

Stephen Gill (*editor*)
GLOBALIZATION, DEMOCRATIZATION AND MULTILATERALISM

Jacques Hersh and Johannes Dragsbaek Schmidt (*editors*)
THE AFTERMATH OF 'REAL EXISTING SOCIALISM' IN EASTERN EUROPE, Volume 1: Between Western Europe and East Asia

David Hulme and Michael Edwards (*editors*)
NGOs, STATES AND DONORS: Too Close for Comfort?

Staffan Lindberg and Árni Sverrisson (*editors*)
SOCIAL MOVEMENTS IN DEVELOPMENT: The Challenge of Globalization and Democratization

Anne Lorentzen and Marianne Rostgaard (*editors*)
THE AFTERMATH OF 'REAL EXISTING SOCIALISM' IN EASTERN EUROPE, Volume 2: People and Technology in the Process of Transition

Laura Macdonald
SUPPORTING CIVIL SOCIETY: The Political Role of Non-Governmental
Organizations in Central America

Stephen D. McDowell
GLOBALIZATION, LIBERALIZATION AND POLICY CHANGE: A Political
Economy of India's Communications Sector

Juan Antonio Morales and Gary McMahon (*editors*)
ECONOMIC POLICY AND THE TRANSITION TO DEMOCRACY: The Latin
American Experience

Ted Schrecker (*editor*)
SURVIVING GLOBALISM: The Social and Environmental Challenges

Ann Seidman, Robert B. Seidman and Janice Payne (*editors*)
LEGISLATIVE DRAFTING FOR MARKET REFORM: Some Lessons from
China

Kenneth P. Thomas
CAPITAL BEYOND BORDERS: States and Firms in the Auto Industry,
1960–94

Caroline Thomas and Peter Wilkin (*editors*)
GLOBALIZATION AND THE SOUTH

Geoffrey R. D. Underhill (*editor*)
THE NEW WORLD ORDER IN INTERNATIONAL FINANCE

Henry Veltmeyer, James Petras and Steve Vieux
NEOLIBERALISM AND CLASS CONFLICT IN LATIN AMERICA: A
Comparative Perspective on the Political Economy of Structural Adjustment

International Political Economy Series
Series Standing Order ISBN 0–333–71110–6
(*outside North America only*)

You can receive future titles in this series as they are published by placing a standing order.
Please contact your bookseller or, in case of difficulty, write to us at the address below with
your name and address, the title of the series and the ISBN quoted above.

Customer Services Department, Macmillan Distribution Ltd
Houndmills, Basingstoke, Hampshire RG21 6XS, England

Beyond UN Subcontracting

Task-Sharing with Regional Security Arrangements and Service-Providing NGOs

Edited by

Thomas G. Weiss
Brown University
Providence
Rhode Island

First published in Great Britain 1998 by
MACMILLAN PRESS LTD
Houndmills, Basingstoke, Hampshire RG21 6XS and London
Companies and representatives throughout the world

A catalogue record for this book is available from the British Library.

ISBN 0–333–69247–0 hardcover
ISBN 0–333–72508–5 paperback

First published in the United States of America 1998 by
ST. MARTIN'S PRESS, INC.,
Scholarly and Reference Division,
175 Fifth Avenue, New York, N.Y. 10010

ISBN 0–312–21051–5

Library of Congress Cataloging-in-Publication Data
Beyond UN subcontracting : task-sharing with regional security
arrangements and service providing NGOs / edited by Thomas G. Weiss.
p.   cm.
Includes bibliographical references and index.
ISBN 0–312–21051–5 (cloth)
1. International police.   2. Non-governmental organizations.
3. Security, International.   I. Weiss, Thomas George.
KZ6374.B49 1998
060—dc21   97–22770
                                                                  CIP

This book is printed on paper suitable for recycling and made from fully managed and sustained forest sources.

10   9   8   7   6   5   4   3   2   1
07   06   05   04   03   02   01   00   99   98

Printed and bound in Great Britain by
Antony Rowe Ltd, Chippenham, Wiltshire

In memory of Joaquín Tacsan

Contents

List of Tables

Preface

The ever-burgeoning demand for helping hands from United Nations (UN) soldiers and other personnel led former Secretary-General Boutros Boutros-Ghali in his 1995 *Supplement to An Agenda for Peace* to write that the 'increased volume of activity would have strained the Organization even if the nature of the activity had remained unchanged'. As well as the volume and nature having changed, financial juggling has become a perpetual challenge as states fail to meet their obligations. Accumulated total arrears hovered around something like \$3.5 billion in 1996, which equalled about three times the regular United Nations budget.

The disparity between demand and supply along with inadequate finances point to a 'strategic overstretch' by the UN of the type that Paul Kennedy attributes to empires in his *The Rise and Fall of the Great Powers*. The clearest diagnosis of the world organization's ills after its fiftieth anniversary is over-extension. The United Nations can cut back on activities or choose to accentuate and actively pursue as a strategy a recent trend toward relying upon regional arrangements or major states for military services, on the one hand, and upon non-governmental organizations (NGOs) for the provision of services, on the other.

Most partisans of multilateralism and supporters of the UN system argue that pursuing global governance requires, first and foremost, strengthening global institutions. The starting point for this volume is different: global governance – defined as better ordered and more reliable responses to problems that go beyond the individual or collective capacities of even powerful states – can also be fostered by a better division of labour between universal membership and other intergovernmental and non-governmental institutions. As such, strengthening the UN system necessitates that the world organization do what it does best, or at least better than other institutions, and devolve responsibilities when other institutions are in a position to respond effectively.

This research project was designed to shed light on this alternative approach, which is captured in the subtitle and title of this volume. The first part contains two frameworks for analysis. There follows in the second and third parts post-Cold War case studies about the 'UN task-sharing with regional security arrangements and service-providing NGOs' (the subtitle) in order to determine whether we have taken steps toward or away from better global governance. A word is in order about the term 'subcontracting',

xi

which might well have had quotes around it in the title as well. A 'subcontractor' follows orders from and is accountable to the general contractor. This is an accurate description for some NGO endeavours *vis-à-vis* the United Nations, but regional security arrangements do not subordinate themselves, either formally or practically, to the world organization.

Task-sharing by the United Nations requires great care to avoid any unnecessary dilution of universal multilateral institutions. 'Tempering collaboration' was the original working title for this volume but was abandoned because authors were concerned about ambiguity. However, this image is worth mentioning here because an assessment of recent experience with the UN's devolving responsibilities illustrates both costs and benefits. Just as steel can be made to have more appropriate characteristics of hardness and elasticity, so too can the world organization. If the fundamental aim is to foster global governance rather than parochial institutional agendas, it is necessary to determine both the appropriate timing and mixture of heating and cooling the fervour of proponents for regional arrangements, NGOs and the United Nations, respectively.

The precise details and patterns of interaction lead toward lessons for the future in the conclusions to this volume in order to move 'beyond UN subcontracting' (the main title). The crucial insights about the differences between UN 'subcontracting' to NGOs and regional arrangements came from my good friend and colleague, Edwin 'Rip' Smith. He forced me through the rigours that he requires of his contract students at the USC Law School, which was one of the important intellectual benefits of having collaborated on drafting the key synthetic chapter to this volume. Needless to say, I am extremely indebted to him for his help in framing the issues as well as the conclusions.

By way of introduction, the reader is no doubt aware that in the security arena the United Nations has attempted a number of times in the past five years to devolve responsibilities toward regional arrangements, and with varying results. The logic behind Chapter VIII of the Charter has been brought back on the policy agenda by the UN's over-extension. In theory, regional arrangements are preferable to universal ones for three reasons. Their territories and economies are most impacted by war and migration, and thus their interests will lead them to act rather than remain on the sidelines. They understand better local cultures and actors because of their shared backgrounds and experience, and thus they can be more effective in the field. Their agendas are not overcrowded with every global problem, and thus they can focus better on the crisis at hand.

In practice, however, recent performances in the security arena by regional arrangements have been chequered. Perhaps most importantly, critics question the plausibility of major powers' consistently acting altruistically on behalf of a larger community of states rather than pursuing unacceptably narrow and self-interested objectives. In short, does UN 'subcontracting' provide a blue fig leaf and legitimacy to gunboat diplomacy?

Case studies of the UN's collaboration with regional groups in the former Yugoslavia, Liberia, Central America and Haiti, and Georgia shed light on these issues with respect to the North Atlantic Treaty Organization (NATO), the Economic Community of West African States (ECOWAS), the Organization of American States (OAS), the Commonwealth of Independent States (CIS) and the Organization for Security and Cooperation in Europe (OSCE). The geographical and institutional range provides an initial basis on which to evaluate both the theory and recent practice of UN 'subcontracting' for security and to make policy recommendations.

In terms of providing services, NGOs are reputed to be more flexible, forthcoming, responsive and cost-effective than UN institutions. Their links to the grassroots mean that they can customize their activities rather than 'wholesale' them as the UN does. At the same time, their energy may lead to frenzy and confusion. Planning and evaluation are often valued less than the next assignment. Impatience with bureaucratic constraints often reflects a naivety that lends itself to manipulation. Independence is valued so intensely as to miss opportunities for cooperation. Again, theory and practice do not necessarily overlap. Some NGOs are biased and unprofessional. In short, how do the costs compare with the benefits of – and here the term is more accurate – 'subcontracting'?

Case studies about the UN's efforts to channel additional resources to NGOs, which parallel those of many bilateral donors to privatize the administration of their official development assistance (ODA), focus on four key types of activities: relief in war zones; election monitoring; development assistance; and environmental action. These activities clearly do not exhaust the range of NGO activities, but they do provide a representative sample that provides insights about the desirability and feasibility of relying upon NGOs rather than the international civil service for certain tasks.

I owe a profound debt of gratitude to many for making this collection possible. First and foremost, appreciation is in order to The John D. and Catherine T. MacArthur Foundation for the generous grant to the Academic Council on the United Nations System (ACUNS), which made feasible commissioning research and sponsoring discussions to improve the written products.

Preface

I also wish to acknowledge the contribution of three institutions. Outlines were discussed in May 1996 in Halifax, Nova Scotia, at Dalhousie University's Centre for Foreign Policy Studies, where Tim Shaw and his colleagues were congenial hosts. And drafts were presented in December 1996 in Providence, Rhode Island at Brown University's Thomas J. Watson Jr Institute for International Studies, where Tom Biersteker and my other university colleagues contributed both intellectually and financially to this endeavour. The chapters in this volume first appeared in mid-1997 as a special issue of the *Third World Quarterly* (Vol. 18, No. 3), and I am as always grateful for the encouragement of its insightful editor, Shahid Qadir.

Along with the other contributors who profited substantially from reflections and comments made by participants at the December conference, I would wish to acknowledge helpful suggestions from: Jarat Chopra, Roger A. Coate, Ben Fred-Mensah, Fen O. Hampson, P. Terrence Hopmann, W. Andy Knight, Charlotte Ku, Ed Luck, Denis McLean, Ellen Messer, Larry Minear, Craig N. Murphy, Amir Pasic, Linda C. Reif, Benjamin Rivlin, Michael Stopford, James S. Sutterlin, Peter Uvin and Ruth Wedgwood.

Participants in events organized by ACUNS have been spoiled over the last five years by the impeccable administrative arrangements resulting from the extraordinary competence and dedication of Program Coordinator Melissa Phillips; this research endeavour was no exception. We are also indebted to Laura Sadovnikoff who made possible the timely and accurate production of this collection of analyses about such a crucial new phenomenon in world politics.

Finally and in solidarity with his extended family in their grief, I would like to dedicate this book to the memory of Joaquín Tacsan. He died tragically in a November 1996 airline crash in Nigeria, where he was pursuing research about the comparative dimensions of regional conflicts. At the time of his death, Joaquín was the director of the Center for Peace and Reconciliation of the Arias Foundation for Peace and Human Progress. His essay for this collection is, in the words of his caring wife Irene Aguilar de Tacsan, 'Joaquín's last contribution to the science he so dearly loved'. Those of us who had the privilege of knowing him professionally through this project, as a board member of ACUNS or as a friend will miss his gentleness and wisdom.

Thomas G. Weiss
Providence, Rhode Island
March 1996

Notes on the Contributors

Clement E. Adibe is Assistant Professor at DePaul University in Chicago, Illinois. He was formerly a Killiam Post-doctoral Fellow at Dalhousie University, where he taught political science. His research interests include international peace and security, regional integration and political economy, international organization and African politics. His recent publications include *Managing Arms in Peace Processes: Somalia*, and 'Africa and global developments in the twenty-first century' (published in *International Journal*, 51 (1), with Timothy M. Shaw).

Muthiah Alagappa is Senior Fellow and Director of the Center for the Study of Politics and Security at the East-West Center in Honolulu. His research interests include international relations in the Asia-Pacific region, regional institutions, democratization, and political authority and legitimacy in Southeast Asia. His most recent publications include *Asian Conceptions of Security: Ideational and Material, Political Legitimacy in Southeast Asia: The Quest for Moral Authority*, 'Systemic change, security and governance in the Asia-Pacific Region' and *Democratic Transition in Asia: The Role of the International Community.*

Vikram K. Chand is Visiting Assistant Professor of Government at Wesleyan University. He was formerly a Post-doctoral Fellow at the Watson Institute for International Studies at Brown University. His research interests focus on democratization, the building of democratic institutions and the role of international NGOs in political change. He is currently completing a book entitled *Constructing Citizens: Mexico's Political Awakening*, which is based on four years of fieldwork in Mexico. He has served as a consultant to the Mexican Elections Project at the Carter Center and was a member of three international delegations to study electoral reform in Mexico and observe the 1994 presidential elections. He received his PhD from the Department of Government at Harvard University.

Mark Duffield is Senior Lecturer in the School of Public Policy at the University of Birmingham. His research interests include the political economy of internal war, the organizational adaptation of aid agencies to working in conflict situations, the impact of humanitarian aid on the dynamics of conflict and the globalization of public welfare. Between 1985 and 1989 he served as Oxfam's country representative for Sudan.

Leon Gordenker, a long-time observer of international organization, is Professor Emeritus of Politics at Princeton University. He is also Research Associate of the Center of International Studies at Princeton and Research Fellow of the Netherlands Institute of Advanced Study in the Humanities and Social Sciences. Among Gordenker's recent publications are: *The UN Tangle: Policy Formation, Reform, and Reorganization, NGOs, the UN and Global Governance* (edited with Thomas G. Weiss), *International Cooperation in Response to AIDS* (with Roger A. Coate, Christer Jönsson and Peter Söderholm), *The Challenging Role of the UN Secretary-General* (edited with Benjamin Rivlin) and *The United Nations in the 1990s* (with Peter R. Baehr).

Sheila Jasanoff is Professor of Science Policy and Law and founding chair of the Department of Science & Technology Studies at Cornell University. Her research interests include comparative and international environmental regulation, interactions between science, technology and the law, and the implications of social studies of science for science and technology policy. Her recent publications include *The Fifth Branch, Learning From Disaster: Risk Management After Bhopal* (edited) and *Science at the Bar.*

Dick A. Leurdijk is Senior Research Fellow at the Netherlands Institute of International Affairs, 'Clingendael' in The Hague. He specializes in the areas of international peace and security, regional conflicts and humanitarian intervention. He is the co-author (with Johan Kaufmann and Nico J. Schrijver) of *The World in Turmoil: Testing the UN's Capacity* and *Changing Global Needs: Expanding Role for the United Nations System.* He is an editor of *International Peacekeeping* (Germany). His most recent publications include *A UN Rapid Deployment Brigade: Strengthening the Capacity for Quick Response* and *The United Nations and NATO in Former Yugoslavia, 1991–1996: Limits to Diplomacy and Force.*

S. Neil MacFarlane is Lester B. Pearson Professor of International Relations and Director of the Centre for International Studies at the University of Oxford. He was previously Professor of Political Studies and Director of the Centre for International Relations at Queen's University. He has published widely on the international relations of the former Soviet region, and his research interests include the evolution of the post-Soviet international system, domestic politics, civil unrest and regional conflict in the Caucasus, and ethnic conflict and international security. He has just completed (with Larry Minear) a study of international humanitarian action in Nagorno Karabakh.

Ian Smillie has served, since 1983, as an independent development consultant for such organizations as the Organization for Economic Cooperation and Development, the Aga Khan Foundation, Winrock International Foundation, CARE and the International Union for the Conservation of Nature. He is the founder of the Canadian nongovernmental organization, Inter Pares. His most recent publications include *Mastering the Machine: Poverty, Aid and Technology* and *The Alms Bazaar: Altruism Under Fire – Nonprofit Organizations and International Development.*

Edwin M. Smith is Leon Benwell Professor of Law and International Relations at the University of Southern California Law School. In 1995, he was appointed by President Clinton as a member of the Scientific and Policy Advisory Committee of the US Arms Control and Disarmament Agency. His most recent publications include *The United Nations in a New World* Order (with Michael G. Schechter) and 'Changing conceptions and Institutional Adaptation' in Keith Krause and W. Andy Knight (eds), *The United Nations in the Twenty-First Century.* He is the chair of the Board of Directors of the Academic Council on the United Nations System.

Joaquín Tacsan, Director of the Center for Peace and Reconciliation of the Arias Foundation for Peace and Human Progress in San José, Costa Rica, died tragically in an airline crash in Nigeria in November 1996. Prior to 1994, he served as special advisor to Dr Oscar Arias Sánchez. Tacsan also taught classes on the relationship between international law and political science at the University of Costa Rica, and was the author of *The Dynamics of International Law and Conflict Resolution.* He was a member of the ACUNS Board of Directors.

Thomas G. Weiss is Research Professor and Director of the Research Program on Global Security at Brown University's Thomas J. Watson Jr Institute for International Studies. He also serves as Executive Director of the Academic Council on the United Nations System. Previously he held several UN posts (at UNCTAD, the UN Commission for Namibia, UNITAR, and ILO) and served as Executive Director of the International

Peace Academy. He has authored or edited some twenty-five books on various aspects of international organization, conflict management, North–South relations and humanitarian action. His most recent books are *Humanitarian Challenges and Intervention: World Politics and the Dilemmas of Help* with Cindy Collins (Westview Press, 1996), *The News Media, Civil War, and Humanitarian Action* with Larry Minear and Colin Scott (Lynne Rienner, 1996), and *NGOs, the UN, and Global Governance* (Lynne Rienner, 1996), edited with Leon Gordenker.

List of Abbreviations

AC	Civic Alliance
AFL	Armed Forces of Liberia
AG	Administrator-General
ASEAN	Association of Southeast Asian Nations
AWACS	Airborne Warning and Control System
BBC	British Broadcasting Corporation
CAS	Close Air Support
CIAV	Commission for International Support and Verification
CIS	Commonwealth of Independent States
CISPKF	Commonwealth of Independent States Peacekeeping Force
CITES	Convention on International Trade in Endangered Species
CSCE	Conference on Security and Cooperation in Europe
CSO	Civil Society Organization
DHA	Department of Humanitarian Affairs (United Nations)
EC	European Community
ECHO	European Community Humanitarian Office
ECOMOG	ECOWAS Ceasefire Monitoring Group
ECOSOC	Economic and Social Council
ECOWAS	Economic Community of West African States
EEC	European Economic Community
EEZ	Exclusive Economic Zone
EU	European Union
FMLN	Farabundo Martí National Liberation Front
GCC	Gulf Cooperation Council
GDP	gross domestic product
GONGO	government-organized NGO
GRO	grassroots organization
IAHRC	Inter-American Human Rights Commission
ICJ	International Court of Justice
ICTY	International Criminal Tribunal for the Former Yugoslavia (United Nations)
ICVA	International Council of Voluntary Agencies
IDP	internally displaced person
IFE	Federal Election Institute
IFOR	Implementation Force (former Yugoslavia)

IGO	intergovernmental organization
IGNU	Interim Government of National Unity
INPFL	Independent National Patriotic Front in Liberia
IPTF	International Police Task Force
LDC	London Dumping Convention
LNTG	Liberian National Transitional Government
LPC	Liberian Peace Council
MIC	methyl isocyanate
MICIVIH	International Civilian Mission in Haiti
MINUGUA	UN Mission in Guatemala
MOU	memorandum of understanding
NAC	North Atlantic Council
NAFTA	North American Free Trade Agreement
NATO	North Atlantic Treaty Organization
NDI	National Democratic Institute
NED	National Endowment for Democracy
NFZ	No-Fly Zone
NGO	non-governmental organization
NPFL	National Patriotic Front of Liberia
NRDC	Natural Resource Defense Council (US)
OAS	Organization of American States
OAU	Organization of African Unity
ODA	official development assistance
OECD	Organization for Economic Cooperation and Development
ONUC	United Nations Operation in the Congo
ONUCA	UN Operation in Central America
ONUSAL	United Nations Observer Mission in El Salvador
ONUVEN	United Nations Observer Mission to Verify the Electoral Process in Nicaragua
OSCE	Organization for Security and Cooperation in Europe
PAN	National Action Party
PRD	Democratic Revolutionary Party
PRI	Institutional Revolutionary Party (Mexico)
PSC	public service contractor
PVO	private voluntary organization
RRF	Rapid Reaction Force
SCF	Save the Children Fund
SFOR	Stabilization Force (former Yugoslavia)
SIDA	Swedish International Development Agency
SMC	ECOWAS Standing Mediation Committee

SNC	Supreme National Council
SRSG	Special Representative of the UN Secretary-General
SNTE	National Teacher's Union (Mexico)
SWAPO	South-West African People's Organization
ULIMO	United Liberation Movement for Democracy in Liberia
ULIMO–J	United Liberation Movement for Democracy in Liberia – Faction led by Johnson
ULIMO–K	United Liberation Movement for Democracy in Liberia – Faction led by Kromah
UN	United Nations
UNCED	UN Conference on Environment and Development
UNCIVPOL	United Nations Civilian Police
UNDP	United Nations Development Programme
UNEAP	United Nations Electoral Assistance Programme
UNHCR	United Nations High Commissioner for Refugees
UNICEF	United Nations Children's Fund
UNIFEM	United Nations Development Fund for Women
UNO	National Opposition Union (Mexico)
UNOC	United Nations Operation in the Congo
UNOMIG	United Nations Observer Mission in Georgia
UNOMIL	United Nations Observer Mission in Liberia
UNONGO	UN-organized NGO
UNOSOM	United Nations Operations in Somalia
UNPROFOR	United Nations Protection Force in the Former Yugoslavia
UNSC	United Nations Security Council
US	United States
USAID	United States Agency for International Development
WCED	World Commission on Environment and Development
WEU	Western European Union
WFP	World Food Programme (UN)
WWF	World Wildlife Fund

Part I
Frameworks for Analysis

1 Regional Arrangements, the UN, and International Security: a Framework for Analysis

Muthiah Alagappa

Under the Charter the Security Council has and will continue to have primary responsibility for maintaining international peace and security, but regional action as a matter of decentralization, delegation and cooperation with United Nations efforts could not only lighten the burden of the Security Council but also contribute to a deeper sense of participation, consensus and democratization in international affairs. Regional arrangements and agencies have not in recent decades been considered in this light. ... Today a new sense exists that they have contributions to make.

(Boutros Boutros-Ghali, 1992)

Termination of the Cold War reinvigorated the United Nations (UN) and simultaneously reinforced the trend toward security regionalism. The new-found unity of the Security Council enabled the world organization to act in a relatively large number of conflicts, and in the process raised the expectations with regard to its 'primary responsibility for maintaining international peace and security'. The UN had several successes – the Gulf War, Cambodia, Mozambique, El Salvador and Haiti – but there have also been several tragic failures – Somalia, Bosnia and Rwanda. These failures and the growing political, financial and operational problems have greatly tempered the earlier enthusiasm and support. Unable to meet the ever-increasing demand for help, the United Nations has actively explored task-sharing and cooperation with other intergovernmental (IGOs) and non-governmental organizations (NGOs) as well as coalitions led by major global and regional powers. Regional institutions (regional arrangements and agencies) have been increasingly looked upon as one way of addressing the growing gap between demand and supply, and reducing the burden on the United Nations. In the words of Boutros Boutros-Ghali 'regional arrangements or agencies in many cases possess a potential that should be utilized'.

The role of regional institutions (constituted under Chapter VIII of the UN Charter) in maintaining international peace and security has commanded renewed attention in policy and intellectual communities from the mid-1980s. Such interest has become more pronounced in the post-Cold War era. Regionalization of international politics, collapse of the Cold War security architecture, inability of any one state or organization to manage the resulting world order, the growth of regional powers and the desire on their part as well as other regional states to seek greater control over their strategic environment, and growth of economic regionalism are some of the reasons that underscore this growing interest and attention.[1] They inform, in various degrees, the attempt to broaden and deepen regional security arrangements and agencies in Europe, to update and revitalize those in Latin America and Africa, and to forge new ones in Asia.

Unlike in the formative years of the UN when regional arrangements were seen as competing with and detrimental to the universal approach embodied in the UN,[2] it is now widely accepted that global and regional institutions can and should work together in promoting international peace and security. Regional actors have a deep interest in conflict management in their respective regions, and they can provide legitimacy, local knowledge and experience, and some resources, especially in the form of personnel. However, they also suffer several limitations including a lack of mandate, the difficulty of maintaining impartiality and forging common positions, limited resources and organizational shortcomings. Regional institutions often require the support and involvement of the United Nations in managing conflicts. The latter has the mandate, legitimacy, structure and greater access to resources and is often the most impartial and preferred means for extra-regional involvement in local conflicts. Thus, the need and rationale for task-sharing and cooperation between the UN and regional organizations is clear, and there have been many instances of such cooperation in the course of the last decade – notably in the former Yugoslavia, Liberia, Georgia, Central America and Haiti, the cases analysed in this volume. Such cooperation, however, has not always been smooth, and in several cases has produced tension.

Effective task-sharing between the UN and regional institutions requires an understanding of the possibilities and limitations of each as well as the development of principles, rules and procedures to govern such a partnership. This has been difficult in practice. Regional institutions vary widely in terms of purpose, structure and capacities. And, often several regional and subregional institutions with overlapping responsibilities exist in a region. Further, the type and intensity of conflicts vary widely. It is impossible to decide in advance as to which would be the most appropriate regional institution for managing a specific conflict. This 'choice' and consequently the basis for task-sharing and cooperation with the UN have often been *ad hoc* and quite distinct as demonstrated by the four case studies in this volume – the North Atlantic Treaty Organization (NATO) in former Yugoslavia, the Economic Community of West African States (ECOWAS) in Liberia, the Commonwealth of Independent States (CIS) and the Organization for Security and Cooperation in Europe (OSCE) in Georgia and the Organization of American States (OAS) in Central America and Haiti.

Although it is difficult to formulate and adhere strictly to a division of labour that would be applicable to each and every, or even most occasions, this does not preclude a general analytically oriented discussion of the basis for task-sharing between the UN and regional institutions. Working on the hypothesis that UN task-sharing with regional security arrangements can contribute to the maintenance of international peace and security, this chapter seeks to develop an analytical framework to investigate the following questions. What are the roles and strategies available to regional institutions in managing peace and security? What are possibilities and limitations of regional institutions in managing domestic and international conflict in their respective regions? What factors determine the effectiveness of regional institutions? What criteria should be deployed in determining the division of labour between the UN and regional agencies? Finally, how should coordination and accountability be achieved when regional institutions cooperate with the UN in maintaining international peace and security? We begin with the definition and discussion of some key terms.

DEFINITIONS

As observed by Gareth Evans,[3] there is no shared vocabulary and even the meanings of commonly used terms differ with audiences. It is therefore crucial to define and develop a common set of concepts to guide enquiry.

Regional arrangements and agencies

Considerable effort was made in the intellectual community in the 1960s and early 1970s to define regions and regional subsystems.[4] Comparatively less effort was devoted to defining *regionalism*.[5] And almost no effort was made to define regional arrangements and agencies. The UN Charter, which is the initiator of these terms, does not define them. Notwithstanding this, the meaning of regional arrangements is similar to that of regionalism. Both relate to cooperation among regional states to enhance their national well-being through collective action. Building on this, 'regional arrangements' or 'regionalism' (these two terms are used interchangeably in this paper) may be defined as 'cooperation among governments or non-governmental organizations in three or more geographically proximate and interdependent countries for the pursuit of mutual gain in one or more issue-areas'. Although NGOs can undertake regional cooperation, the concern in this paper and hence the ensuing elaboration is on cooperation among governments. Regionalism can be issue-specific – a collective self-defence arrangement (alliance) to confront a specific external threat, or a collective security arrangement to maintain order among member states, or a nuclear-free regime to regulate nuclear activities. Or, it can encompass an issue-area or a number of issue-areas.[6] Often, as for example in the case of the OAS, the Organization of African Unity (OAU) and the Association of Southeast Asian Nations (ASEAN), it is a broad framework within which several specific regimes and accompanying bureaucratic organizations in a number of issues and issue-areas can and do nest.[7] 'Regional agencies' refer to formal and informal regional organizations (with physical and organizational infrastructure, staff, budget, etc.) with responsibility for implementing regional arrangements. Regional agencies or organizations are usually coterminous with regional arrangements but not necessarily so. The term 'institutions' is used in this paper to cover both arrangements and agencies.

Peace and security

The United Nations, which has as its principle purpose the maintenance of international peace and security, neither defines these terms nor specifies the relationship between them. They appear to be used rather loosely and often interchangeably. Peace and security carry distinct meanings within the academic community, but there is no agreed definition. The schism and debate between the proponents of negative and positive peace has been a central feature of peace studies.[8] Similarly, there is an ongoing debate in security studies over the definition of security. Realists insist on a definition in terms of an international structural problem whose focus is international military threats to the political survival of the state. Others have argued for broadening the referent, scope and approach to security.[9] We cannot resolve the definitional problems in this paper.

The dependent variable in this paper is 'security', which is defined as 'the protection and enhancement of values deemed vital for the political survival and well-being of a community'. This definition is deeper and broader than Realist definitions of security but not indiscriminately so. The security referent in this definition is community which usually, though not always, is the nation-state.[10] Communities at the subnational, regional and global levels may also be referents of security. The definition excludes non-human entities like the international economic system or the ecological system as security referents in their own right because of the logic that security is for and about people who normally provide for their security by organizing themselves into communities. The focus on political survival and especially the well-being of a community enables the inclusion of non-conventional issues as security concerns either because of their impact on political survival or because of their consequences for the well-being of the community. Such issues, however, must be vital. Only those concerns that are grave and urgent, that require the mobilization of a substantial part and ultimately, if necessary, all of a community's intellectual and material resources, should be labelled as security concerns.

This definition does not seek to include or exclude on the basis of specific issues, dimensions, nature and type of problems, threats or means, but on the basis of the gravity and urgency of issues or problems. This approach sidesteps the unresolvable debate between the proponents of narrow and broad conceptions of security. It permits considerations of security at the intra-state and international levels, and does not limit the pursuit of security only to competitive means with emphasis on military power. It, however, restricts the scope of security to political problems with zero-sum and distributional characteristics. This is necessary to keep the exercise manageable. It should be noted here that this definition is much broader than allowed for by Realists and incorporates some features of the minimalist or negative definition of peace.

Sources of insecurity

Most states are confronted with internal and international sources of insecurity. For analytical purposes these sources of conflict may be discussed separately, but in reality they are often interconnected. The international source of insecurity is rooted in anarchy, a condition that is taken by Realists to be the fundamental fact of international political life.[11] In a system of sovereign states, there can be no central political authority. The structure of the system is necessarily anarchic, with each state retaining the right to judge its own cause and decide on the use of force. The incentives for aggression, risk of tension, conflict and war in such a system are high. In arming for their security, states set in motion a vicious circle.

Attempts to increase the security of one state undermine the security of another, creating a security dilemma.[12]

This structural aspect, a 'tragic consequence' of the desire for state autonomy, however, is only one of the two component layers that constitute the security dilemma.[13] The second component is more intentional and dynamic, a product of state policy rooted in the ideological beliefs and goals of the state and in its orientation toward the international political and territorial status quo. A policy seeking revolutionary change, hegemony or domination will intensify the struggle for power and sharpen the insecurity caused by the anarchic structure. Although these two layers of the security dilemma (structural and policy driven) are often intertwined in practice, distinguishing them is analytically useful in investigating when, why and how regionalism can promote international security.

Domestic sources of insecurity are rooted in problems of political identity, legitimacy and socio-economic inequality. The idea of the nation as the basis of political community and the related construct of the nation-state have now become universal norms. But the nation is an 'imagined community', and, in many cases, the idea of the nation on the basis of which the state is constituted is not deep-rooted.[14] Supposedly, colonial states have in many cases been transformed into nation-states. The arbitrary state boundaries drawn by the colonial powers resulted in 'multiethnic territorialisms' that had no political rationale for existence other than as dependencies of the metropolitan powers.[15] With the dissipation of the unity fostered by anticolonial nationalism and experience of 'internal colonialism', ethnic, racial, linguistic and religious consciousness has been on the rise in some countries, contributing to disenchantment with the nation and nation-state rooted in the colonial state.[16]

Dissonance between power and legitimate authority is a second domestic source of conflict. This is relevant to states in which the normative and institutional frameworks for the acquisition and exercise of political power are not well established. In situations where the exercise of state power is not rooted in moral authority, the legitimacy of the regime (political system) as well as that of the incumbent government is likely to be contested by rival claimants to power on the basis of competing ideologies, promise of better performance or greater force.[17] In the absence of accepted mechanisms and procedures to manage them, such competition is likely to translate into extra-legal and violent means including *coups d'état*, rebellion and revolution. Political legitimacy has and is likely to continue to be an acute and persistent problem for most modern states.

Large and growing socio-economic inequality is yet another source of domestic conflict. Socio-economic grievances can fuel peasant rebellions or protests and strikes by farmers and industrial workers, but their consequences are likely to be limited unless they feed into the conflicts over political identity or legitimacy. Often there is an overlap. Economically backward regions provide fertile ground for the development and support of separatist movements or for political organizations that challenge the legitimacy of incumbent regimes and governments on the basis of competing ideologies or promises of better performance.

Insecurity and conflict at the international level are inherent in the principle of anarchy, which underpins the international system and cannot be resolved as long as sovereign political units (states or some other entities) exist. At the domestic level, the problems of political identity, legitimacy and socio-economic grievances are rooted in the nation- and state-formation processes, and they cannot be resolved quickly. Creation of political identities takes decades if not centuries; the cultivation of political legitimacy is unending; and the attainment and maintenance of socio-economic equality requires continuous monitoring and action. These problems are not amenable to a once-and-for-all solution. Still, though the sources of conflict cannot be eliminated, they can nevertheless be managed and ameliorated.

Conflict management

Although in practice they overlap, for analytical purposes conflict management may be divided into three stages: prevention, containment and termination. In 'conflict prevention', the goal is to forestall conflict situations and prevent the outbreak of hostilities or other forms of disruptive behaviour. Conflict prevention will require the redefinition of the identity, interests and capabilities of the communities concerned. In 'conflict containment', the goal is to deny victory to the aggressor and to prevent the spread of conflict. Denial of victory includes stopping aggressors short of attaining their full goal and persuading them to undo their action. Preventing the spread of conflict includes stopping horizontal escalation in which other communities and issue-areas become involved. It may also be directed to halt vertical escalation up the ladder of violence, including the use of weapons of mass destruction.

In 'conflict termination', the goal is to halt and bring hostilities to a satisfactory conclusion through settlement or resolution. A satisfactory conclusion includes defeating the aggressor and re-establishing the *status quo ante*, achieving a compromise through splitting the difference or removing the source of the conflict. 'Conflict settlement' focuses on achieving an agreement to end the use of violence and resolve the more immediate and overt dimensions of the conflict.[18] 'Conflict resolution', however, seeks to remove the source of conflict altogether. This requires changes in the goals, attitudes and perceptions of the conflicting parties. While these two aspects of conflict termination are not mutually exclusive, conflict resolution usually follows conflict settlement and requires long-range political and economic strategies to alter, if not transform, the underlying dynamics of the conflict. In a sense, this bring conflict management back to conflict prevention.

REGIONAL INSTITUTIONS: ASSETS, ROLES AND STRATEGIES

In theory, regionalism should facilitate communications and socialization, information sharing, increase in consensual knowledge and growth in power through the pooling of resources and collective action.[19] Based on these assets, regional institutions should be able to avail themselves of one or more of the following interconnected strategies: norm-setting, assurance, community-building, deterrence, non-intervention, isolation, intermediation, enforcement, and internationalization. Norms can define identities of states as well as regulate their behaviour. Through norm-setting, regional institutions can influence the collective expectations and the internal and international behaviour of member states in the political, economic and security arenas.

Assurance strategies can increase transparency, reduce uncertainty, limit and regulate competition and thus help to build confidence and avoid unintended outbreak and escalation of hostilities. The purpose of assurance strategies is to mitigate the security dilemma and minimize and regulate the use of force, not to eliminate it. Community-building strategies take this one step further and seek to eliminate the role of force in the resolution of political disputes. The culmination point is a security community in which 'there is real assurance that the members of the community will not fight each other physically but will settle their disputes in some other way'.[20] Deterrence strategies – collective security, collective defence – seek to deter aggressive behaviour on the part of member states as well as non-member states.

Collective security comprising political, diplomatic, economic and military measures is the more appropriate measure for maintaining order among member states since it is not directed against a specific country or group of countries which are identified as posing a threat.[21] Collective defence (alliances like NATO and the now defunct Warsaw Pact), based on an identified common threat, is more appropriate in dealing with external aggression. These two strategies are not, however, mutually exclusive, as illustrated by the provisions of the Rio Treaty. Assurance, community-building and deterrence strategies are primarily concerned with conflict prevention, although many of the specific arrangements, particularly alliance and collective security, have a role in conflict containment and termination as well.

Non-intervention is an option when, for whatever reason, a regional institution does not seek to become involved in a particular conflict. Closely linked to non-intervention, but quite distinct, is isolation, the purpose of which is to prevent geographical spillover or widening of the conflict through the involvement of other parties. The intent in adopting these strategies may be to allow the protagonists to resolve a conflict among themselves, or to preserve a future intermediation role for a regional institution. Intervention refers to direct and active involvement in a conflict through the application of a regional organization's collective political, economic and military resources to contain and terminate conflict. Intervention can be undertaken to enforce collective security and collective defence or to keep the peace among the warring parties. Collective security and collective defence are implemented against an identified aggressor. Peacekeeping, the interposition of forces between belligerents to prevent further fighting, is undertaken to provide a cooling off period and to facilitate mediation.

Intermediation and internationalization are two strategies applicable to conflict termination. Intermediation refers to a non-partisan and usually non-coercive approach to settlement. Regional institutions may urge conflicting parties to use regional or global mechanisms and procedures for pacific settlement of disputes, or they may attempt to play a more direct and active role by engaging in conciliation and mediation.[22] The strategy of internationalization becomes relevant when conflict prevention, containment and termination are beyond the capabilities of the regional arrangements or when extra-regional actors become involved. Through internationalization, regional organizations can mobilize the resources of external actors and organizations in support of their strategies, while denying the same resources to their adversaries.

The possible relevance of these strategies for managing internal and international conflicts and enhancing the security of member states is summarized in Table 1.1. Discussion in the ensuing sections highlights some critical aspects with regard to the possible roles and tasks of regional institutions in conflict management.

Table 1.1 Regional Institutions and Security: a Framework for Analysis

	Tasks	Measures/strategies
Domestic conflicts – Issues of contention: identity, legitimacy, socio-economic grievances		
Conflict prevention	1. Protection of individual and minority rights. 2. Support for socio-political development. 3. Support for economic development. 4. Early warning.	1. Norm-setting. 2. Redress by regional institutions. 3. Encourage and facilitate dialogue. 4. Preventive deployment. 5. Collective inducement and sanctions. 6. Regional economic cooperation. 7. Maintain a stable and conducive regional environment.
Conflict containment	1. Prevent escalation. 2. Prevent torture, killing and genocide. 3. Humanitarian relief.	1. Preventive deployment. 2. Enforce sanctions. 3. Isolate conflict. 4. Peacekeeping. 5. Internationalize conflict. 6. Humanitarian assistance.
Conflict termination	1. End violence. 2. Negotiate and guarantee settlement. 3. Election monitoring. 4. Address underlying issues.	1. Encourage dialogue. 2. Intermediation. 3. Enforcement action. 4. Encourage and support long-range strategies for nation and state building. 5. Internationalization.

Table 1.1 (Continued)

Tasks	Measures/strategies
Conflict among member states – issues of concern: security dilemma, specific issues in dispute, aggressive behaviour by member states	
Conflict prevention	
1. Ameliorate security dilemma.	1. Foster development of normative context that rejects threat and use of force as an instrument of state policy.
2. Deter aggressive behaviour.	2. Build regimes – assurance and regulatory.
3. Build a society leading eventually to a community of nations.	3. Regional dispute resolution mechanisms.
4. Encourage dispute resolution.	4. Collective security arrangement.
	5. Regional integration measures.
Conflict containment	
1. Deny victory to aggressor.	1. Enforce collective security arrangements.
2. Prevent escalation.	2. Isolate conflict.
3. Humanitarian relief.	3. Peacekeeping.
	4. Internationalization.
	5. Humanitarian assistance.
Conflict termination	
1. Stop armed conflict.	1. Encourage dialogue among parties to conflict.
2. Negotiate and guarantee settlement.	2. Intermediation.
3. Resolve dispute.	3. Enforcement action.
	4. Internationalization.

Table 1.1 (Continued)

Tasks	Measures/strategies
Conflicts with external actors – issues of concern: security dilemma, specific issues in dispute, aggressive behaviour by external actors	
Conflict prevention	
1. Ameliorate security dilemma.	1. Dialogue and negotiations.
2. Deter aggressive behaviour.	2. Security regimes – assurance and regulatory.
3. Encourage dispute resolution.	3. Collective self-defence.
Conflict containment	
1. Deny victory to aggressor.	1. Implement collective self-defence.
2. Prevent escalation.	2. Internationalization.
3. Humanitarian relief.	3. Humanitarian assistance.
Conflict termination	
1. Defeat aggressor.	1. Implement collective self-defence.
2. Negotiate settlement.	2. Internationalization.
3. Resolve dispute.	3. Intermediation.

REGIONAL INSTITUTIONS AND CONFLICT MANAGEMENT

The ability of regional institutions to manage conflict depends, in part, upon the type of armed conflict that is to be managed. Three in particular concern this analysis.

Domestic conflicts

Conflicts at the domestic level pose serious security problems for many countries including some developed ones. Domestic conflicts often spill over into neighbouring countries and/or invite major power intervention, threatening regional security as well. Yet the basis on which governments enter into regional cooperation often precludes any formal role for regional institutions in the management of internal armed conflicts.

The principles of sovereignty and non-intervention form the cornerstones of regional arrangements like the inter-American system, the OAU and ASEAN.[23] Based on these principles, regional institutions have been deliberately excluded from domestic conflict management (OAU, ASEAN) or accorded a role subject to the invitation of member states (ECOWAS, and until recently the OAS). The sanctity of the principle of non-intervention, however, is now under challenge. A growing number of Western policy-makers and scholars make the case for intervention by the international community on humanitarian grounds and to protect democratic regimes.[24] Although this case is contested in many quarters, some change, particularly with regard to gross violation of human rights, may be in the offing.[25] Beginning in 1993 by giving priority to the goal of safeguarding democracy in the hemisphere, the OAS relaxed the commitment to the principle of non-intervention. In what has come to be known as the Santiago commitment, the foreign ministers of the OAS pledged to adopt 'timely and expeditious procedures to ensure the promotion and defence of representative democracy'. The OAS has since condemned the coup in Guatemala, Haiti and Peru and has applied economic sanctions to back its demand for return to democratic rule in these countries. While the Santiago commitment emphasizes the protection of democratic regimes at the expense of the principle of non-intervention, the latter is far from dead.[26]

Humanitarian considerations and incipient rethinking of the basis of political community are also forcing a re-examination of the principle of non-intervention in Africa. Nevertheless, this crucial principle is very much still in evidence and effectively precludes any direct intervention by regional and other international institutions until armed conflicts erupt.

16 *Muthiah Alagappa*

Often the conflict prevention role of regional institutions in relation to domestic conflicts has to be indirect, and relevant strategies may include norm-setting, the development of collective regional identities that may mitigate internal identity conflicts, the prevention of external meddling in domestic conflicts, and the creation of a stable and conducive environment for the economic development of member states. Early warning systems, and mechanisms and procedures to encourage the pacific settlement of domestic disputes, may also be part of the inventory. Once a conflict has erupted, regional institutions have the options of non-intervention, isolation, intervention or mediation and conciliation.

Non-intervention has been the preferred strategy of most regional institutions for a variety of reasons: adherence to the principle of non-interference in domestic affairs; a lack of invitation from the incumbent government; a lack of capability; the intractability of the conflict; the anticipated human and material costs, especially if recent experiences have been negative (Britain's experience in Northern Ireland influenced its and several other European Union (EU) members' approach to the ongoing conflict in Bosnia; the OAU's experience in Western Sahara and Chad influenced its approach toward the Liberian conflict); difficulty in forging a common position (the EU in relation to Yugoslavia); difficulty in determining aggression and aggressor; the tension between competing principles (territorial integrity versus self-determination in the case of Yugoslavia, or non-intervention versus the promotion of democracy in several Latin American cases); a firm belief that external actors can have only a marginal impact on the resolution of domestic conflicts and that these have to be resolved by domestic contestants even if the political, economic and human costs are high. The OAU, for example, has traditionally restricted its involvement to internal conflicts related to decolonization and apartheid. A common position was not difficult to formulate in these situations. It did not intervene in the numerous other internal conflicts on the continent.

Concurrent with non-intervention, regional organizations often seek to isolate conflicts to prevent external interference and escalation, urging contestants to resolve the conflict by themselves. This has been the preferred option in ASEAN. In February 1986 when the Philippines was confronted with a critical situation which 'portended bloodshed and civil war', the other ASEAN member states called upon all Filipino leaders to join efforts to pave the way for a peaceful resolution.[27] But as demonstrated in the case of the Philippines as well as by the ECOWAS experience in Liberia, isolation can be rather difficult. Domestic contestants will appeal and, in the absence of unanimity in the international community, are likely to receive external support.

Non-intervention in the context of endemic internal conflict, as in Africa, projects an image of regional institutions as irrelevant and useless. The OAU's reputation in and out of Africa has suffered much because of its reluctance to become involved in domestic conflicts. Such considerations are pushing it to become more involved. But intervention too carries its own limitations and dangers. Difficulty in forging and maintaining unity among member states, difficulty in maintaining the neutrality of the intervention force, the limited authority and capability of regional institutions, a lack of financial resources and difficulty in arriving at and implementing an international settlement limit the containment and termination roles of regionalism.

The above discussion suggests several observations. First, regional institutions are severely limited as agents of domestic conflict management. Preclusion from domestic politics and the complex and intense dynamics of domestic conflicts severely limit their possibilities for conflict prevention. They may have a relatively greater role in conflict containment (isolation) and termination (mediation), but this is likely to be limited to a select few situations. Even then regional institutions may have to enlist the support of the UN or other external actors. Second, to the extent that regional institutions do have a role in domestic conflict management, their status quo character leads them to favour incumbents. Governments tend to support one another. As former Tanzanian president Julius Nyerere is reported to have said, 'The OAU exists only for the protection of the African Heads of State.'[28] Similarly, the primary rationale for the Gulf Cooperation Council (GCC) is the protection of the incumbent monarchs and their conservative kingdoms.[29] Even non-intervention and isolation, as noted above, are likely to work in favour of the incumbent power holders. Third, instead of containing and terminating domestic conflict, regionalism can also prolong and intensify it. By strengthening the hand of the government, as for example in Burma, regional support increases the persecution and insecurity of groups seeking political change.

For the most part, international actors and dynamics, including those at the regional level, will have only an indirect impact and will be relevant only to the extent that they influence the domestic political discourse and affect the power resources of the domestic contestants. In light of the dilemmas and limitations, the optimal strategies of regional institutions in dealing with domestic conflicts would appear to be non-intervention, isolation, diplomatic pressure urging peaceful settlement of the dispute, offering good services and enlisting the support and role of the United Nations or a key external power.

Conflict among member states

Regionalism has its greatest value at the intramural level when the policy-driven power struggle component of the security dilemma has abated. In this situation, regional strategies can be effectively deployed to reduce the uncertainty inherent in anarchy and the misperception that can issue from it. Because of the commitment of member states to the status quo, regionalism can be particularly effective in conflict prevention. Through the construction of security regimes in the areas of confidence- and security-building and pacific settlement of disputes, and promoting defensive defence, it can mitigate the negative effects of anarchy. The resulting secure environment can foster cooperation in other issue-areas, increase interdependence, alter the cost-benefit calculus in favour of peaceful resolution of disputes and contribute to the forging and consolidating of shared norms and values. This will further strengthen international society and in the long run make for the development of a pluralistic security community.

Regionalism is much less useful in coping with the policy-driven power struggle component of the security dilemma. When the latter operates un-abated, as is the case at the intramural level when hostilities break out among member states and most of the time at the extramural level, the collective power that regionalism can bring to bear will be the crucial determinant of its role in conflict prevention, containment and termination. The power of a regional organization should, in theory, be greater than that of individual states. But the realization of this potential will be dependent upon the unity of purpose among member states and their willingness to pool national power and act collectively on the issue of concern. Even when these stringent conditions are met, the power of the collective may still be insufficient to redefine the interests and goals of the parties to the conflict. Usually regional organizations are strong only in terms of diplomatic power, which can be useful in mobilizing international support and structuring international, especially UN, action.

To be effective in terms of deterrence, however, diplomatic power must be complemented with economic and military power. This will require a regional organization to ally or align with one or more major powers or seek the assistance of the UN. Though the diplomatic power of a regional institution can be deployed to harness international power in support of its policies, success will depend on the pattern of relations among the major powers and the congruence of interest the regional institution can establish with the target actor. The internationalization strategy will also constrain the freedom and flexibility of regional institutions. Generally, the effectiveness of a regional institution in conflict containment and termination is much more limited than its effectiveness in conflict prevention. And because of its partisan role in conflict containment, its conflict termination role may be even more limited.

Conflicts with extra-regional states

The security goal of regional institutions here is the protection of member states from insecurity created by other states and organizations. There is no sense of community at this level, and regional institutions would have to deal with countries that are not necessarily committed to the status quo. Some may even be categorically opposed and seek to overthrow it. Regionalism could be perceived by these countries as directed against them, provoking counter-groups and exacerbating the security dilemma. In this situation it may not be possible to implement far-reaching assurance strategies. Limited regimes to avoid mutually undesirable outcomes, such as that between Israel and Egypt after the 1973 war, may however, be feasible.

Conflict prevention at the extramural level has to address both aspects of the security dilemma, with power being much more significant in the reduction of insecurity. In theory, regionalism can and should enhance the power (defined broadly to encompass military, economic and diplomatic power) of the collective. In practice, regional institutions, especially among developing countries, seldom command the required power and/or a common threat perception for an effective alliance. They can seek to enhance their power through alliance or alignment with extra-regional powers, as for example the ASEAN countries with China to contain the Vietnamese and Soviet threats, but there is the possibility that the interests of regional states may be overridden by those of the major powers. Beijing's own objectives of punishing Vietnam and containing the Soviet threat overrode ASEAN's concerns and its peace proposals on several occasions. Even the EC has not been exempt from this. During the Cold War, American interests and policies frequently took priority over Western European concerns.

Although militarily weak, regional institutions may be relatively strong in diplomatic or economic power. If such power constitutes critical mass, then they can play a critical role in shaping the rules of the larger regional game, as with the European Community (EC) in relation to Eastern Europe in the post-1989 period and ASEAN in relation to Indochina. Even when the power of regional institutions does not constitute critical mass, they may be able to take the initiative in constructing the larger regional order, as is currently the case with ASEAN's successful initiative in creating the ASEAN Regional Forum (ARF) to begin a dialogue on security matters in the Asia-Pacific region. But for this to be possible, the status quo has to be acceptable or at least tolerable to all the major powers, and they must support, or at least not oppose such initiatives. The abatement of the struggle for power among the major countries is a necessary precondition for such initiatives to succeed.

The diplomatic power of regional institutions can also be deployed to contain extramural conflict. It may be particularly useful in influencing UN debate and action. The arms embargo against the former Yugoslavia was sanctioned by the Security Council at the request of the European Union. Indeed, the UN became involved in trying to negotiate an end to that conflict at the European Community's urging. Similarly, the support of the OAS was crucial in getting the Security Council to impose sanctions on Haiti. The OAU successfully pushed for UN sanctions against territory under the control of Charles Taylor in Liberia. Diplomatic power, however, is only enabling, providing regional institutions with the power of initiative. It cannot guarantee success. That will still depend on the disposition of non-member states, the dynamics of the larger international system and the competence of member states in harnessing the power of external states in the service of their cause.

Effectiveness of regional institutions

As noted earlier the roles, tasks and strategies identified in Table 1.1 should in theory be available to all regional institutions. Their feasibility in practice and the effectiveness of regional institutions in conflict management, however, are contingent upon a number of factors, and therefore likely to vary considerably across institutions. Five factors – the type of institution and commitment to it; shared interests in relationship to a specific armed conflict; institutional capacity; resource availability; and legitimacy and credibility – appear to be crucial in determining the effectiveness of regional institutions.[30]

In ascertaining effectiveness, one must begin with the purpose, scope and commitment of an institution, which will determine whether and to what extent a regional institution can become involved in conflict management, and the roles and tasks that it can undertake. The purpose and scope of an all-inclusive multipurpose regional organization like the OAS or OAU will differ from subregional ones like ECOWAS and ASEAN, which in turn will differ from specific task-oriented institutions like NATO. Further, it is necessary to explore what roles and tasks are allowed or prohibited by the principles and purposes of the charters of these institutions and whether practice has deviated. This will help ascertain the likely roles in conflict management and the legal basis for them. Intimately connected to the purpose and scope is the identification with an institution and commitment to the norms, rules and procedures governing regional order. The stronger the identification and commitment from member states, the more effective the regional institution and vice versa.

Commitment of member states, however, will often vary by issue. Thus shared interests in a specific conflict and common purposes with regard to strategy and outcome are crucial in the effectiveness of regional institutions. In their absence, even a strong regional organization like the European Union will be inhibited from playing an effective role, as was the case in Bosnia.

Institutional capacity refers to the ability of a regional institution to make decisions, as well as the existence of organs, rules and procedures to implement them. Of concern here are the capacity and efficacy to collect, collate and analyse data, the principles and procedures to make decisions, the necessary subsidiary organs to carry out these decisions, command, control and communications capabilities, and administrative and logistics support.

Closely linked to institutional capacity is the availability of financial and manpower resources. Financial capacity is crucial, as are manpower resources. They include trained mediators and negotiators, military and police forces, civilian administrators and NGOs. Financial and manpower resources and military strength will circumscribe the types of roles and tasks that a regional institution may be able to undertake.

To be effective, regional institutions must command the respect and authority of the parties to the dispute in concern. For this to be the case, they must be perceived to be impartial and strong, and with a good track record. Recognition and support by other regional and global institutions as well as cooperation with them may also enhance credibility. Lack of coordination and especially competitive behaviour by other institutions may undermine legitimacy and credibility.

Strength in these areas will enhance the role and effectiveness of regional institutions in managing conflicts, but they by no means guarantee success. As noted earlier, regional institutions have considerable potential, but their actual role in conflict management has been much more limited. Regionalism has to be viewed as part of a package that includes national self-help, regional and global balances of power, alliance with extra-regional powers and the UN collective security system. Often regional institutions will have to enlist the involvement and support of the UN or other extra-regional actors.

REGIONAL INSTITUTIONS AND THE UNITED NATIONS

The Charter, assigning primary responsibility for maintaining international peace and security to the Security Council, envisions a hierarchy with regional arrangements serving global interests as defined by the council. It requires regional institutions to keep the Security Council fully informed of activities undertaken or contemplated with regard to the maintenance of international peace and security. The single exception relates to the provision for collective defence under Article 51. Even here, the Security Council must be informed of the exercise of this right which is allowed only until the Security Council takes action. In practice, however, the relationship between the UN and regional institutions has been rather loose and subject to considerable variation across institutions. On occasion, the UN and some regional institutions have interacted as envisioned in the Charter. But there have also been occasions when regional institutions were used to circumvent and/or undermine the United Nations. During the Cold War, American- and Soviet-led regional alliances played key roles in maintaining international peace and security, with the United Nations on the periphery. Even now the hierarchy envisioned in the Charter does not hold. The UN is still not the key player where the security concerns of major powers, especially those of the Permanent Five members of the Security Council, are concerned. The world organization can act in support of but not against them. The UN is not in a position to dictate to regional institutions, although it can deploy its moral authority and access to resources to influence regional institutions in certain situations.

The United Nations and regional institutions may occasionally be able to cooperate, one serving the interests of the other. At other times they may compete. Tension is always present in interactions between the UN and regional institutions, even when they are cooperating. Each may derive benefits from cooperating with the other, but both will also incur costs especially in terms of their purpose and autonomy. Often, each will try to preserve its independence while attempting to use the other to serve its own purposes. This tension can only be managed, not eliminated. The actual relationship between the UN and regional institutions will vary by specific institution, issue and context. A flexible approach is needed, along with some general principles or criteria to facilitate the interaction of the United Nations and regional institutions in situations when it is in their mutual interest to cooperate. Of particular relevance here is the basis for division of labour between the two institutions as well as the means to ensure accountability.

Division of labour

The earlier abstract discussion of conflict management suggested that prevention is perhaps the strong suit of regional institutions. At the intra-state level, they can play an indirect role in conflict prevention as well as encourage the pacific settlement of disputes. Regional institutions should be particularly strong in preventing the outbreak of armed conflicts among member states, but less so in preventing conflicts initiated by extra-regional actors. Regional institutions, for a number of reasons, are likely to be less strong in conflict containment and even weaker in conflict termination. This suggests that regional institutions may have a comparative advantage and therefore should take the lead in conflict prevention, while the UN or other actors may be better able to take the lead in the other stages of conflict management. This functional division of labour, however, is an abstract one that should be modified for specific cases. Several factors should be taken into account in ascertaining which institution is better placed to take the lead, and which kinds of support should be provided by other institutions:

- *Depth of interest and consequences*. Regional institutions will usually have greater interest as they will be most affected by the outcome of regional conflicts. Further, a global institution like the UN may not have equal concern with all conflicts. It would therefore appear logical for regional institutions to take the lead. But this logic may be negated by other considerations.
- *Acceptability*. This is a crucial consideration for non-acceptance by one or more parties to the conflict will undermine the potential of an operation. As regional institutions are close to a conflict and their members are likely to have vested interests, it is difficult for them to remain impartial, at least for any length of time. Consequently they may be less acceptable to one of more parties to the conflict.
- *Institutional capacity*. The organizational capacity to make decisions and implement them is critical. The components of this capacity have been identified earlier and will not be repeated here. A further capacity question to consider is whether an institution can handle an additional responsibility or whether is it already fully stretched, if not overburdened.
- *Resource availability*. Which institution has or can harness the necessary financial, human and military resources necessary to carry out the operation, and for how long? It is possible that one institution may be

strong in one resource and weak in another. This will indicate who can
provide what better.

• *Consequences for an institution.* What will be the consequences of
taking on this new responsibility for the institution? Will its credibility
be enhanced or undermined? Although it may be difficult to correctly
anticipate the consequences, it is a question that must be given due
consideration. Taking on a responsibility which is unlikely to succeed
can damage the institution and negate its other positive benefits.

Consideration of these factors provide a basis to decide who should take
the lead role and what support can be provided by the other institution.
Often, however, the division of labour is not decided a priori. It evolves
over time, sometimes fortuitously. Further, the lead role may pass from
one institution to another in the course of a conflict. The key requirement
is to remain flexible and make adjustments as required by the situation.

When the UN and a regional institution are cooperating in conflict management, the ultimate responsibility, and hence ultimate political control,
must rest with the Security Council. All other responsibilities may be
shared or delegated. The UN or a regional institution must take the lead
role in managing a certain operation with the other limiting itself to providing support. There should be no ambiguity as to who is in control.
Otherwise, not only will the success of the operation be hampered, it may
also make for tension between institutions, complicate the chain of
command, and present enormous problems of coordination and accountability.

Accountability

When a regional institution is engaged in conflict management with the
endorsement and support of the United Nations, it must remain accountable to the Security Council. Accountability means 'the ability to ensure
that a mission subcontracted by the international community to a powerful
state (or regional institution) reflects collective interests and norms and
not merely the national imperatives and preferences of the subcontractor'.[31] Accountability applies to mission and objectives, the principles
governing the conduct of the operation including impartiality and the use
of force, and the utilization of resources provided by the United Nations
which must retain oversight and not lose control of the operation. At the
same time, however, it must not seek to micro-manage an operation that is
being led by a regional institution. A proper balance between losing
control and micro-managing has to be struck. Accountability may be

difficult to achieve in practice especially if a major power is the driving force of a regional institution. The leverage available to the UN to ensure accountability is limited to its moral authority and at times the resources that it can make available. The latter is only a consideration with respect to regional institutions in the developing world. It is therefore important to define clearly mission, objectives and principles at the outset, and make UN endorsement and continued support conditional upon strict adherence to the initial terms. That changes to the initial terms can only be authorized by the Security Council must also be stipulated at the outset.

One or more of several measures may be employed to ensure accountability. First, the initial authorization of a mission should be for a specific, often limited, duration. Each extension will have to be re-authorized by the Security Council. This would provide an opportunity for the council to exercise oversight and retain control over the mission. Second, UN personnel may be injected into the command and control system to provide guidance and assistance, as well as to report back to the UN. Third, a separate joint body comprising personnel from the UN, a regional institution and other interested parties may be constituted to oversee the implementation of a mission. Fourth, the UN may appoint a special envoy to undertake the same function. The choice of measures will depend on the situation and the degree of oversight sought. This cannot be determined without reference to context.

A related issue is action when UN terms are violated or if the delegated power and authority have been abused. Here the options available to the world organization are limited. It can withdraw its endorsement, but this may not be possible if the target institution has influence in the Security Council. The only option then would be not to re-authorize the mission. But for this to be possible, the initial endorsement must be for a limited duration and must expire at the opportune moment. Failing this, the UN may have to resort to mobilizing international norms and opinion through the General Assembly and/or attempt to persuade the regional institution or actor to comply with the initial mission, goals and principles.

CONCLUSION

Approaches to international security in the post-Cold War world have to be multilayered, comprising several arrangements and actors. No single arrangement or actor will be sufficient. Regional institutions and the United Nations can each play an invaluable role in conflict management, but there are clear limitations for both. Task-sharing and cooperation

could help overcome some of these limitations. An effective partnership
between global and regional institutions depends on a good understanding of the possibilities and limitations of each, an effective division of
labour, and accountability of the various institutions involved in managing a specific conflict. Although no firm basis can be applied to all occasions and flexibility is required, this chapter has set forth an analytical
framework to investigate and understand the possible roles and limitations of regional institutions, identified factors that must be considered in
the division of labour between global and regional institutions, and suggested some ways of ensuring accountability when regional institutions
cooperate with the United Nations in maintaining international peace
and security.

NOTES

1. For an elaboration, see Muthiah Alagappa, 'Regionalism and conflict man-
    agement: a framework for analysis', *Review of International Studies*, 21 (4),
    1995, pp. 359–87.
2. For a good account of the deliberation on regionalism versus globalism in
    the context of the formulation of the UN Charter, see Inis J. Claude, Jr, 'The
    OAS, the UN, and the United States', *International Conciliation*, 547,
    March 1964, pp. 3–60. See also his *Swords into Plowshares: The Problems
    and Progress of International Organization* (New York: Random House,
    1971), pp. 102–17.
3. Gareth Evans, 'The United Nations: Co-operating for Peace', address to the
    Forty-Eighth General Assembly of the United Nations, 27 September 1993.
4. For an overview of the effort to define a region, see Bruce M. Russett,
    'International regions and the international system', in Richard A. Falk and
    Saul H. Mendlovitz (eds), *Regional Politics and World Order* (San
    Francisco: W. H. Freeman, 1973), pp. 181–7. On the effort to define a re-
    gional subsystem and specify the necessary and sufficient conditions for it,
    see William R. Thompson, 'The regional subsystem: a conceptual explica-
    tion and a propositional inventory', *International Studies Quarterly*, 17 (1),
    1973, pp. 89–117.
5. Among the few definitions of regionalism are those by Donald J. Puchala
    and Stuart I. Fanagan, and by Joseph Nye. See Puchala and Fanagan,
    'International politics in the 1970s: the search for a perspective',
    International Organization, 28 (2), 1974, p. 259, and Nye, *International
    Regionalism* (Boston: Little, Brown, 1968), p. vii.
6. On issues and issue-areas, see Ernst B. Haas, 'Why collaborate? Issue-
    linkage and international regimes', *World Politics*, 32 (3), 1980, pp. 364–7.
7. On 'nesting', see Vino Aggarwal, *Liberal Protectionism* (Berkeley:
    University of California Press, 1985), p. 27.

8. On negative and positive peace and the debate among peace studies scholars, see Johan Galtung, 'Violence, peace and peace research', *Journal of Peace Research*, 6 (6), 1969, pp. 167–91; and Carolyn M. Stephenson, 'The evolution of peace studies', in Michael Klare and Daniel Thomas (eds), *Peace and World Order Studies: A Curriculum Guide*, 5th edn (Boulder, Colo.: Westview Press, 1989), pp. 9–19.

9. See Muthiah Alagappa, 'Defining security: a critical review and appraisal of the debate', in Muthiah Alagappa (ed.), *Asian Conceptions of Security: Ideational and Material* (forthcoming).

10. There is a growing body of literature that questions the effectiveness of the sovereign state and its continued relevance as the referent unit of security. It should be acknowledged here that (a) the scope of state sovereignty in a number of issue-areas like human rights, monetary and financial matters, and production is becoming substantially limited; that (b) non-state actors (subnational and international) have proliferated and in some cases play a central role in domestic and international regulation in the specific issue-area of their concern; and that (c) the state can protect as well as oppress its citizens. These developments, by no means uniform across states, should be given due consideration in analysis and policy-making, but they should not be interpreted as eclipsing the importance of the state. The sovereign state continues to be the most effective unit with respect to political identity and allegiance as well as to the fulfilment of the security and welfare functions, and it is the principal actor in the international system. The proliferation of secessionist movements, while reflective of the weakness of the constitution of specific states, is not indicative of the obsolescence of the state. On the contrary, it is a vindication of the state's continued vitality. The goal of the secessionist movements is to create new states in which the fit between ethno- or religious-nation and state will be closer and in which their ethnic or religious group will become the *Staatsvolk*, the dominant ethnic group that controls state power.

11. See Kenneth N. Waltz, *Theory of International Politics* (New York: Random House, 1979), pp. 102–28.

12. On the security dilemma, see John H. Herz, 'Idealist internationalism and the security dilemma', *World Politics*, 2 (2), 1950, pp. 157–80; Robert Jervis, *Perception and Misperception in International Politics* (Princeton, NJ: Princeton University Press, 1976, pp. 72–6; and Barry Buzan, *People, States and Fear: An Agenda for International Security Studies in the Post-Cold War Era* (Boulder, Colo.: Lynne Rienner, 1991), Chapter 8.

13. The two components of the security dilemma derive from Waltz's three-image analysis of world politics. He posits the third image (the structure) as describing the framework of world politics and as the permissive cause of war, and the first and second images (man and the state) as the forces of world politics, the immediate or efficient causes of war. See his *Man, the State and War* (New York: Columbia University Press, 1959). Barry Buzan terms the two components as the power dilemma and the security dilemma, and their combination as the power-security dilemma. See his *People, States and Fear*, pp. 294–8.

14. Benedict Anderson *Imagined Communities* (London: Verso, 1992), p. 6. See also Clifford Geertz, *The Interpretation of Cultures* (New York: Basic Books, 1973), pp. 317–19.

15.   For a discussion of the formation of national-territorial states in the Third World, see Anthony D. Smith, *State and the Nation in the Third World* (New York: St. Martin's Press, 1983), Chapter 7.

16.   The phrase 'internal colonialism' is used by Michael Hechter, *Internal Colonialism: The Celtic Fringe in British National Development* (Berkeley: University of California Press, 1975).

17.   For an expanded discussion of the problem of political legitimacy, see Muthiah Alagappa (ed.), *Political Legitimacy in Southeast Asia: The Quest for Moral Authority* (Palo Alto, Calif.: Stanford University Press, 1995), Chapters 1–3.

18.   For the differences between conflict settlement and resolution, see C. R. Mitchell, *The Structure of International Conflict* (New York: St. Martin's Press, 1981), pp. 275–7.

19.   This and the next section draw extensively on Alagappa, 'Regionalism and conflict management'.

20.   See Karl Deutsch, *Political Community and the North Atlantic Area* (Westport, Conn.: Greenwood, Press, 1957), pp. 5–7.

21.   See Claude, *Swords into Ploughshares*, pp. 245–85. See also Jerome Slater, *A Re-evaluation of Collective Security: The OAS in Action*, Mershon National Security Program Pamphlet Series No. 1 (Columbus: Ohio State University Press, 1965), pp. 9–23; George W. Downs (ed.), *Collective Security Beyond the Cold War* (Ann Arbor: University of Michigan Press, 1994); and Thomas G. Weiss (ed.), *Collective Security and Changing World Politics* (Boulder, Colo.: Lynne Rienner, 1993).

22.   On intermediation, qualifications required, and the intervenor's repertory of practice, see Oran R. Young, *The Intermediaries* (Princeton: Princeton University Press, 1967), pp 50–79.

23.   For a discussion of the evolution of the principle of non-intervention in the inter-American system, see G. Pope Atkins, *Latin America in the International Political System* (Boulder, Colo.: Westview Press, 1989), pp. 215–18.

24.   See Laura W. Reed and Carl Kayson (eds), *Emerging Norms of Justified Intervention* (Cambridge, Mass.: American Academy of Arts and Sciences, 1993).

25.   On the growing force of human rights regime in Latin America, see Kathryn Sikkink, 'Human rights, principled issue-networks, and sovereignty in Latin America', *International Organization*, 47, Summer 1993, pp. 411–41. On the weakness of the regime in Africa, see Claude E. Welch, 'The OAU and human rights: regional promotion of human rights', in Yassin El-Ayoutty (ed.), *The Organization of African Unity Thirty Years On* (Westport, Conn.: Greenwood Press, 1994), pp. 53–76.

26.   Richard J. Bloomfield, 'Making the Western hemisphere safe for democracy? The OAS defense-of-democracy regime', *The Washington Quarterly*, 17 (2), Spring 1994, pp. 157–69, quote at p. 162.

27.   'ASEAN Joint Statement on the Situation in the Philippines', in *ASEAN Document Series 1967–1986*, issued by the ASEAN Secretariat in Jakarta, 1986, p. 469.

28.   Yassin El-Ayoutty, 'An OAU for the future', in El-Ayoutty (ed.), *The Organization of African Unity Thirty Years On*, p. 179.

29.   According to R. K. Ramazani, 'the overriding pre-GCC concern of Saudi Arabia with the security and stability of the House of Saud and other royal families' contributed to the creation of the GCC. See his *The Gulf Cooperation Council: Record and Analysis* (Charlottesville: University of North Carolina Press, 1988), pp. 1–11.

30.   For a similar discussion of a somewhat different list of factors, see Michael Barnett, 'Partners in peace? The UN, regional organizations, and peace keeping', *Review of International Studies*, 21 (4), 1995, pp. 420–24.

31.   Jarat Chopra and Thomas G. Weiss, 'The United Nations and the former Second World: coping with conflicts', in Abram Chayes and Antonia Chayes (eds), *Preventing Conflict in the Post-Communist World* (Washington, DC: The Brookings Institution, 1996), p. 529.

2 Devolving Responsibilities: a Framework for Analysing NGOs and Services

Leon Gordenker and Thomas G. Weiss

Five essays in this volume examine the work of non-governmental organizations (NGOs) in specific sectors of important international concern. This introduction to those chapters sets out common groundwork for their enquiry. The common working hypothesis is based on an earlier research project[1] that included a series of functional case studies[2] touching on efforts by the United Nations (UN) and associated agencies to channel resources to NGOs:

> As part of a 'privatising'[3] of world politics and the emergence of a global civil society, bilateral and multilateral organisations are increasingly relying upon NGOs. To the extent that this is true and either beneficial or detrimental for enhanced global governance – that is, working for or against better solutions to or management of problems that extend beyond the capacity of individual states – a policy prescription would follow: this trend could and should be either accelerated or attenuated.

At least five basic questions are implied in the working hypothesis and the earlier research. These questions are explicitly posed here, along with some plausible policy notions that emanate from them. The following chapters provide fuller illustrations and partial answers to the questions regarding relief in war zones, election monitoring, development assistance and environmental action. Generalizations, to the extent that they are defensible, are drawn together in the concluding essay to this volume. In all of the studies, the central phenomenon under observation is the practice by intergovernmental organizations (IGOs) of 'contracting out'[4] work to NGOs that is intended to fulfil the mandates of both the intergovernmental and non-governmental organizations.

IS 'NGO' A USEFUL CATEGORY FOR EXAMINING
CONTRACTING FOR SERVICES BY THE UNITED NATIONS?

In the UN system, the role of NGOs was originally defined primarily in a
legal sense as opposed to a functional one. The legal definition, based on
Article 71 of the UN Charter and the rules of procedure embodied in
Resolution 1296 (XLIV) that the Economic and Social Council
(ECOSOC) adopted in 1968, treats NGOs as either consultative bodies
related to ECOSOC or to the official governing bodies for other UN
organizations and bodies.[5] NGO participation in setting agendas and in
making appearances to advocate policies fell under strict intergovernmental control. These legal rules increasingly have become obsolete and
difficult to adapt to changing conditions. They hardly ever represented the
variety of actual relationships which could be portrayed as a continuum
ranging from dependency, interdependence and independence to isolation
and virtual opposition.

NGOs have increasingly exploited another sort of relationship that
neither was envisaged nor fitted under the ECOSOC parliament-style
definition. It has the attributes of conventional business and is nothing new
for IGOs. In this sense, NGOs are vendors of goods and services on the
basis of a contract that would be similar to those enforceable in national
courts. This capacity, for which there is a rich array of examples in a
growing literature,[6] includes much of the subject matter for the cases in
this volume. It involves a wide variety of links including everything from
treaty-like multilevel, multiparty contracts between NGOs and donor governments and IGOs, to NGOs selling simple services to recipient governments, to long-term deals between international and grassroots NGOs.[7]

The NGOs considered here are non-profit organizations – that is, they
are private in form but public in purpose. Thus, a great many private organizations that do business with the United Nations and make profits are excluded. However, the term 'NGO' does need to encompass two groups
whose acronyms have entered the lexicon of contemporary international
affairs: 'public service contractors' (PSCs) – that is, market-oriented non-
profit businesses serving public purposes – and 'private voluntary organizations' (PVOs) – driven more by concern with values than with bottom
lines and markets.[8] More and more NGOs appear to function as hybrids of
PSCs and PVOs, combining both strong market skills and orientation with
a clear social commitment.

Furthermore, on some occasions entities representing industrial or other sectoral interests have developed relationships with IGO personnel and have tried to affect the policy process. Such sectoral groups do not aim directly at profit-making, but they find their sole support in profit-making industry and commerce. How far such interest groups conform to what is understood as 'NGO' remains controversial.

Even such a general description and definition leaves a great deal of uncertainty about precisely what NGOs, in fact, could do under which circumstances, which specific qualities that they possess, and which types of contracted and subcontracted services are appropriately assumed by them. It also implicitly raises and leaves open the question as to whether increased public financing through contracts may weaken the NGO capacity for independent initiatives. This concern involves a central preoccupation of NGO partisans for whom autonomous activity defines their very *raison d'être*. In this regard, some UN institutions and some NGOs have already developed relationships of fairly standard sorts,[9] and others employ variants of them. Whether such standard relationships in fact limit initiatives remains unclear. The whole subject is well worth further exploration.

Advocacy organizations

Intergovernmental bodies of the UN system may well encounter the most uncertainty and difficulty in entering into contracts for services with NGOs whose core functions are to advocate particular policies or ideologies, which without embarrassment some describe as a global 'conscience'.[10] The inherently controversial nature of their missions, which seek to oppose existing governmental policies and eventually to change them, may pose particularly dramatic issues in regard to human rights or the environment. Yet in these fields, international agendas have been in large part affected or even determined by NGOs whose values are clear and are anything except neutral. They spur visceral resistance and defensiveness from governments that they criticize. More likely than not, governments subjected to such criticism will attempt to restrain UN relationships with highly critical and influential NGOs. As a result, the UN will not be likely, or perhaps well-advised, to experiment with organizations, however willing, whose experience or scope has not already demonstrated the capacity to render the services sought rather than merely to have advocated new policies and pressed for their adoption.

NGO size and scope

The size and scope of NGOs no doubt affects their abilities to relate to the United Nations. Coalitions and federations of large organizations may be more convenient partners for the administrators of large international agencies than atomized forms of non-governmental organizations. Furthermore, solid performance in one functional or geographical arena makes larger NGOs familiar to bilateral and IGO administrators who subsequently are more likely to call on them for other assignments. The need to be 'competitive' for contracts also incites NGOs to abandon any sectoral or geographical specialization in favour of a more comprehensive organizational structure. The expansion of subcontracts from larger to smaller NGOs (especially toward local ones) is desirable and possible, although there are precious few analyses of the problems of 'scaling down'.[11]

Terminology and definition

The term 'NGO' obviously evokes mixed reactions. For those who opine that governments inherently are wicked or incompetent, it may be attractive. For those who believe that government can serve socially useful purposes, it tends to define an opposition. Moreover, the practice of intergovernmental organizations with regard to NGO relationships makes clear that it is a topic characterized by dynamic developments and lagging organizational and legal adaptations.

Nevertheless, the conventional terminology of 'NGOs', 'IGOs' and 'governments' is employed here simply because it is familiar and calls attention to a body of practice. Its use is neither intended to prejudge the value of NGOs nor to insist on an immutable definition. Indeed part of the rationale for the examination of NGO contracting with IGOs is the hope that further clarification of the relationship will emerge.

WHAT CAN NGOs DO BETTER THAN IGOs?

Transnational NGOs can operate with a minimum of filtration of their services through governmental channels. Such an operational style is widely regarded as according with the general acceptance of social decision-making through the operation of markets. This idea may oversimplify the behaviour of NGOs, which in fact display a wide range of approaches to

relations with official institutions as well as to competition for creating
and managing them.

The cultural normal operating style of NGOs encourages a large number
of informal contacts. These involve governmental personnel and that of
other NGOs. Information is exchanged among them. In what is quite
likely a growing number of cases, NGO personnel join IGO staffs and vice
versa for varying periods. Consequently NGOs individually and working
in concert may have access to more complete, less managed information
about their terrain of work than either IGO or governmental agents.

NGOs do not necessarily depend on governmental establishments for the
execution of their policies, as is the case for most recommendations and programmes emanating from organizations of the UN system. NGOs can,
moreover, choose to give effect to international policies and programmes
while avoiding the incapacities, malfeasances or domination of both the
donor and recipient governments that play different and sometimes
conflictual roles as member states in IGOs and their governing bodies.

Governmental grasp

Except for the unusual case of humanitarian intervention, NGOs hardly
can operate completely outside of governmental grasp; but neither does
their work, if tactfully done, necessarily openly derogate from or erode
governmental authority. Governments tend to be extremely sensitive about
what national civil servants perceive as avoidance or interference with legitimate authority. NGO operations in connection with a UN programme
therefore can involve long, detailed negotiations aimed at dispelling novelty
and ignorance and setting operational modes and forestalling difficulties
about the application of authority. Consequently, working out standard,
model memoranda of understanding (MOU) for use among UN organizations, potential recipient countries and prospective NGO subcontractors
could perhaps streamline wasteful procedures and unnecessary frictions.

Other considerations of a less business-like character may have a
bearing (both positive and negative) on reactions by recipient governments. Many are at least ambivalent and often hostile about the formation
of grassroots and intermediary NGOs, for which development efforts
provide a considerable experience.[12] Some governments harbour suspicions of the expatriates whom NGOs usually employ to supervise or
inspect activities. This suspicion easily develops into accusations of espi-
onage against NGOs. In other instances, NGO practices conflict with such
local practices as paying bribes to governmental counterparts or ignoring
women's right in respect of local cultural norms. Beyond that, some

governments support legal preferences for domestic businesses and con-tractors, which reduces the freedom of operation for international NGOs.

Yet operations by such outsiders and their personnel are usually subject to fewer restraints from diplomatic protocol than is the case for programmes directly administered by bilateral or intergovernmental aid agencies; their activities always involve formal representation in capitals and official approval from the host authorities. The demands of diplomatic protocol may constrain their wish to innovate. In contrast, NGOs usually emphasize getting on with the job over the niceties of diplomacy.

Prickly issues

NGOs have the indisputable capacity to pose thorny questions and ensure especially intense surveillance in places where recipient governmental au-thority is contested or abusive. Human rights, the environment and relief in war zones figure prominently among these issues. They pose such far-reaching challenges that governmental and intergovernmental personnel have far greater difficulties than usual in openly seeking changes in gov-ernmental practice or supporting the arguments of the opposition. The extent to which NGOs are seen as an extension of the United Nations or as an alternative whose relevance is looked upon askance or with favour by local authorities is influenced by such factors as the following.

Inimical policies
The policies that the UN itself has adopted in a highly politicized (such as a security) situation may be regarded by one or more opposing parties, whether unarmed or armed, as inimical and unacceptable. Any NGOs in-volved in executing or rightly or wrongly associated with contested inter-governmental initiatives would come under similar suspicion, and their personnel could also be endangered. Consequently, in tense, controversial or dangerous situations, NGO involvement would be limited by the general organizational policies and restrictions of each organization and by the willingness of NGO personnel to be involved.

Intense conflict
In arenas of intense armed conflict among politically driven factions in both intra- and inter-state wars, the ability of NGOs to gain access to clients, either through governments or directly to individuals, may be as severely limited as for IGOs. No non-governmental organization is really well equipped to operate on anything but a very small scale where fighting is active, although some traditional and long-standing relationships may

actually open the way to the delivery of some services even in highly
politicized contexts. This has been the case, for example, for some NGOs
operating in Afghanistan and Somalia.

Threat to sovereignty

Some secretive or repressive governments claim that NGO operations routinely violate the reserved areas of domestic jurisdiction and represent a
serious threat to the state. This is hardly more than a primitive fiction. The
purported threat to sovereignty is often used by insecure governments or
political authorities whose own legitimacy is already shaky and whose
grasp of their territories and people has already been loosened. NGOs
practically always work with explicit or tacit permission from local authorities. If none exists, as in the case of imploding or failed states, there
can hardly be a violation of sovereignty. At the same time, changes in the
content and procedures of world politics over the last decade have created
subtle pressures on state sovereignty by both international and indigenous
NGOs. Economic malpractice, structural adjustment policies, and the
wave of liberalization and democratization have meant that NGOs have
expanded their delivery functions to take in some social services formerly
provided by state authorities. This often takes place with the encouragement of donors and within a climate that sometimes verges on blind
infatuation with privatization.[13]

Rather than displacement of sovereignty from the state to NGOs, the
real issue when the government fails to function has to do with the effect
of NGO programmes on the future of governing arrangements. It is con-
ceivable that an NGO programme could instil entirely new values in the
population that it encounters. This in turn could deeply affect the eventual
character of governing structures.

Special advantages

Non-governmental organizations can offer distinct benefits regarding the
use of their personnel in a contractual devolution of operational responsibility from the UN system. Some NGOs, especially the larger ones that
have actively sought to augment the professional qualifications of their
staffs, include highly trained and experienced personnel. They could serve
– in fact, many have already served – in field operations of various types
of organizations (governmental, intergovernmental or non-governmental).
Many NGO staff members have capacities and expertise in policy-making
and overall supervision of transnational programmes that are at least as
substantial as those of international civil servants. More specific study and

knowledge of the extent to which there is movement from NGO to UN employment, and vice versa, would make clear how comparable staffs may be and to what extent learning from one type of institution is applied in another.

From the point of view of international organizations, NGO personnel are available without the customary long recruitment process and without long-term contracts. Their numbers can be expanded and contracted far more easily than is the case with permanent staff appointed to intergovernmental secretariats or even those serving on limited-term UN contracts. Their assignment is not subject to the vagaries of geographical distribution that inhibit UN appointments. The costs of employing NGO personnel through their organizations are also likely to be lower than those of international civil servants – less than half on average, although the senior staff of prominent NGOs may be as well paid as UN officials.

This expertness and flexibility could thus be particularly advantageous when Western parliaments insist upon the restructuring and continual adaptations that are relevant to organizational shibboleths for many domestic audiences. These often are administratively awkward for an international civil service founded on the Nobelmaire principles, applied since the earlier days of the League of Nations, which hold that international officials should be paid at a rate comparable with the best of the national civil services and engaged for permanent tenure. As for the use of NGOs, rather than commercial organizations, the conceptual rationale points to the perceived disadvantages (that is, profits) of the latter in the provision of public goods. At the same time and from the point of view of costs, flexibility and efficiency, market forces are at work that contribute to treating NGOs as preferable to governmental and intergovernmental bureaucracies.

WHAT ARE THE MOST IMPORTANT CONSTRAINTS THAT APPLY TO BRINGING NGOs INTO UN PROGRAMMES?

The most general constraints, mentioned earlier, arise from the inherently dynamic, variegated nature of the relationship between the United Nations, NGOs and host governments. Still others relate to the specific context of using NGO services, of which four come specifically to mind.

Policy-making

International policy-making without active and direct NGO participation may limit the latter's interest in and understanding of UN programmes. A variety of methods from parallel forums for global *ad hoc* conferences to joint working groups have evolved over the last quarter century. If, however, particular NGOs effectively participate in policy-making, the result could be jealousy or misunderstanding among them and non-participating NGOs (particularly local NGOs without transnational part-ners). Moreover, there is almost always opposition from insecure governments that insist, with few exceptions, on unsullied state participa-tion in making and administering the policies and programmes of UN organizations.

NGO autonomy

The degree of autonomy that they will enjoy in carrying out internation-ally approved programmes is also a recurring question for NGOs. Given their emphases on voluntary activities, distance from 'politics' and inde-pendence, they are likely to press for a minimum of supervision from both governments and intergovernmental organizations. But in order to justify contracts to non-governmental organizations, governments and IGOs also have to answer to their constituencies and fiscal authorities about the quality of the programmes sponsored by them but actually carried out by NGOs. The debate that arose during the Cold War among NGOs about the pluses and minuses of public financing will doubtless resume, perhaps with the same intensity in light of the increasing resources being chan-nelled to them from public sources. It would bring into renewed usage an almost forgotten acronym, GONGOs (government-organized NGOs), while a new and even more awkward acronym, UNONGOs (UN-organized NGOs), may become more familiar. In that light, it may be expected that NGO directors will seriously weigh the benefits and costs of contracts to determine whether their terms of engagement as primary contractors for donors result in an unacceptable loss of autonomy or of flexibility to play catalytic roles.[14]

Programme execution

Appropriate methods and procedures for executing programmes and the adequacy of expatriate staff also can become issues for NGOs. Generally, IGOs have greater strength in designing policies and implementing pro-jects than in evaluating their results, and this generalization applies to NGOs with at least as much salience as they weigh the relative merits of providing concrete assistance versus evaluating previous policies, projects and programmes. Financial backers as well as NGOs are proud of their activist 'culture', which creates an almost visceral unwillingness in principle to devote scarce resources to research and reflection. This reluctance raises questions as to the degree that any learning from experience takes places and is transmitted to others in the field or to succeeding generations.

At the same time, the tradition of voluntary service in the NGO culture may result in the recruitment of well-intentioned individuals who for one reason or another fail to adapt to field conditions or otherwise to render satisfactory services. Their presence can lead to friction with the local government and distress among IGO supervisors. Furthermore, specific operational problems – for example, related to accounting for expenditures, reimbursement procedures, restrictions of budget modifications and cultural sensitivities – may come to loom large in the provision of public services by some non-profit agencies. An additional element of complexity arises from the growing practice among donors of earmarking finances for programmes or projects and demanding strict accounting for the use of their contributions. Such provisions can require expensive adaptations that add little but trouble to field operations. In addition, the use of NGO personnel in dangerous situations raises issues of liability that have not been fully explored.

These are structural weaknesses, or strengths according to true-believers. Most emanate from the dominant operational styles of NGOs and may come to constrain the expansion of contracting or to foster the consolidation and homogenization of non-governmental organizations.

Government reactions

Pressure from government representatives may develop in the decisional organs of IGOs concerning the devolution of operations to NGOs, even if in principle it is agreed that letting and supervising contracts falls within the legitimate purview of international secretariats. NGOs may find themselves scrutinized and criticized in new ways when governmental delegations make representations, complain, protest and generally display opposition to the activities of NGOs that have been contracted for work by a particular UN organization. Moreover, it can be expected that in those national governmental organs that examine contributions to UN budgets, additional pressure can develop to control options and activities by NGOs as ancillary to policies and financing that are for whatever reason under domestic attack.

WHAT CAN BE DONE TO IMPROVE THE ACCOUNTABILITY OF NGOs?

Contracting to NGOs has become a substantial business, but this market is now essentially unregulated. As in the case for devolving responsibility to regional organizations for activities to preserve international security that forms the other focus for this volume,[15] the need to enhance and ensure international accountability to the authority authorizing a contract to an NGO will undoubtedly involve increasing pressures to oversee the conduct of those that accept contracts.[16]

Rules of the game exist even in the most free market as, for example, anti-cartel rules and prohibition against price-fixing by vendors of products. The idea that a need exists for international 'anti-trust legislation' is far-fetched.[17] Yet the question arises as to whether NGOs will eventually be driven to self-regulation or will be regulated by governments (in countries where NGOs work or are incorporated) or by the United Nations. Among the emerging issues are the following.

NGO governance

ECOSOC rules for consultative status provide that accredited NGOs be democratically governed. This provision has not, in fact, ever been enforced or even understood. For the most part and in spite of their lofty rhetoric, NGOs are formed by members and leaders who act on their own initiative – that is, they are self-appointed. Once an organization is established, its leadership is selected by internal processes that might in some instances be nothing more complicated than appointing acquaintances and coopting successors. Nevertheless, a great many NGOs that are not really democratic are perfectly competent to offer services – for example, university research institutes. Moreover, NGOs are probably no less accountable than many other members of civil society – for example, business and the media – or even than governments and UN organizations.

It is likely, however, that the internal policy-making and governing practices among NGOs varies from casual to rule-bound, from inherently autocratic to exemplarily democratic. To what extent internal governance structures of NGOs are actually consequential for accepting contracts and for subcontracting requires additional scrutiny.

As mentioned earlier, nobody knows to whom NGOs are answerable. This lack of democratic legitimacy, however, does not mean that NGOs cannot be consulted by UN personnel before technical decisions are made on matters with which NGOs are concerned or expert. In this narrower sense, NGOs could make up some of the gap in representation that the diplomatic nature of the UN creates. In other words, the presence of NGO contractors could help make the United Nations better informed and more representative of changing world politics and popular opinion even if not truly more democratic in decision-making. This does not mean, however, that NGOs can therefore simply be expected to serve as a surrogate for a popular representative organ in the absence of what is often referred to in proposals as a 'People's General Assembly'.

UN oversight

More contracting to NGOs raises serious questions about responsibility and accountability, but the United Nations is not now really equipped organizationally to deal with them. There is no popular representative organ on either side of the relationship between the UN and NGOs. In light of the present poor public profile of the world organization in much of the Western world, will increased contracting to NGOs weaken or strengthen the credibility and authority, such as they are, of the United Nations?

Measuring accountability

General accountability is a topic that encompasses much unexplored territory, even for those NGOs that have developed policies that circumscribe their work with IGOs. Little empirical information is available to answer such basic questions as: What kind of contracts may be accepted? How are NGO personnel permitted to operate in conjunction with a contract with an IGO? Would accreditation be sensible, and if so by whom? To what extent are they equipped to take the wishes and auditing practices of the end-users (that is, clients or recipient governments or political authorities) into account rather than primarily those of financial backers? What provisions are there for financial responsibility? What research and development products are involved in the operations of an NGO? To what degree is an NGO prepared to work in coalitions or federations?

Toward a new model?

As for accountability and responsibility, contracting for NGO services allows, in theory at least, a clear separation between overall policy (that is, the formulation of norms, principles, decisional procedures) and supervision, on the one hand, and the actual operational conduct of programmes, on the other. In light of changing world politics and with increased cost-effectiveness in mind, a clearer alternative model could be developed: the UN could exclusively orchestrate policy and monitoring, while NGOs could deliver specific contracted activities. Whatever the exact nature of the division of labour between IGOs and NGOs, there will undoubtedly be a growing role for NGOs' structuring their own collaboration and professionalism through *ad hoc* mechanisms or standing voluntary consortia like the Geneva-based International Council of Voluntary Agencies (ICVA) or the Washington-based InterAction.[18]

It probably would be futile to try to organize comprehensive structures for generally relating NGOs to the United Nations for the convenience of administrators, but perhaps this could be attempted for specialized matters or on particular occasions or in specific geographical arenas. *Ad hoc* arrangements of this kind are subject matter for policy leaders who build coalitions rather than for bureaucracies that follow rules. Could we anticipate the rise of a new kind of coalition leader growing out of increasing delegation of activities to NGOs?

WHAT ARE WE LEARNING ABOUT THE RELATIONSHIPS AMONG NGOs, IGOs AND WORLD CIVIL SOCIETY?

NGOs may be developing and increasingly playing a profound, even crucial, role in fostering and creating a world civil society. It is characterized by multiple organizational and personal relationships largely outside the purview of state control. Such relationships ebb and flow and hardly conform to conventional conceptions of authority and hierarchy. They rest rather on specific choices of activities and policies, which can be linked in dynamic coalitions in a highly pluralistic context. If this is so, then the nature of IGO programmes and projects will necessarily be affected. Moreover, a broader process of change affecting attempts at global governance through IGOs that depend mainly on intergovernmental cooperation would simultaneously also be initiated. These developments, even if they prove short-lived or incomplete, will challenge conventional understandings and analyses of world politics.

Contracts between the United Nations system and non-governmental organizations to help carry out international programmes offer the observer an accessible and practical lens through which to view and analyse the processes that foster world civil society in our era. In acting as contractors, NGOs could extend the reach and scope of IGO programmes, bringing them closer to the ultimate recipients and thereby enlisting their collaboration. If such potentials take root, private groups would increasingly be brought into contact with UN programmes. This could be expected to enhance the legitimacy of such activity and give a concrete tone to UN programmes that otherwise would have a distant relationship to ultimate consumers.

In the process, NGOs might well pioneer in forming a new kind of transnational society in which individuals and their voluntary associations replace IGOs and governments as the immediate sources of various social services now usually associated with the territorially based state. In advancing such an outcome, NGOs would presumably have the advantage of sensitivity to social changes and their causal dynamics. If they were to surpass governments in the quality or even quantity of certain social services, they would collectively serve as substantial agents of change although the contribution of any particular NGO might have only modest proportions.

As agents of change, non-governmental organizations would establish new and essential lines of communications to introduce ideas, train individuals and help create alternative institutions. There is good reason to conclude that NGOs already have set up lines of communications among themselves that skirt the familiar dimensions of the state and its control devices. These channels may already be taking up some of the gaps opened by the end of the Cold War and would support tendencies towards nurturing a wider sense of human community. Yet if NGOs openly attempt, as UN contractors, to use their activities to modify substantially governmental policies or transform local social mores, they may create new controversies and frustrate the achievement of their own aims. By proceeding tactlessly, they could in fact stimulate and ultimately renew the strength of governmental authority whose exercise they oppose. This would also tend to block the acceptance by incensed government personnel of the international programmes that NGOs have contracted to execute.

The dynamism and variety in the NGO universe ensures that no monolithic march in any direction may be expected. Yet it is that very untidiness which can irritate diplomats and administrators that opens opportunities for collaboration with IGOs on a contractual basis. If these opportunities also include dangers to the autonomy of NGOs as well as governmental authority, they may also include the prospect of a change in the nature of international relations. With those prospects in mind, the five case studies of NGOs in action are an analytical step toward understanding the dynamics in world civil society at the dawn of the twenty-first century.

NOTES

1. Leon Gordenker and Thomas G. Weiss, 'Pluralizing global governance: analytical approaches and dimensions' and 'NGO participation in the international policy process', in Thomas G. Weiss and Leon Gordenker (eds), *NGOs, the UN, and Global Governance* (Boulder Colo.: Lynne Rienner, 1996), pp. 17–47 and 209–221.

2. In ibid., see Felice D. Gaer, 'Reality check: human rights NGOs confront governments at the UN', pp. 51–66; Andrew S. Natsios, 'NGOs and the UN system in complex humanitarian emergencies', pp. 67–82; Ken Conca, 'Greening the UN: environmental organizations and the UN system', pp. 103–19; Christer Söderholm and Peter Jönsson, 'IGO-NGO relations and HIV/AIDS: innovation or stalemate?', pp. 121–38; and Martha Alter Chen, 'Engendering world conferences: the International Women's Movement and the UN', pp. 139–55.

3. This term is in quotes because it means the provision of public goods financed with public resources but carried out by private organizations; this should be distinguished from the enchantment with the notion of eliminating public services altogether. For a discussion, see Steven R. Smith and Michael Lipsky, *Non-Profits for Hire: The Welfare State in the Age of Contracting* (Cambridge, Mass.: Harvard University Press, 1993); and Lester Salamon and Helmut Anheier, *The Emerging Sector: An Overview* (Baltimore Md.: The Johns Hopkins Institute for Policy Studies, 1994).

4. This phrase refers to the mutually agreed devolution of obligations from an intergovernmental body to an NGO. It may take the form of a specific, legally binding contract or may result from an informal agreement. The latter sometimes is only tacit but nevertheless real. Such devolution usually involves quite specific tasks and in principle excludes the duty of making authoritative social decisions.

5. For further discussion, see Gordenker and Weiss, 'Pluralizing global governance', pp. 21–3.

6. For an annotated bibliography, see Weiss and Gordenker (eds), *NGOs*, pp. 227–40.

7. See Peter Sollis, 'Partners in development? The state, NGOs, and the UN in Central America', in ibid., pp. 189–206; and Paul Nelson, *The World Bank and Non-Governmental Organizations* (New York: St. Martin's Press, 1995), especially Chapters 4–6.

8. David Korten, *Getting to the 21st Century: Voluntary Action and the Global Agenda* (West Hartford, Conn.: Kumarian Press, 1990), especially pp. 102–5.

9. See Nelson, *The World*, pp. 71–4 for the example of the World Bank.

10. For example, see Peter Willetts (ed.), *The Conscience of the World: The Influence of Non-Governmental Organizations in the U.N. System* (London: Hurst, 1996).

11. See Peter Uvin, 'Scaling up the grassroots and scaling down the summit: the relations between Third World NGOs and the UN', in Weiss and Gordenker (eds), *NGOs*, pp. 159–76.

12. See Ian Smillie, *The Alms Bazaar: Altruism Under Fire – Non-profit Organizations and International Development* (London: IT Publications, 1995).

13. See Antonio Donini, 'The bureaucracy and the free spirits: stagnation and innovation in the relationship between the UN and NGOs', in Weiss and Gordenker (eds), *NGOs*, pp. 83–101.
14. See a series of essays in David Hulme and Michael Edwards (eds), *Too Close for Comfort? NGOs, States and Donors* (West Hartford, Conn.: Kumarian Press, forthcoming).
15. See S. Neil MacFarlane and Thomas G. Weiss, 'Regional organizations and regional security', *Security Studies*, 2 (1), Autumn 1992, pp. 6–37; and Jarat Chopra and Thomas G. Weiss, 'Prospects for containing conflict in the former Second World', *Security Studies* 4 (3), Spring, 1995, pp. 552–83.
16. See Michael Edwards and David Hulme (eds), *Beyond the Magic Bullet: NGO Performance and Accountability in the Post-Cold War World* (West Hartford, Conn.: Kumarian Press, 1996).
17. See Antonio Donini, 'Surfing on the crest of the wave until it crashes: intervention in the South', draft forthcoming. This theme is also present in his *The Policies of Mercy: UN Coordination in Afghanistan, Mozambique, and Rwanda* (Providence, RI: Watson Institute, 1996), Occasional Paper No. 22.
18. See Cyril Ritchie, 'Coordinate, cooperate, harmonize? NGO policy and operational coalitions', in Weiss and Gordenker (eds), *NGOs*, pp. 177–88.

Part II
Regionalism and
International Security

3 Before and After Dayton: the UN and NATO in the Former Yugoslavia
Dick A. Leurdijk

There is no doubt that the development of the relationships between the United Nations (UN) and the North Atlantic Treaty Organization (NATO) has been very much affected by the Yugoslav crisis, both before and after the signing of the Dayton Peace Agreement.[1] The experience of cooperation is relevant for a better understanding of the complex relationships within the UN's system of collective security as well as between the UN and regional organizations. There was no blueprint nor any 'arrangement' which regulated such mutual relationships. Furthermore, the cooperation before and after Dayton took place under fundamentally different conditions of subcontracting. This reflects the fact that the international community's involvement in the falling apart of the former Yugoslavia made the Balkan region a testing ground for international politics that required new definitions of crises, analyses and responses. The evolving UN and NATO forms of cooperation had an experimental character. These contacts would have been unthinkable during the preceding years of the Cold War. The Atlantic Alliance chose not to identify itself as a regional organization under Chapter VIII of the UN Charter, thereby excluding any Soviet infringement in NATO's security matters. The central question is whether subcontracting, as applied in the former Yugoslavia, set precedents for future relationships between the UN and regional organizations, particularly in terms of division of labour and accountability.

UN AND NATO: THE INSTITUTIONAL FRAMEWORK

An analysis of the role of NATO in the former Yugoslavia conflict should be made in the broader context of the relationship between the UN and regional organizations, including Chapter VIII. From the NATO perspective, it is necessary both to look at the NATO Treaty and the policy decisions on its future 'new missions', taken in the aftermath of the Cold War.

One of the main issues in current international relations debates concerns the role that regional organizations can play in maintaining international peace and security. The increasing demands on the UN have led to an overload of commitments. Given its lack of resources, the UN has been obliged to acknowledge its inability to do the job alone and it has appealed to regional organizations for assistance. In consecutive annual reports, the Secretary-General paid special attention to the possible functions regional organizations could perform. In his 1992 annual report, then Secretary-General Boutros Boutros-Ghali acknowledged the role of those organizations in many of the cases in which the UN had been active:

> My aim is to see that in any new division of labour, the United Nations retains its primacy in the maintenance of international peace and security, while its burden is lightened and its mission reinforced and underlined by the active involvement of appropriate regional agencies. The exact modalities of this division of labour remain to be worked out, as regional organizations, no less than the United Nations itself, redefine their missions in the post-cold-war period.[2]

In his thought-provoking *An Agenda for Peace*, Boutros-Ghali stressed that regional organizations clearly possess a potential that should be utilized; in this context, he even spoke of 'a new complementarity'.[3] On a later occasion, he pointed out that in establishing the United Nations in 1945, the founding fathers chose an 'uneasy compromise' between regionalism and internationalism. Thus, while Article 51 of the UN Charter recognized 'the inherent right' of individual and collective self-defence, 'until the Security Council has taken the necessary measures for maintaining international peace and security', Article 52 recognized the existence of regional accords or organs for dealing with situations which might threaten international peace and security at the regional level, assuming their activities are consistent with the principles of the UN Charter. Article 53 even introduced the possibility of close working relationships between the UN and regional organizations for the specific purpose of 'enforcement action', stating: 'The Security Council shall, where appropriate, utilize such regional arrangements or agencies for enforcement action under its authority.' Only after the end of the Cold War at the initiative of the UN was this 'hidden potential' invigorated, mainly as a consequence of the situation in the former Yugoslavia in the first half of the 1990s.

During the Cold War, NATO had been primarily a collective defence organization, aimed at preserving the territorial integrity of its member states against external threats. Article 5 of the North Atlantic Treaty identified the commitments that the Allies accepted, that is, exercising the right of individual or collective self-defence recognized by Article 51 of the UN Charter: 'The Parties agree that an armed attack against one or more of them in Europe or North America shall be considered an attack against them all.'

The end of the Cold War resulted in a new political and strategic environment in Europe and the world. As the importance of NATO's classical collective defence task diminished, the Western Alliance had to adapt from deterring a clearly defined threat to coping with what emerged to be an unpredictable and unstable security environment that required 'new thinking' in terms of analyses, responses and missions. 'Peacekeeping' became a key concern in the course of 1992 as a consequence of two factors: the general policy debates on NATO's future tasks, and the implications of the war in the former Yugoslavia for the Western Alliance. At both levels a number of basic questions were raised: Is NATO a regional organization under Chapter VIII of the UN Charter? Has NATO legal competence to act 'out-of-area'? Has NATO the competence to engage in what could be termed 'non-Article 5 activities' ('new missions'), if there is no armed attack as mentioned in Article 5? And if so, should the North Atlantic Treaty be adapted?

Some of these issues reflected discussions preceding the establishment of the Alliance in 1949.[4] In the debate about the Preamble to the Treaty in the 1940s, France took the view that the pact was both a regional arrangement within the meaning of Chapter VIII as well as a collective defence system under Article 51. The British objected strongly to any reference to the UN Charter's Chapter VIII in the Preamble to NATO's constitution, fearing that all action taken would be subject to the veto of the Security Council.[5] All the representatives, including the French, agreed in the end to omit any specific reference in the Preamble, or in any of the Articles of the Pact, to Chapter VIII of the Charter. After difficult discussions, it was finally agreed that the Parties to the Pact, in their public statements, should stress the relationship of the Pact to Article 51 but should avoid saying that it was connected with Chapter VIII or other Articles of the UN Charter.[6]

In 1992, the question of peacekeeping among the Allies was controversial, not so much because of legal issues but because of France's politically motivated objections against giving NATO a new role or strengthening the alliance in general.[7] In June, NATO endorsed the principle of participation in peacekeeping, in particular by making available its assets to the Conference on Security and Cooperation in Europe (CSCE). The modalities of this endorsement had to be worked out, guaranteeing a continuation of the debate on: the 'out-of-area syndrome', the available infrastructure and military means, including troops, the geographic proximity of the Yugoslav crisis, and the national interests of NATO's individual members, including their national agendas. Six months later, on 17 December, the member states of NATO responded to a letter from the UN Secretary-General to his NATO counterpart:

> We confirm today the preparedness of our Alliance to support, on a case-by-case basis and in accordance with our own procedures, peacekeeping operations under the authority of the UN Security Council, which has the primary responsibility for international peace and security. We are ready to respond positively to initiatives that the UN Secretary-General might take to seek Alliance assistance in the implementation of UN Security Council Resolutions.[8]

While rejecting any form of automaticity and stressing its autonomous position, NATO expressed its willingness, in principle, to provide assistance on an *ad hoc* basis as it recognized the Council's political primacy. In fact, this statement reflected the 'full consensus' among the Allies, and only formally confirmed what, in the meantime, was already taking place in the field.[9]

One of the characteristics of NATO's involvement in the former Yugoslavia has been pragmatism. Taking into account its potential as a military organization, NATO's capabilities (expertise, logistics, infrastructure, means of communication, AWACs and forces) could be used for non-Article 5 operations. Accordingly, within a relatively short period of time, beginning in May 1992, NATO gradually expanded its involvement in support of the United Nations. In December 1992, the Western Allies noted that, 'For the first time in its history, the Alliance is taking part in UN peacekeeping and sanctions enforcement operations.' In May 1993, only five months later, NATO was already active at different levels: the enforcement of a maritime embargo; the enforcement of the no-fly zone over Bosnia; the contribution in terms of personnel and equipment to establish a command and control element for the UN Protection Force (UN-PROFOR) headquarters in Bosnia-Hercegovina; and the development of contingency planning concerning prevention of spillover of the conflict. Such plans included the protection of personnel on the ground, the monitoring of heavy weapons, the establishment of 'secure areas' and, finally, contingency planning for the implementation of a possible UN 'peace plan' for Bosnia.

These activities laid the foundation for further cooperation between the world organization and NATO, both before and after Dayton, though under different formats. In April 1996, NATO's Secretary-General Solana finally gave an additional argument for out-of-area actions, arguing that with the end of the Cold War NATO could 'return to its original, broader ambition of becoming an instrument for our well-being and stability: it can move from safeguarding security to promoting it.' He added, 'Nowhere has this new role of NATO become more visible than in Bosnia.' In this way, NATO's involvement in implementing the Dayton Peace Agreement was agreed.

NATO IN THE FORMER YUGOSLAVIA BEFORE DAYTON: CASES OF UN SUBCONTRACTING

In the case of the former Yugoslavia, the UN legitimized NATO to carry out tasks in the Adriatic to enforce compliance with sanctions. However, UNPROFOR had neither the mandate nor the means to execute these tasks. Similarly, the council subcontracted the enforcement of the no-fly zone over Bosnia and Hercegovina to NATO.

NATO's involvement in the Yugoslav crisis began on 16 July 1992 with operation 'Maritime Monitor'. For the first time in its history, NATO ships entered the Adriatic Sea and began monitoring compliance of resolutions on 'a general and complete embargo on all deliveries of weapons and military equipment to Yugoslavia' (Security Council Resolution 713) and on economic sanctions against the Federal Republic of Yugoslavia (Serbia and Montenegro) (Security Council Resolution 757). Though the resolutions were adopted under Chapter VII of the UN Charter, the NATO mission started as a simple monitoring operation. In November 1992, the Security Council enlarged the sanctions regime and in April 1993, it decreed a total embargo on land, at sea, in the air and on the Danube, authorizing member states 'to use the necessary means commensurate with the circumstances'. Although NATO recognized that allied ships involved in the Adriatic blockade could find themselves in a combat situation, no major incidents occurred. Following the initialling of the Dayton Accord on 21 November 1995, operation 'Sharp Guard' was adapted in accordance with suspending economic sanctions and phasing out the arms embargo. In June 1996, the Security Council decided to lift the arms embargo completely. On 1 October 1996, following the certification of the elections in Bosnia and Hercegovina, the Council lifted all economic sanctions, a decision which terminated operation 'Sharp Guard'.

Exactly three months after the initiation of the first action at sea, NATO started a similar monitoring action in the air, after the Security Council had established 'a ban on military flights in the airspace of Bosnia-

Hercegovina'. The concept of operations provided for combining the deployment of military observers, drawn from UNPROFOR, at airfields with information obtained from 'technical sources' (that is, NATO's AWAC aircraft). In March 1993, Security Council Resolution 816 strengthened the ban on military flights. Acting under Chapter VII, member states were authorized, 'acting nationally or through regional organizations or arrangements, to take all necessary measures in the airspace of Bosnia and Hercegovina, in the event of further violations, proportionate to the specific circumstances and the nature of the flights'. As in the case of the embargoes, the monitoring was followed by enforcement. The ban could be implemented by the use of force, but under certain conditions. Operation 'Deny Flight' began on Monday, 12 April 1993.

The operation differed in one key respect from its maritime counterpart. At sea, NATO alone was responsible for the operational tasks. In executing operation 'Deny Flight', NATO for the first time in the Yugoslav crisis was obliged to cooperate closely with UNPROFOR. For this reason, liaison officers were exchanged, with NATO officers stationed in UNPROFOR headquarters. This arrangement later was replicated for 'close air support' and 'air strikes'.

As anticipated in Resolution 816, the rules of engagement for the operation turned out to be highly circumscribed; they disappointed many who had hoped for tougher measures. In the meantime, the question was raised as to whether the Allies were slowly moving towards stronger military commitments in the former Yugoslavia and what consequences that could have for the safety of UN personnel. The United Kingdom and France, in particular, were reluctant to back up the no-fly zone, taking into account the possibility of reprisals against their UN troops on the ground. This debate explained why a new military option ('close air support') was introduced on 4 June 1993, and provided the use of airpower for the safety of UN personnel.

On the morning of 28 February 1994, almost one year after 'Deny Flight' had become operational, NATO aircraft shot down four Serbian aircraft that violated the no-fly zone. In carrying out the Western Alliance's first military action since its establishment 45 years earlier, it was the first time that NATO planes opened fire over Bosnia. Operation 'Deny Flight' ended on 20 December 1995, with the transfer of authority from UNPROFOR to the Implementation Force (IFOR).

In a second innovation, NATO provided air power for purposes authorized by the Security Council and in support of UNPROFOR in implementing its mandate, both in terms of 'close air support' and 'air strikes'. As Boutros-Ghali noted, this raised 'unprecedented issues of command

and control', such as the 'dual key' arrangement which led to much controversy between the UN and NATO. In the absence of a precise agreement as to the circumstances justifying the use of force, each organization responded to its own priorities, which frequently were at loggerheads. Under this arrangement, UN and NATO, until the fall of Srebrenica in mid-1995, operated with little success. Only after a fundamental review of the arrangement did the cooperation between the two institutions under Operation 'Deliberate Force' become successful. This illustrated that both organizations can cooperate effectively, depending upon agreed conditions and priorities.

The process of subcontracting in the former Yugoslavia before Dayton was preceded and accompanied by the presence of UN peacekeepers. The establishment of UNPROFOR on 21 February 1991 was originally intended to contribute to the implementation of a peace plan for Croatia. But UNPROFOR gradually expanded its mandate in terms of its area of operation (from Croatia to Bosnia-Hercegovina and Macedonia), strength (from an initial 10,000 troops to a force of some 52,000) and tasks. This development in the first half of 1992 led Boutros-Ghali to challenge the Security Council's preoccupation at the time with the conflict in the former Yugoslavia as a 'rich man's war', at the expense of other conflicts in Africa such as Somalia.

UNPROFOR's primary task in Bosnia was to support the provision of humanitarian assistance, with the UN High Commissioner for Refugees (UNHCR) acting as the 'lead agency' in what would become 'one of the worst humanitarian emergencies of our time'.[10] Gradually, the Security Council's involvement led to an unprecedented series of resolutions, covering such issues as humanitarian assistance, an arms embargo, economic sanctions, a no-fly zone, safe areas, international humanitarian law and the mandate of UNPROFOR. In this almost permanent process of adaptation, the UNPROFOR peacekeeping personnel become involved in such elements of peace-enforcement as ground monitoring at airfields as part of the no-fly zone, in 'deterring attacks' on safe areas and in the implementation of exclusion zones, including the control of the heavy weapons placed by the parties in designated weapons collection points. This mixture caused much conceptual and operational confusion, with serious consequences both for the UN and NATO and for their cooperation.

In a number of cases, the developments on the battlefield isolated so-called Muslim enclaves from the outside world. The deliberate attacks on the civilian population, including the 'strangulation' of cities like Sarajevo, and the sheer number of casualties led to deep feelings of dismay and frustration in the international community. The position of these enclaves in terms of their status as 'safe areas' would become the key issue for the involvement of both the UN and NATO in the years before Dayton.

The Security Council's safe area policy was based on Resolution 836, as adopted on 4 June 1993. Acting under Chapter VII and concerned by continuing armed hostilities in Bosnia, it decided 'to ensure full respect for the safe areas'. These areas were established by the Council when it declared in an earlier resolution that 'Sarajevo and other such threatened areas, in particular the towns of Tuzla, Zepa, Gorazde, Bihac, as well as Srebenica, and their surroundings' should be treated as safe areas and should be free from armed attacks. Under Resolution 836, the mandate of UNPROFOR was extended to enable it to 'deter attacks' against the safe areas. The resolution, furthermore, authorized UNPROFOR, 'acting in self-defence, to take the necessary measures, including the use of force, in reply to (a) bombardments against the safe areas, or (b) to armed incursions into them, or (c) in the event of any deliberate obstruction in or around those areas to the freedom of movement of UNPROFOR or of protected humanitarian convoys.' And it decided, in a separate paragraph, that member states, acting nationally or through regional organizations, may take 'all necessary measures, through the use of air power, in and around the safe areas to support UNPROFOR' in the performance of its tasks. Thus formulated, Resolution 836 became one of the most controversial decisions of the Security Council, with repercussions far outside UN headquarters.

It was against this background that the safe areas had to be kept 'safe'. Questions were raised about both the interpretation of the relevant resolutions and the political, legal and military implications of the concept of 'safe areas', including the consequences for both UNPROFOR and NATO, and their mutual relationships. There was conceptual confusion about the linkage between peacekeeping and peace-enforcement; the definition of the safe area 'regime' in terms of its legal status, its political aims, its size, its disarmament and its demilitarization; the gap between goals and the necessary military means (including a 'credible air strike capability' to be provided by NATO). As a result, NATO and the UN developed the concepts of 'close air support' and 'air strikes', closely related to the 'dual key' arrangement. This reflected and contributed to serious disagreements on the conditionality of the use of force, both in protecting the safe areas and the safety of UNPROFOR's blue helmets.

The dual key provided both organizations with the right to veto the use of air power. While NATO never questioned the political primacy of the Security Council, it simultaneously underlined its own autonomy. There was no automaticity in implementing UN resolutions. Under the circumstances prevailing in Bosnia before Dayton, the dual key formula, however, implied two separate but not separable command chains. This arrangement led to many misgivings about mutual relations, which basically reflected the different intentions of the organizations. The UN position on the use of air power mainly could be explained out of concern for the safety of the UN personnel and possible negative effects on the peace talks and the provision of humanitarian assistance. NATO's main concern was to maintain its credibility as an effective military organization. Due to their vulnerability, UN blue helmets were used on several occasions as human shields or taken hostage, by way of reprisals, in an effort to prevent the use of more air power. In May 1995, finally Boutros-Ghali considered UNPROFOR's position 'untenable'. NATO already seriously considered the option of a withdrawal of the UN force, implying the fall of the safe areas. The Security Council, however, decided to strengthen UNPROFOR within its mandate, by establishing the so-called Rapid Reaction Force (RRF), after close consultations with NATO and the countries providing the troops.

A third variant of subcontracting, closely related to the safe area policy, concerned the accomplishment of tasks that were not authorized specifically by the Security Council. The primary examples were NATO's enforcement of 'exclusion zones' around the safe areas that required the presence of UN 'forward air controllers' on the ground. The concept of the exclusion zones in February 1994 was formulated not in New York, but in Brussels at NATO headquarters. The massacre at a marketplace in Sarajevo in February 1994 forced the UN Secretary-General to call for NATO to authorize air strikes. In implementing this call, the NATO Council formulated an 'ultimatum', aimed at the withdrawal, or regrouping and placing under UNPROFOR control, of the heavy weapons of Bosnians and Serbs located in an exclusion zone. A similar ultimatum was used in Gorazde in April 1994 to prevent its fall. The success of the 'Sarajevo model' underlined the need to redefine the 'safe area' concept, including the exclusion zones, and even raised the question of the feasibility of extending the concept to other parts of Bosnia.

The numerous dilemmas of this policy (especially the safety of UN personnel versus the lives of those living in the areas and the repercussions of the use of force for the UN soldiers) would strain the relationships between the UN and NATO in the months that followed in other safe areas such as Bihac and Sarajevo. The decisions, in the aftermath of the fall of Srebrenica in July 1995, that attacks against the remaining safe areas would lead to 'a firm and rapid response from NATO air forces', were also taken in Brussels, without any formal consultations with New York. At the same time, the adaptation of the dual key arrangement consisted of excluding from the chain of command the UN's political representative, Yasushi Akashi, who generally was seen as the 'bad genius' and was blamed for holding back the use of force by NATO airplanes. This proved to be another decisive element of the prelude to operation 'Deliberate Force', in which the UN and NATO together determined the terms of the ceasefire. Together with the US initiative at the diplomatic level, the combination of diplomacy and force effectively led to the Dayton Peace Agreement.

NATO IN THE FORMER YUGOSLAVIA AFTER DAYTON: ANOTHER CASE OF SUBCONTRACTING

After Dayton, the Security Council authorized the member states 'acting through or in cooperation with' NATO to establish a multinational IFOR to assist in the implementation of the territorial and other military related provisions of the peace agreement. The IFOR-role under NATO's command, as applied under the Dayton Peace Agreement, was another innovative model calling upon NATO's potential. Among other things, IFOR required close cooperation between NATO and non-NATO members, and between military and civilian authorities in the field. IFOR experience will have a profound impact on the further development of the political, conceptual and operational thinking – with a view to the future role of NATO in support of non-Article 5 operations, and in the perspective of what these days is described as the 'new NATO' preoccupied with 'new missions'.[11]

In the case of Bosnia, from the start of the negotiations to a political settlement, it had been clear that to guarantee its implementation, a large military force would be required. This was a cornerstone of both the Vance-Owen and Owen-Stoltenberg plans. In this context, planning for such an endeavour became part of NATO's agenda and added a new dimension to the evolving relationship between the UN and NATO. In the spring of 1993, the UN Secretary-General asked NATO to provide him with the results of its contingency planning. (NATO had already developed a first plan for a force of about 75,000 troops to ensure respect of the Vance-Owen plan.) In August 1993, NATO decided in principle to participate in the implementation of a settlement under the authority of the Security Council, if asked to do so. Politically sensitive issues soon became clear. For the US, sending ground troops would be acceptable only in the context of a peace settlement. Moreover, Washington's participation would require also the consent of the parties, a NATO command, a clear timetable and enforcement powers.

In the aftermath of the fall of Srebrenica, the US took the initiative in new efforts to find a political settlement. Assistant Secretary of State Richard Holbrooke would become the final architect of the Dayton Peace Agreement, building upon earlier proposals, in particular the 'peace plan' of the Contact Group of July 1994. This included a unitary state with two entities, the 51:49 per cent parameter and the confederal option. After three and a half years of war, on 14 December 1995, the parties put their signature under 'The General Framework Agreement for Peace in Bosnia and Hercegovina', with eleven annexes divided into a military and civilian component. This reflected the built-in division of labour in the implementation of the Peace Agreement between the military authorities under NATO leadership and the civilian authorities, and led by High Representative Carl Bildt. Conceptually, the framework of the Dayton settlement was a mixture of peace-enforcement, peacekeeping and post-conflict peacebuilding.

In December 1995, the NATO Council endorsed the military planning for IFOR, stating that the operation would attest to its capacity to fulfil its new missions of crisis management and peacekeeping. IFOR was elaborated at NATO headquarters in Brussels which was totally outside the UN framework. Richard Holbrooke negotiated the provisions of the peace settlement and NATO worked out the modalities for IFOR, including the command and control arrangements, participation of non-NATO countries and a mission definition. IFOR would function as an integral part of the Dayton Peace Agreement, the terms of which clearly reflected American involvement. For instance, sending IFOR 'for a period of approximately one year' was a prerequisite for the Clinton administration to win approval for American participation in IFOR from an unwilling Republican majority in Congress.

Under the Dayton Agreement, the parties invited the Security Council to authorize member states or, regional organizations and arrangements to establish a multinational military implementation force. The agreement laid down IFOR's tasks and enforcement powers, which thus received the parties' consent. Following the signing of the Bosnian Peace Agreement, the Security Council, acting under Chapter VII of the UN Charter, gave the authorization to establish IFOR under unified command and control and composed of ground, air and maritime units from NATO and non-NATO nations to ensure compliance with the relevant provisions of the Peace Agreement. The following day, 16 December 1996, the North

Atlantic Council (NAC) approved the overall plan for IFOR and directed that NATO commence Operation 'Joint Endeavour'. UN Secretary-General Boutros-Ghali, on 20 December 1995, in a letter to the Council, formally confirmed the end of UNPROFOR's existence after the transfer of authority from UNPROFOR to IFOR. He also announced the termination of all the enforcement measures previously adopted by the Security Council. This effectively ended the authorization to take enforcement measures under the pre-Dayton UN regime, including its safe areas policy.

NATO's Acting Secretary-General spoke of the 'most challenging operation in its history', adding: 'This is indeed a historic moment for the alliance – our first-ever ground force operation, our first-ever deployment "out-of-area", our first-ever operation with our PfP (Partnership for Peace) partners and other non-NATO countries.' The force would have a unified command and be NATO-led under the political direction and control of the North Atlantic Council and operate under NATO rules of engagement. Thus, IFOR's authority to use force legally was based both on the Dayton Peace Agreement and Security Council Resolution 1031, and reflected a deliberate policy choice of deploying IFOR with enforcement powers as a necessary condition for a credible performance. In this respect, IFOR differed fundamentally from UNPROFOR's peacekeeping character.

NATO's principal tasks were related to the military aspects (cessation of hostilities, withdrawal of foreign forces, redeployment of forces, prisoner exchanges), regional stabilization and the inter-entity boundary line. Operation 'Joint Endeavour', which would become 'the largest and most complex operation NATO has ever undertaken', consisted of five phases. IFOR's first priority was to establish a secure environment, for both the military and civilian organizations, including a rapid build-up of combat power. Once the execution of the purely military tasks was accomplished, the beginning of the 'transition to peace' made it possible for IFOR to pay more attention to civilian tasks, which were to be executed in close cooperation with a number of other international bodies, such as the High Representative, the International Police Task Force (IPTF), UNHCR, the Organization for Security and Cooperation in Europe (OSCE) and the International Criminal Tribunal for the former Yugoslavia (ICTY). In addition to its primarily military tasks, IFOR had a number of so-called 'supporting tasks'. The crucial question was how far NATO would go in these tasks, most notably with regard to war criminals. The formal position soon became that 'IFOR will assist, to the extent possible within its mandate and available resources, the civilian part of the implementation process.' This reflected both a fear for 'mission creep' and the related issue of possible casualties among the military.

The transfer of authority to IFOR ended UNPROFOR, but the UN's involvement was not over. The Peace Agreement assigned the UN two principal responsibilities: continued coordination of humanitarian assistance and the lead role for dealing with issues relating to refugees and displaced persons, tasks to be performed by UNHCR, and help for the parties to carry out their law enforcement responsibilities, a task assigned to the IPTF – as part of the UN Mission in Bosnia and Hercegovina (UNMIBH). Apart from the authorization to establish IFOR, the Security Council under the Dayton Agreement and by a separate resolution established a UN International Police Task Force as an unarmed, monitoring and advisory force – in a traditional peacekeeping capacity. On this basis, the IPTF could not be seen as an operational police force with the powers to apprehend indicted war criminals for it had no authorization and little means.

One of the most contentious provisions of Dayton was the ban on holding a public office by persons under indictment by the Criminal Tribunal for the former Yugoslavia. The North Atlantic Council determined that neither the Dayton Peace Agreement nor Resolution 1031 provided a clear mandate for IFOR to arrest indicted war criminals. After several months of discussion, NATO and the ICTY signed a 'memorandum of understanding', codifying the procedures for the detention and transfer of persons indicted for war crimes to the ICTF and for IFOR support to ICTY investigation teams in Bosnia. This confirmed the NAC's policy of 'arrest on sight', refusing an active 'man-hunt'.

National elections, which took place on 14 September 1995, were a cornerstone of the Dayton implementation process. The most critical phase of this process, according to Carl Bildt, would be the period following the elections when a number of crucial developments would take place: the certification of the election results ('imperfect and debatable, but overall acceptable'); 'institution-building' in terms of setting up common institutions, such as the presidency; the further implementation of the civilian components of Dayton; the termination of IFOR's mandate; and the debate on IFOR's follow-up force. The modalities for such a force were extensively discussed at NATO's headquarters, but the Security Council again would be invited to authorize its deployment and mandate. In Resolution 1088 of 12 December 1996, the Security Council authorized the establishment for a planned period of 18 months of a multinational Stabilization Force (SFOR) as the legal successor to IFOR under NATO command to fulfil similar tasks as its predecessor, but with more emphasis on the civilian component and with half the number of soldiers (30,000).

CONCLUSION

Relations between the UN and NATO in the former Yugoslavia, both
before and after Dayton, have provided numerous cases of subcontracting. Before Dayton, the international community aimed to establish a
peace settlement; after Dayton, the goal was to help implement the Peace
Agreement. In both timeframes, several types of 'burden-sharing' have
applied to the execution of particular tasks. The use of the term 'subcontracting' in those cases is appropriate because regional organizations are
requested or invited by the Security Council to execute tasks within terms
set by the Council. In terms of subcontracting, the extremely complicated
model – conceptually, politically and militarily – that applied before
Dayton was exceptional and will not easily be repeated.

Similarly, the post-Dayton model, with the deployment of several thousands of well-armed troops having peace-enforcement powers and operating under a single command structure, is also highly unusual although for
different reasons. With a peace agreement in force, peacekeeping was possible. But under the influence of the United States, the choice was peace-
enforcement under NATO command. At the same time, the model as
applied under Dayton may have set a precedent for future cases of subcontracting. It would be in line with ideas as proposed by former UN
Secretary-General Boutros-Ghali.[12] Essentially, he accepted the idea that
the Secretary-General should restrict himself to managing peacekeeping
operations. But peace-enforcement should be authorized by the Security
Council, presumably by contracting more ambitious, complex or comprehensive operations to multinational forces, either led by major powers
with special interest in the dispute in question or under the command of a
regional organization. This approach has already been used in cases of humanitarian intervention during the past few years, such as in Somalia,
Rwanda and Haiti.

In the years before Dayton, the terms for the cooperation between the
UN and NATO were determined only gradually. There was no blueprint;
under the influence of the course of the conflict, both organizations were
forced to develop working relationships in the field, taking into account
the presence of UN peacekeepers on the ground. The experimental character of subcontracting as applied at this stage was underlined by its different
formats in a very dynamic decision-making process: the enforcement of
economic sanctions at sea and the enforcement of a no-fly zone in the air
executed by NATO without any UN involvement; the use of different
forms of NATO air power ('close air support' and 'air strikes') on the
basis of the 'dual key' arrangement; and the enforcement of 'exclusion

zones' by NATO, without explicit authorization by the Security Council, while requiring the cooperation of UN blue helmets. After Dayton, the lead role of the Security Council was replaced by the North Atlantic Council, which became the key policy-making instrument under the Dayton Peace Agreement. In both cases it was possible for the Security Council to delegate functions relating to the maintenance of international peace and security to regional organizations or arrangements without transferring its own political primacy as provided in Article 24 of the UN Charter. Before Dayton, NATO responded to invitations of the Security Council; after Dayton, the Council merely legitimized IFOR and SFOR under the terms as set out in the Dayton Peace Agreement.

The involvement of the international community in the former Yugoslavia has made that part of the Balkans a testing ground for international diplomacy. NATO's presence in the former Yugoslavia provided pragmatic answers to many of the theoretical questions posed in the first chapter as regards an analytical framework to analyse the relationship between the UN and regional institutions. NATO's main strategy in the former Yugoslavia has been the willingness to use force, if necessary, for tasks determined by the Security Council. Given UNPROFOR's presence in the area before Dayton, most of these tasks were executed in close co-operation with the world organization. After Dayton, NATO was supposed to work closely together with other international organizations in the civilian sphere. In terms of its effectiveness, NATO illustrated the contribution of a specific task-oriented regional organization with respect to peace and security. At the same time, its performance in the former Yugoslavia raised questions about the legal justification of both NATO's 'new missions' and its actions 'out-of-area'. NATO possessed the institutional capacity for taking and implementing decisions, including the North Atlantic Council, whose decisions are taken after close consultations with NATO's military authorities. NATO had the requisite financial, manpower and military-operational capabilities.[13] Finally, NATO commanded the respect and authority of the parties to the dispute, but with different success under different conditions before and after Dayton.

As for the division of labour between the UN and regional organizations, political and the military analyses are essential. In line with the UN Charter and the provisions of the Washington Treaty, NATO always recognized the Security Council's political primacy and its primary responsibility for maintaining international peace and security. At the same time, NATO stressed its own autonomous role, sometimes even denying that it acted as a 'subcontractor'.

Before Dayton, two military components were involved: UNPROFOR and NATO. This structure reflected on the one hand that the UN was over-stretched by some twenty to thirty thousand blue helmets, and on the other hand that NATO possessed an under-utilized capacity to enforce deci-sions. The dual key arrangement, while respecting organizational auton-omy, undermined effectiveness because of the different intentions and interests of both organizations, the vulnerability of UNPROFOR's func-tioning in a hostile environment, different interpretations of mandates and the prevailing conceptual confusion. The conditionality of the use of force thus became a key issue. An adaptation of the arrangement finally resulted under operation 'Deliberate Force'.

After Dayton, the Security Council authorized, at the request of the sig-natories of the Dayton Peace Agreement, the deployment of IFOR and SFOR under the conditions set out in the document to ensure the imple-mentation of the military aspects (acting under Chapter VII). These condi-tions included NATO-led forces from both NATO and non-NATO countries under a unitary command and control structure as well as the pursuit of 'supporting tasks' with civilian organizations, including the High Representative, UNHCR, OSCE, ICTY and the IPTF, and a number of non-governmental organizations (NGOs). The IFOR Commander had the authority to do what he judged necessary, including the use of military force, to protect IFOR and to carry out the responsibilities, but the opera-tion was under the political guidance of the North Atlantic Council and not the Security Council.

A last principle concerning the relationship between the UN and re-gional organizations concerns accountability. Normally, this term con-notes that a regional organization should be accountable for its performance to the Security Council because of the latter's responsibility and political primacy. This leaves the Security Council itself non-account-able. The Council, for its part, does not discuss extensively the modalities of failed operations, such as in Somalia, Rwanda or the former Yugoslavia. In this perspective, the fall of Srebrenica, followed by the most serious case of genocide in Europe since the Second World War, raises the question of the political responsibility that never became part of the agenda of the Security Council.

Before Dayton, given the close cooperation between UNPROFOR and NATO, the issue of accountability was irrelevant. Apart from the evolving contacts between the Secretaries-General and irregular contacts among the officials of both organizations, there were no formal mechanisms for con-sultations. Both organizations were pragmatically supposed to work closely together, including the operationalization of the dual key arrangement and the establishment of the Rapid Reaction Force.

After Dayton, NATO, in accordance with Resolution 1031, regularly reported to the UN about the progress made in implementing the Peace Agreement. In December 1996, NATO's Secretary-General, in a letter addressed to his UN counterpart, sent the thirteenth and final report (two pages only) on IFOR operations to the members of the Security Council.[14] This reporting entails only a formal requirement and can hardly be taken seriously in terms of accountability.

Notwithstanding the variety of attempts at cooperation between the UN and NATO in the former Yugoslavia, the experiment can be seen as the cautious beginning of a development of principles and criteria to govern collaboration between the universal United Nations and regional institutions. In adopting Resolution 1031, the Security Council recognized 'the unique, extraordinary and complex character of the situation in Bosnia and Hercegovina, requiring an exceptional response'. This was an accurate summary of the models of subcontracting between the UN and NATO in the former Yugoslavia, both before and after Dayton.

NOTES

1. For a more comprehensive treatment of the subject, see Dick A. Leurdijk, *The United Nations and NATO in Former Yugoslavia, 1991–1996; Limits to Diplomacy and Force* (The Hague: Netherlands Atlantic Commission/ Netherlands Institute of International Relations, 'Clingendael', 1996).
2. Boutros Boutros-Ghali, 'Report on the Work of the Organization' (New York: United Nations, September 1992), p. 44.
3. Boutros Boutros-Ghali, *An Agenda for Peace,* A/47/277-S/24111, New York, June 1992, para. 64.
4. See Sir Nicholas Henderson, *The Birth of NATO* (London: Weidenfeld & Nicolson, 1982), pp. 101–5.
5. Article 53 of the UN Charter states that all enforcement action under regional arrangements was subject to the authorization of the Security Council, and Article 54 requires that all activities taken under regional arrangements must be reported to the Security Council.
6. This understanding was embodied in the agreed minutes of interpretation. Under paragraph 7, it was said: 'It is the common understanding that the primary purpose of this Treaty is to provide for the collective self-defense of the Parties ... It is further understood that the Parties will, in their public statements, stress this primary purpose, recognized and preserved by Article

66 *Dick A. Leurdijk*

51, rather than any specific connection with Chapter VIII or other Articles of the United Nations Charter'. Thus, the use of the term 'primary purpose' leaves room for other purposes.

7. *Atlantic News*, 2428, 3 June 1992, p. 2, and 2433, 17 June 1992, p. 1.
8. 'Final Communiqué, Ministerial Meeting of the North Atlantic Council, NATO Headquarters, Brussels – 17th December 1992', in *Atlantic News*, 2484, Annex, 19 December 1992.
9. The term 'full consensus' was used by Secretary-General Manfred Wörner during his final press conference. *Atlantic News*, 2484, 19 December 1992.
10. 'Report of the Secretary-General pursuant to Security Council Resolutions 757, 758 and 761, 1992, 10 July 1992', Document S/24263.
11. General George A. Joulwan, 'SHAPE and IFOR: adapting to the needs of tomorrow', *NATO Review*, 2, March 1996, pp. 6–9.
12. Boutros Boutros-Ghali, *Supplement to An Agenda for Peace: Position Paper of the Secretary-General on the Occasion of the Fiftieth Anniversary of the United Nations,* A/50/60-S/1995/1, 3 January 1995, paras 84–9.
13. David Lightburn, 'NATO and the challenge of multifunctional peace-keeping', *NATO Review*, 2, March 1996, pp. 10–14.
14. Document S/1996/1066, 24 December 1996.

4 The Liberian Conflict and the ECOWAS–UN Partnership
Clement E. Adibe

The internationalization of the Liberian conflict is owed mainly to two factors. The first is the beleaguered attempt by Liberia's neighbours, acting under the aegis of the Economic Community of West African States (ECOWAS), to prevent the regional spread of the conflict through direct political and military intervention.[1]The second was the decision by the United Nations (UN), following the euphoric reception of *An Agenda for Peace* in 1992, to demonstrate global support for 'the efforts of the people of Liberia to establish peace in their country'[2] Thus internationalized, the Liberian conflict set the stage for an experiment in international politics. For the first time ever, 'the United Nations would undertake a major peacekeeping operation with another organization, in this case a sub-regional organization.'[3] The Liberian case provides a useful empirical basis for evaluating the idea of task-sharing between the United Nations and regional arrangements – and by extension with the non-governmental organizations (NGOs) discussed later in this volume – in accordance with the spirit of Article 33 of the UN Charter. Accordingly, this essay evaluates the effectiveness of the ECOWAS–UN partnership in responding adequately to the conflict in Liberia by answering three critical questions: What led to the ECOWAS–UN partnership in Liberia? What was the nature of this partnership? What lessons may be drawn from this pioneering partnership?

ECOWAS FAILURE AND UN INVOLVEMENT

The United Nations was invited to join the search for peace effort in Liberia only *after* ECOWAS had failed to make any appreciable progress towards conflict resolution. According to David Wippman, attempts made in 1990 to place the Liberian crisis on the Security Council's agenda failed, 'in part because of opposition by Côte d'Ivoire, and because the

Council's members shared the US view that the problem should be solved by Africans'.[4] What is the explanation for the organization's change of position on this matter? The ECOWAS *volte-face* reflected its beleaguered efforts to contain the Liberian conflict through direct diplomatic and military intervention.

The failure of diplomatic intervention

ECOWAS did not expect that its intervention in Liberia would be a long-drawn-out affair. Rather, it envisaged a short, surgical 'police action'. Indeed, the nature of the conflict itself suggested a seemingly simple solution. After all, the immediate cause of the problem was the guerrilla 'incursion' into Liberia's northern territory by a band of rebels, numbering about a couple of hundred 'Gio *tribesmen*'.[5] In the view of the military rulers of Liberia's neighbours, most notably Nigeria, Sierra Leone and Guinea, the rebel incursions were an act of thuggery that should have been repelled quite easily by the Armed Forces of Liberia (AFL). Consequently, AFL's failure to contain these raids suggested a fundamental weakness in the ability of the central government in Monrovia, headed by President Samuel Doe, to govern effectively. One solution would be to shore up the Doe regime through the provision of arms and ammunition and, if need be, military advisers. Indeed, Nigeria and the United States did precisely that until it became obvious by the summer of 1990 that the 'incursions' were not uncoordinated acts by some 'tribesmen'. Rather, the Doe government was facing a well-planned military rebellion led by an opposition militia, the National Patriotic Front of Liberia (NPFL), which had recruited massively from the ranks of the discontented throughout Liberia.[6] With rebel forces by occupying two-thirds of Liberia's territory, the Doe government helpless and reduced to a tenuous control of a few perimeter areas around the presidential mansion, and the civilian survivors of the conflict fleeing in large numbers to neighbouring countries, regional attention turned to the feasibility of establishing a politico-military presence in Liberia.

ECOWAS took on the Liberian challenge barely five months after the initial outbreak of armed conflict. At the outset, the United States was expected to intervene as the patron of the Liberian state throughout much of its history. Washington was, however, preoccupied with changes in the international system due to rapid political changes in the former Soviet bloc. Many observers expected that early reports emerging from West Africa in the middle of spring 1990 alleging that NPFL rebels were trained and equipped by Libya would trigger strong American reaction culminating in the direct military intervention advocated by European ambassadors.[7] In many ways Washington reacted strongly, for the US soon began consultations with its African 'allies' with a view to orchestrating a regional response to the Libyan threat. However, the dynamics of the war changed quite sharply by the end of spring 1990 due to a series of massacres targeting foreign nationals in Liberia, by government and rebel forces alike.

Washington's response to this development was to deploy forces to evacuate American citizens and privileged foreigners residing in Liberia. Vocal Liberians, pan-Africanists and the African press saw this action as a clear indication of the growing trend toward the marginalization of Africa by the West in general. In particular, the action was seen as proof of America's insensitivity to the plight of Africans. If the world had abandoned Africa because the Cold War had ended, the prescription was clear: Africa must act in the spirit of pan-Africanism to save one of its own from self-destruction. Naturally, the Organization of African Unity (OAU) was looked upon for leadership. Not surprisingly, according to Chike Akabogu, Africa's premier regional arrangement 'merely dusted up its Articles on non-interference in the internal affairs of member-nations'.[8] However, for the new OAU leadership comprising President Yoweri Museveni of Uganda as chairman and former Tanzanian foreign minister, Salim Ahmed Salim, as secretary-general, the norm of non-intervention did not apply to the *sui generis* character of the Liberian conflict.[9] Their tactic was to approach Nigeria, the dominant West African state, to lead a regional force into Liberia within the framework of ECOWAS.

General Ibrahim Babangida, Nigeria's military ruler at the time, seized on the opportunity not only to exercise statesmanship but also to divert national and international attention away from mounting socio-economic problems and political abuses at home. As chairman of ECOWAS, he convened a meeting of ECOWAS heads of state and government in Banjul in May 1990 to discuss his blueprint for the establishment of an 'ECOWAS Standing Mediation Committee [SMC] to settle disputes and conflict situations within the Community'.[10] The summit accepted the proposal and constituted the membership of the SMC as follows: The Gambia, Ghana, Mali, Nigeria and Togo.[11] At its inaugural meeting in July, the committee discussed the Liberian conflict and agreed on a peace plan with the following features:[12] the establishment of an immediate ceasefire by the warring parties; the establishment and deployment of an ECOWAS Ceasefire Monitoring Group (ECOMOG) to monitor the observance of the ceasefire by all sides to the conflict; an agreement by the parties to the establishment of an Interim Administration in Monrovia, pending the election of a substantive government; and an agreement by the parties to constitute a substantive government through nationwide elections to be monitored by ECOMOG.

According to official reports of the ministerial conference, there had been a substantial disagreement between members of the SMC, on the one hand, and the parties to the conflict, on the other, about key elements of the proposed peace plan. The issues in dispute were: the desirability and timing of the ceasefire; the desirability and composition of an interim government; and the usefulness of deploying a regional peacekeeping force.[13] The inability to find a common ground on these issues led eventually to the breakdown of talks between ECOWAS and Liberia's warring parties over methods to resolve the conflict peacefully. It was the way that ECOWAS reacted to its initial failure to negotiate a ceasefire between the warring factions that resulted in uncontrolled mayhem in Liberia. The problem began with the frustration of the ministers of the SMC with Charles Taylor, whom they viewed contemptuously as the principal cause of their failure in Banjul. According to the SMC ministerial report:

> It became clear [to] the Ministerial Meeting ... that the NPFL was holding on firmly to its initial position of demanding the departure of President Doe before it could consider any of the other essential issues. Indeed, the Committee gained the distinct impression that the NPFL had opted for a military solution. In the light of this, the Ministerial Meeting decided ... to request that another course of action be considered to bring the Liberian crisis to a speedy and peaceful end.[14]

Quite to the surprise of many diplomatic observers, the ministerial conference proceeded with the formation of a Sub-Committee on Defense Matters 'to consider issues relating to the military arm of the proposed ECOWAS Monitoring Group (ECOMOG) in Liberia'.[15] After only two days of meeting in Freetown between 18 and 20 July 1990, the subcommittee emerged with a blueprint of an ECOWAS military intervention force. In presenting the blueprint to the chairman of the ECOWAS summit, General Ibrahim Babangida, the ministers urged their heads of government 'to bring the Liberian crisis to a *speedy* and peaceful end'.[16] This call was heeded two weeks later when the leaders of the SMC states, meeting in Banjul, between 6 and 7 August, adopted *Decision A/DEC.1/8/90*, which contains the following elements of what would later be known as the ECOWAS Peace Plan for Liberia:[17] the immediate cessation of hostilities by all factions; the formation and immediate deployment of ECOMOG to Liberia; the generalized disarmament of the warring parties by ECOMOG; an embargo on the importation and acquisition of arms by the warring parties in Liberia; the formation of an Interim

Government of National Unity pending the conduct of general elections; and the establishment of an atmosphere for the conduct of general and presidential elections in Liberia.

Viewed from the perspective of diplomacy, the ECOWAS Peace Plan was a recipe for disaster in Liberia. Very little negotiation took place between members of the SMC and the factions in Liberia, particularly the NPFL whose leader, Charles Taylor, accused ECOWAS of essentially handing him down a set of instructions to roll back his forces from Monrovia. Defiant and agitated, Taylor insisted that the NPFL 'took up arms, got rid of Doe, and took more than 95 percent of the country' and so had earned the *right* to rule Liberia.[18] To this claim, ECOWAS accused Taylor of being 'arrogantly intransigent', and declared its intention to proceed with its Liberian initiative with or without the support of the factions.[19] In the words of the president of Guinea, one of the proponents of the Peace Plan: 'We do not need the permission of any party involved in the conflict to implement the decisions reached in Banjul. So, with or without the agreement of any of the parties, ECOWAS troops will be in Liberia.'[20]

Why was ECOWAS so impatient with the course of diplomacy in Liberia? Two factors account for the organization's diplomatic débâcle in Liberia. The first is the organization's lack of experience in the diplomacy of multilateral security. If, as is often the case, foreign policy is a reflection of domestic politics, there is nothing about the domestic politics of the states of the SMC – all under various forms of authoritarian rule – to inspire confidence in the success of diplomacy.[21] The second reason relates to calculations of self-interest by proponents of the ECOWAS Peace Plan. This was coldly expressed by Obed Asamoah, Ghana's foreign minister: 'The Liberian situation – assumed international dimensions because several thousand Ghanaians, Nigerians and other nationals [had] been holed up in Liberia and [were] suffering because of the fighting.' Furthermore, he argued, the heavy economic toll of the refugee and humanitarian situation on Liberia's neighbours made a quick intervention by ECOWAS an imperative that could not be accomplished by the grinding wheels of diplomacy. In echoing the Guinean president, Asamoah insisted that members of ECOWAS 'do not have to look at the interest of warring factions alone but also at the interests of the neighbouring countries. So many countries have been saddled with refugees. Are they to continue to carry this burden because one particular faction in Liberia wants to carry out its ambition?'[22]

The ECOWAS diplomatic initiative in Liberia was bound to fail even before it had begun. While ECOWAS was convening a conference of

Liberian exiles in The Gambia in the last week of August 1990 to elect an
interim government, the factions in Liberia were vowing to oppose the
Peace Plan. The eventual selection of Amos Sawyer, an exiled Marxist
professor at the University of Liberia, to head the interim government in
Monrovia served only to crystallize opposition to the ECOWAS plan. In
what was described as 'a sudden new-found confidence', even Samuel
Doe, the embattled president of Liberia, accused ECOWAS leadership of
'meddling in Liberia's internal affairs', just as the NPFL contended that
'the ECOWAS discussion of an interim government showed complete and
total disregard for the constitution and sovereignty of Liberia'.[23] With
ECOWAS bent on a single-minded effort to push through its Liberian initiative, the NPFL warned that 'if there was any attempt at peacekeeping
from any part of the world, [it] would not allow that force to enter'.[24] The
stage was now set for a military showdown between ECOWAS and the
Liberian factions.

The failure of military intervention

The speed with which ECOMOG was constituted and deployed suggests
that the ECOWAS leadership did not give diplomacy a chance. At their
meeting in August 1990 in Bamako, the heads of government of the SMC
states endorsed the plan to establish ECOMOG as the principal instrument
for implementing the Liberian Peace Plan. The legal instruments establishing the force stipulate that ECOMOG be composed of military contin-
gents drawn from the member states of the SMC as well as from Guinea
and Sierra Leone. It bestowed on the force commander the power 'to
conduct military operations for the purpose of monitoring the ceasefire,
restoring law and order to create the necessary conditions for free and fair
elections to be held in Liberia'. Unlike UN resolutions authorizing the establishment of peacekeeping forces, the ECOWAS decision left the duration of the ECOMOG mission open-ended: ECOMOG operations 'shall
commence forthwith' (that is, 7 August 1990) and 'shall remain in Liberia,
if necessary, until the successful holding of general elections and the
installation of an elected government'.[25]

One week after the mission was authorized, ECOMOG forces drawn
from Nigeria, Ghana, Guinea, The Gambia and Sierra Leone began to as-
semble at Queen Elizabeth Quay in Freetown, Sierra Leone, for onward
deployment in Monrovia.[26] Under the initial command of Ghanaian
General Arnold Quainoo, ECOMOG troops landed in Monrovia on
24 August 1990, to commence what they dubbed 'Operation Liberty'.[27] In
the absence of any prior ceasefire agreement with the warring factions, the

West African forces came under fire as they came ashore in Monrovia. According to an eye-witness account:

> On landing, nothing had changed at the diplomatic level to raise bright hopes for ECOMOG in the task ahead. And so, the force had to inch ahead against all the persistent odds. The fierce fighting we sensed on the high sea between the NPFL rebels of Charles Taylor and the INPFL forces of Prince Johnson did not subside. Even as sea men struggled to anchor the ships and off-load their contents, heavy gunfire cracked, interspersed with booms from mortar, lasting for an hour.[28]

ECOMOG forces fought their way into Liberia. To accomplish even the most basic objective of establishing a foothold in Monrovia, ECOMOG had to take on local forces that then controlled the entry point around the Freeport area of Monrovia. As they consolidated and widened their defence perimeter beyond their immediate confines, ECOMOG forces pushed NPFL militia to the outskirts of Monrovia. This move produced three unpleasant consequences which greatly imperilled the mission's chances of success. First, it unnecessarily escalated the conflict by pitting the 'peacekeepers' against one of the parties to the conflict. Second, it diminished the presence and power of one of the local factions, thereby distorting the correlation of forces in the local arena. More to the point, by quickly dislodging NPFL militia from the positions that they had long occupied in Monrovia, ECOMOG forces arbitrarily enhanced the presence of a rival militia, the Independent National Patriotic Forces of Liberia (INPFL). On 9 September, the INPFL took maximum advantage of their enhanced profile to abduct and kill President Samuel Doe on the premises of ECOMOG headquarters.[29] Third, and more significantly, the view of ECOMOG as an impartial arbiter quickly eroded and was replaced by widespread perception within and outside West Africa that ECOMOG had indeed become a factor in the Liberian conflict. This perception was further strengthened by a series of deadly encounters between ECOMOG forces and various Liberian factions from 1990 onwards.

With the death of President Doe in circumstances that seriously undermined the military credibility of ECOMOG, General Babangida and Flt-Lt Jerry Rawlings of Ghana agreed in September to strengthen ECOMOG ground forces to the level of an effective fighting army. Their objective was not to deter the warring factions from launching further assaults on ECOMOG forces. Rather, it was to prepare ECOMOG for peace-enforcement actions designed to restore its prestige as a credible military force. To this end, ECOMOG strength was doubled from 3,500 in August to 7,000 soldiers by the end of September 1990. Furthermore,

ECOMOG was completely reorganized to include all three components of a modern fighting force (the army, navy and air force).

A crucial aspect of the reorganization involved the replacement of Force Commander General Quainoo – who was widely perceived to be 'soft' on the warring militia – with a more aggressive commander, Nigerian General Joshua Dogonyaro.[30] The instruction that was handed down to the new force commander was to ensure the attrition of militia forces by strictly enforcing a complete arms embargo on the warring parties in Liberia. It was reasoned that such a measure would 'prevent arms and ammunition [from] continuing to come into [*sic*] the rebel forces, who were still not subscribing to a ceasefire'.[31] In October, General Dogonyaro launched a campaign to drive out local militia forces from the vicinity of Monrovia into Liberia's heartland. By the time it was concluded in November, the ECOMOG assault described as a 'limited offensive' had inflicted so much collateral damage on Monrovia as to warrant frantic calls by many individuals and organizations, including Western diplomats sympathetic to ECOMOG, for General Dogonyaro's replacement.[32] In the aftermath of this operation, the NPFL withdrew into the safety of Gbarnga, a provincial town in the middle of Liberia. In Monrovia, ECOMOG was able to confine the remnants of INPFL forces and their leader, Prince Johnson, to a small sector of the city. It was in the midst of the illusory peace and normalcy that prevailed in Liberia at the time that ECOMOG committed one of its most serious blunders.

Against the stern opposition of the local militias, ECOMOG took the unprecedented step of installing an alternative government in Monrovia – the controversial Interim Government of National Unity (IGNU), led by Amos Sawyer. Lacking any basis of local support and widely ridiculed as a puppet of ECOWAS, IGNU became a uniting force for the leaders of disparate militia factions whose principal desire was to assume the presidency of Liberia.

By 1992 common opposition to IGNU and ECOMOG had driven many Liberians to join the NPFL, now based in Gbarnga. Emboldened by the growing mass support for his movement and the widening rift between ECOWAS states over the direction of the Liberian mission, Taylor launched 'Operation Octopus', which was a well-calculated military offensive designed to retake Monrovia.[33] To beat back the NPFL, the leadership of ECOWAS agreed to a substantial increase in the force strength of ECOMOG to 11,256 soldiers, up 60 per cent from 1990. By the time the attack was repelled in January 1993, ECOMOG and the NPFL had become so weakened and exhausted that they both expressed a new willingness to embrace a diplomatic solution to the conflict, but this time under the auspices of the United Nations. After a series of meetings that took place in Geneva at the instance of the late President Felix Houphouet-Boigny of Côte d'Ivoire, Liberia's warring parties, ECOWAS, OAU and the United Nations agreed to a new peace plan that was unveiled in Cotonou, in the summer of 1993. The new peace plan called for the dis-arming of the warring factions and the replacement of Amos Sawyer's IGNU with a collective Council of State – the Liberian National Transitional Government (LNTG). The deal also called for the demobil-ization of the warring factions, as well as the election of a substantive government in a nationwide poll. The real novelty of the Cotonou Agreement, however, lay in the establishment of the United Nations Observer Mission in Liberia (UNOMIL) to oversee the implementation of the peace plan in conjunction with an expanded ECOMOG.

THE NATURE OF THE ECOMOG–UNOMIL PARTNERSHIP

The United Nations was invited to step into the Liberian quagmire because of the politico-military stalemate encountered by ECOWAS. Although the ECOWAS–UN alliance was not born out of any mutual enthusiasm for the potential complementarities between the two organizations in the task of conflict resolution in Liberia, the UN worked hard to lay the foundation for possible organizational interdependence. The UN Secretary-General's report of 9 September 1993, on which basis the Security Council estab-lished UNOMIL through Resolution 866, was quite emphatic about the teamwork that was expected from ECOMOG and UNOMIL:

> Since the role foreseen for UNOMIL is to monitor and verify the imple-mentation of the [Cotonou] Agreement, its concept of operation neces-sarily must be parallel to that of ECOMOG. ... UNOMIL would thus ... deploy observer teams in concert with ECOMOG deployment, includ-ing border crossings, airports and seaports. ... [In short], UNOMIL and ECOMOG would collaborate closely in their operations.[34]

For these tasks, the UN Secretary-General recommended a mission comprising 303 military observers.[35] Included in this figure were 41 teams composed of six observers per team, 25 military observers based at the UNOMIL headquarters and eight observers at each of the four regional headquarters. An unspecified number of administrative or support staff were recommended for deployment to assist the military observers.

In accepting the Secretary-General's recommendation on 22 December 1993, the Security Council widened the mandate of UNOMIL to include

social reconstruction, a decision that may have been influenced by a precedent set in Somalia. According to Resolution 866, 'UNOMIL shall com-
prise military observers as well as medical, engineering, communications,
transportation and electoral components.' Its eight-item mandate is no less
extensive than that of the UN Operations in Somalia (UNOSOM). It includes the verification of compliance to the peace agreement, judicial administration of violations, delivering humanitarian assistance, engineering
local elections, rebuilding socio-economic infrastructure, disarming and
demobilizing combatants, and the like. However, notwithstanding the expansion of the tasks of the proposed mission, Resolution 866 maintained
the maximum strength of 303 observers recommended for UNOMIL and
accepted a cost ceiling of $42.6 million for the seven-month duration of
the mission.[36]

The success of UNOMIL was inextricably linked to the success of the
Cotonou Agreement. Like previous agreements before it, however, the
Cotonou Agreement collapsed soon after it was signed with much fanfare.
Attempts to establish a transitional government in Monrovia were frustrated by persistent bickering over the choice of membership. In the security arena, the disarmament programme which called for the surrendering
of all weapons and ammunition by the warring factions to UNOMIL and
ECOMOG forces failed miserably. Not only were no provisions made for
the welfare and rehabilitation of the militia, many of whom were child-
soldiers, UNOMIL failed to attract the level of personnel and material
support necessary to undertake this assignment. Consequently, it resorted
to relying on ECOMOG for initiative as well as logistical support. Not
surprisingly, therefore, UNOMIL quickly lost the trust of local factions
which had remained wary of ECOMOG; it also lost any attraction for
states willing to contribute their forces to the mission. Indeed, by the
spring of 1995, UNOMIL had shrunk from 303 observers drawn from 14
states to 77 observers (see Table 4.1). One year later, all troop-contributing
African states, except Uganda, had withdrawn their forces from UNOMIL,
thereby leaving the mission moribund. Why did this happen?

From the beginning, UNOMIL was not designed to be independent.
UNOMIL was inextricably tied both to ECOMOG as well as the Cotonou
Agreement of 1993. In the words of the UN Secretary-General:

> The role foreseen for the United Nations in the implementation of the
> Cotonou Peace Agreement is *predicated on the assumption that the
> ECOMOG force will be in a position to perform the wide-ranging tasks
> entrusted to it by the Liberian parties.* The United Nations has received
> the necessary assurances in this regard from ECOMOG. None the less, I

Table 4.1   Composition of UNOMIL, April 1995

Country	Troops	Observers
Bangladesh	7	8
China	–	5
Czech Republic	–	6
Egypt	–	7
Guinea-Bissau	–	5
India	–	6
Jordan	–	9
Kenya	2	9
Malaysia	–	8
Pakistan	–	8
Uruguay	–	6
Total	9	77

Source: *The United Nations and the Situation in Liberia* (New York: United Nations Department of Public Information, April 1995), p. 20.

must stress that should the additional troops not be deployed or should some of ECOMOG's troops be withdrawn prematurely, the successful implementation of the Peace Agreement would be in jeopardy. Obviously, *without the necessary support and cooperation of ECOMOG, UNOMIL will not be able to successfully carry out its responsibilities in the peace process.* In such an event, ... I might be obliged to recommend the withdrawal of UNOMIL.[37]

None of these conditions existed on the ground. The Cotonou Agreement failed shortly after it was initialled. Contrary to the letter and spirit of the Agreement, ECOMOG was unable to expand its forces partly because many of the African states were unable to fulfil their pledge to contribute troops for the mission. Worse still, ECOMOG was substantially downsized due to financial and domestic political uncertainties in Nigeria and continuing concerns in Ghana about the seriousness and good faith of the parties to the Liberian dispute. Indeed, by June 1994 Nigeria had reduced its contribution to 6,000 from 11,000 the previous year. With the military temporarily out of power by this time in Nigeria, the civilian-led government of Ernest Shonekan was threatening a complete pull-out from ECOMOG in order to save the tenuous regime from the fiscal and political burden of the beleaguered operation. At the same time, Ghana was completing the phased reduction of its ECOMOG force by 50 per cent, with a promise to end its participation by the end of 1994. By the end of 1993

ECOMOG 'fatigue' was already visible in the key regional states that were sponsoring the mission. This situation was further worsened by the inability of the United Nations to deliver on its promise to render financial and logistical assistance to the states contributing to ECOMOG.[38] The material capacity and political will of ECOMOG states to undertake the tasks entrusted by the Cotonou Agreement eroded.

Despite the failure of the Cotonou Agreement, the Security Council continued to extend periodically UNOMIL, even though the mission's tangible utility had significantly diminished over the years. Although largely unwritten, the present task of UNOMIL is to attempt to provide transparency to the peace process mainly by its presence, even without further material commitments to the Liberian peace process.[39] In the two years since the collapse of the Cotonou Agreement, UNOMIL has used its 'good offices' to encourage efforts to reach new and promising agreements between the warring factions in Liberia. This yielded the Akosombo Agreement of 1994 which, despite President Jerry Rawlings' widely acclaimed personal efforts and initiative, failed to bring lasting peace in Liberia.[40] The collapse of the Akosombo Agreement was quickly followed by the ratification of yet another agreement in Abuja, Nigeria, in August 1995. This agreement was largely the product of political changes in Nigeria which brought about a fundamental attitudinal and policy shift in favour of Charles Taylor and the NPFL from a widely isolated military regime in Abuja.[41]. This new agreement contained the timetable presented in Table 4.2 for ending the Liberian conflict.

For a while it seemed as though the Abuja Agreement would guarantee the lasting peace that had eluded previous conciliation efforts in Liberia. Within weeks of signing the agreement, the thorny problem of constituting the six-member Council of State was finally resolved. The membership of the council included the leaders of the major factions: Charles Taylor from the NPFL, Alhaji Kromah from the United Liberation Movement for Democracy in Liberia (ULIMO) and George Boley from the Liberian Peace Council (LPC).[42] Other members of the Council were Professor Wilton Sankawulo (Chairman), Chief Tamba Taylor and Oscar Quiah (members). However, soon after it was constituted, the collective presidency was plunged into a crisis as a power struggle ensued between its members 'over appointments to positions in government'.[43] Worse still, factional in-fighting also broke out within the United Liberation Movement for Democracy in Liberia between Alhaji Kromah and Roosevelt Johnson, forcing the latter to form his own wing: (ULIMO-J). By the end of 1995, the tension had boiled over to encourage attacks on ECOMOG forces. On 28 December, elements of ULIMO-J ambushed

Table 4.2   The major provisions and timetable of the Abuja Agreement

Dates	*Description of activities*
26 August 1995	Ceasefire takes effect throughout Liberia.
2 September 1995	The six-member collective presidency, the Council of State, is constituted.
16 December 1995	Disarmament begins with the deployment of UNOMIL and ECOMOG forces in territories controlled by the factional militias.
30 January 1996	Disarmament and demobilization of combatants are completed.
Spring 1996	The repatriation and resettlement of refugees and internally displaced persons are underway.
20 August 1996	Presidential and general elections are held throughout Liberia. The presidential election is not open to the chairman of the Council of State. However, other members of the council wishing to run for elective offices may do so only if they resigned their membership three months prior to the date of elections.

Nigerian ECOMOG forces attempting to disarm the militias. This was followed by a heavy artillery bombardment of ECOMOG's base in the
provincial town of Tubmanburg in diamond-rich Bomi County[44]
According to Max Sesay, the attack was caused by the collapse of an 'understanding between Nigerian soldiers and ULIMO-J over diamond
mining areas' controlled by Johnson's forces.[45] Following this incident,
tension increased and security deteriorated very rapidly, leading to the
indefinite suspension of ongoing disarmament operations in the Liberian
hinterland.

In February 1996, fresh clashes broke out between rival factions over
competing claims to territories previously handed over to
ECOMOG–UNOMIL as part of the disarmament process. Ben Asante, a
leading correspondent for *West Africa*, attributed the outbreak of renewed
fighting to the 'circumstantial incompetence' of ECOMOG–UNOMIL
peacekeepers in Liberia.[46] The return to street fighting in Monrovia in
April 1996 led to yet another round of refugee flows and the subsequent
evacuation of foreign nationals by US forces. The renewed violence was
triggered by the decision of the Council of State to dismiss and subsequently arrest Roosevelt Johnson for his alleged responsibility for the violence that erupted in December 1995. The spring disturbances were later

quelled by reluctant ECOMOG forces after much persuasion by Western diplomats.[47] Following the end of the hostilities, a summer meeting was called by ECOWAS in Accra to prevent the complete collapse of the Abuja Agreement. On 17 August the leaders of Liberia's factions agreed to 'a revised version of the Abuja Accord' and appointed Ruth Perry to replace Sankawulo as the chair of the Council of State.[48] The key elements of the revised Abuja Accord were: the implementation of disarmament and demobilization by 31 January 1997; the dissolution of all factional militia by the end of February 1997; general elections by 31 May 1997; and the formation of a national government by 15 June 1997.

From all indications, the revised accord has worked as planned. The disarmament and demobilization phase has proceeded without any major hitches. What is even more striking is that the new accord has been progressively implemented in spite of the United Nations, not because of it. The parties have evolved a *modus operandi* based primarily on the personal chemistry that exists between Charles Taylor and General Sani Abacha, Nigeria's military ruler. This was evidenced by the recent wedding of Charles Taylor, which was attended by the major factional leaders and hosted by Nigeria's foreign minister. Taylor, who has since emerged as General Abacha's favourite, has been highly favoured to win Liberia's presidential elections in the summer of 1997. Should this happen, why was this outcome prevented by seven years of multilateral intervention? What lessons, then, may be learned from this unusual exercise in multilateral partnership and task-sharing?

THE LESSONS OF A FAILED PARTNERSHIP

From the beginning, the United Nations viewed its security partnership with ECOWAS as an experiment. For ECOWAS, the Liberia project was the first of its kind in two significant ways. First, it was the first time that the organization had shifted its focus away from its primary objective of enhancing regional trade relations toward the uncharted waters of security integration. The legal steps for cooperation on military matters had been taken with the adoption of the Defense Protocol of 1978. Amid fears of a Nigerian domination, however, ECOWAS did not confront a security dilemma until the outbreak of the Liberian conflict in 1989. Second, and more significantly, there was no history of task-sharing between ECOWAS and the United Nations. In fact, like many African states since the failure of the United Nations Operation in the Congo (ONUC) in the 1960s, ECOWAS member states avoided UN involvement in their affairs.

That the UN–ECOWAS partnership took place at all, given the circumstances of widespread fears of domination and mistrust, is indicative of progress in African diplomacy in particular, and inter-institutional cooperation in general. What lessons may be learned from this experiment in institutional task-sharing between the United Nations and regional arrangements? The West African experience points to three crucial lessons: the complexity of the geopolitical environment; the nature of command or authority structure; and the character of international support.

The fear of domination and the necessity to steer clear of messy regional geopolitics

ECOWAS violated the cornerstone of every successful peacekeeping mission – strict adherence to the principle of impartiality. Not only must peacekeepers be impartial in their dealings with all parties to a dispute, they must be perceived as such. In Liberia, ECOWAS displayed a complete disregard for this most fundamental tenet. From the beginning, the ECOWAS mission suffered from justifiable concerns about the organization's objectivity in light of the credentials of its sponsors, especially Nigeria and Ghana. In this regard, in West Africa and much of Africa diplomacy has really been about the politics of personality.[49] In the case of Liberia, a complex web of personal ties and 'friendship' involving the principal actors in the conflict – Samuel Doe, Charles Taylor, Ibrahim Babangida, Blaise Compaoré and Jerry Rawlings among others – posed enormous challenges to the presumption of impartiality by ECOWAS.

The conflict in Liberia was the consequence of an organized effort to topple the corrupt despotism of Master-Sergeant Doe. Exiled from Liberia, Charles Taylor and other leaders of the rebellion had sought residence in various capitals in West Africa and, as a consequence, were very well known to various government officials. In one particular instance in the 1980s, the personal ties that had developed between Charles Taylor – then resident in Ghana – and President Rawlings threatened diplomatic relations between Accra and Monrovia, with President Doe accusing Rawlings of 'supporting "dissidents" seeking to overthrow his regime'. However, according to Byron Tarr, the once cosy relationship went sour, with Rawlings incarcerating Taylor in Accra. In 1987, Taylor relocated to Burkina Faso where he was warmly welcomed by Captain Blaise Compaoré, a sworn adversary of Doe.[50] But Doe was not without his own friends in the subregion. He and Nigeria's General Ibrahim Babangida did little to disguise the depth of their mutual affection. In Liberia, Doe named a major highway and a school at the University of Liberia after Ibrahim

Babangida. The latter, using state resources, returned the favour by shower-
ing Doe with largesse. Given these personal networks, individual biases
were carried into the domain of state policy once armed conflict broke out
in Liberia. Taylor was backed unconditionally by his long-time friend,
Blaise Compaoré, the leader of Burkina Faso. Doe, on the other hand,
sought and obtained the support of his President Babangida. On his part,
Flt-Lt Jerry Rawlings of Ghana had no particular reasons to support either
Doe or Taylor. Like his Nigerian counterpart, however, Rawlings did not
want to see Taylor assume the presidency of Liberia although he was far
less enthusiastic than General Babangida about taking actions to prevent
the emergence of Charles Taylor as the president of Liberia.[51] Given these
circumstances, ECOWAS merely became an institutional expression of
these biases as soon as it took on the Liberian mission.[52]

Closely related to the problem of ECOWAS's impartiality in Liberia is
the enigmatic role of Nigeria, West Africa's presumed 'hegemon'.[53] The
ECOWAS case in Liberia underlines the argument made in the theoretical
literature that hegemony is 'Janus-faced' with positive as well as negative
sides.[54] Many students of West African politics agree that Nigeria, which
was central to the formation of ECOWAS, has been the political, military
and financial force behind the organization's mission in Liberia.[55]
Between 1990 and 1996, successive Nigerian governments have spent in
excess of $3 billion on the Liberian mission. Throughout the different
phases of the Liberian mission, the Nigerian troop contribution to
ECOMOG consistently accounted for between 70 and 80 per cent of the
total strength of the force. With such level of commitment, few observers
believe that ECOMOG could have been initiated without Nigeria.

But, as significant as its contribution has been to the initiation and maintenance of the mission, Nigeria has also contributed immensely to the
problems that the ECOWAS mission in Liberia has encountered over the
years. The rigid position adopted by the Nigerian government against
Charles Taylor cost the Liberian mission the support of many ECOWAS
states, especially the francophone members. Moderate states, such as
Senegal and Togo, could not understand why General Babangida had so
much interest in *who* became Liberia's president as a result of the
ECOWAS mediation efforts.[56] According to one Senegalese official,
'Taylor's integrity is in serious doubt, but so is the integrity of Nigerian
leaders. Besides, if the process we (i.e. ECOWAS) are negotiating
produces Taylor as Liberia's leader, why should we not respect that
verdict?'[57] On several occasions between 1990 and 1994, even Ghana,
Nigeria's strongest ally in ECOWAS, expressed similar misgivings and
threatened to pull out of ECOMOG because of General Babangida's per-

sonalization of the Liberian problem around Charles Taylor. How, then, did the UN respond to this acrimonious environment?

As we have seen, the world organization firmly immersed itself in the dirt of West Africa's politics of hegemony by aligning itself so closely to Nigeria and ECOMOG. If it has been difficult to distinguish between the UN and ECOMOG in Liberia, it is because very little effort was made by UNOMIL to formulate an independent initiative. The United Nations accepted the much disputed ECOWAS Peace Plan as the principal plank on which to pursue reconciliation in Liberia.[58] When that agreement failed, the UN jumped quickly to endorse the Cotonou, Akosombo and Abuja Agreements that were similarly 'destined' to failure. In all this, the UN was playing catch-up, thereby raising questions about the world organization's initiative and leadership in the vital area of international peace and security. The obvious lesson from Liberia, therefore, is that if the UN must accept the invitation of regional organizations to intervene in regional conflicts following the exhaustion of local initiatives and options, the world body should invest its resources into crafting an alternative peace initiative rather than merely becoming a rubber stamp for failed plans.

The dysfunctional nature of parallel command structures

Whatever its intended uses, the existence of parallel authority structures hampers the effectiveness of field operations by blurring the hierarchy of command. In Liberia, UNOMIL and ECOMOG maintained parallel command structures. This is especially surprising considering the UN had been invited because of the particular deficiencies of the regional command structure. The weakness of UN deployments in the field frequently challenged the relative autonomy of the UN's chain of command, thus leaving the ECOWAS command structure as the only real source of authority to which Liberia's warring factions frequently referred. Consequently, the subordination of regional command structures to global authority was neither attempted nor achieved by UNOMIL. For this particular reason, UNOMIL was essentially redundant in Liberia as a participant in the process of conflict resolution. The structural parallelism that characterized the command and control apparatus of ECOWAS and the UN in Liberia may be attributed to UNOMIL's weak financial base from the beginning of the mission or mere administrative oversight at the UN Secretariat. Whatever the reason, however, the parallelism for the most part strengthened the position and significance of Nigeria and ECOWAS and it served only to promote the idea and perception that the United Nations was either incapable of peace-enforcement actions or unwilling to undertake such tasks in Liberia.[59] It also provided crucial evidence to support the predictive logic of hegemony theory present in other cases in this volume (especially Georgia), that the UN will tend to defer to regional powers when it is engaged in a partnership with regional organizations, especially in the security issue-area.[60]

The desirability of political conditionalities for supporting regional security initiatives

The ECOWAS experience in Liberia demonstrates the need for better judgement by the United Nations in approving or delegating security tasks to regional organizations. The issue is not whether security tasks should be devolved to regional arrangements. Rather, it is what kinds of security tasks should be devolved to what kinds of regional institutions, and what conditions need be met by them? In such cases as Liberia, where the causes of conflict are to be located in the abuses of despotic regimes, the United Nations is *obliged* to ensure that those states and organizations that are authorized to mediate such conflicts are themselves free from the menace of despotism. As Ofuatey-Kodjoe has argued:

... the notion that a group of states headed by military dictatorships have the right to intervene in another state in order to establish a democratic regime is grotesque. And the notion that these states can in fact achieve that objective by the application of outside force may be only an exercise in wishful thinking.[61]

In West Africa, Nigeria's military rulers used Liberia as a dress rehearsal for their elaborate scheme to consolidate despotic rule in their own country.[62]

In conclusion, those looking for a model of UN burden-sharing with regional arrangements should be directed away from ECOWAS and Liberia. At its best, the UN involvement in Liberia may be characterized as indifferent and purposeless. With the majority of its forces 'stranded' in their home countries because of logistical lapses, UNOMIL relied too heavily on ECOMOG forces even for the most basic tasks. This was the direct consequence of the gross inadequacy of funding for the mission. In 1994 when the Security Council authorized the mission, the Secretariat estimated the cost of the operation at $36.4 million for the initial duration of seven months. However, according to Max Sesay, 'by the end of that year the assessed contributions paid by member states ... amounted to only $5.7 million.'[63] It is hardly surprising, therefore, that many Liberians were unaware of a UN presence in their country. The dismal performance of

UNOMIL should dramatize to the leadership of the United Nations the high cost of half-hearted measures relating to the maintenance of international peace and security. The UN should re-evaluate the wisdom of authorizing missions simply to create the impression that something significant is being done in a desperate environment.

NOTES

1. Established in 1975, ECOWAS is the principal regional economic grouping in West Africa. Its membership of 16 states – francophone, anglophone and lusophone – makes it the largest and by far the most complex subregional organization in Africa. Its members are: Benin, Burkina Faso, Cape Verde, Côte d'Ivoire, The Gambia, Ghana, Guinea, Guinea-Bissau, Liberia, Mali, Mauritania, Niger, Nigeria, Senegal, Sierra Leone and Togo. See S. K. B. Asante, *The Political Economy of Regionalism in Africa: A Decade of the Economic Community of West African States (ECOWAS)* (New York: Praeger, 1986); and C. E. Adibe, 'ECOWAS in comparative perspective', in Timothy M. Shaw and Julius E. Okolo (eds), *The Political Economy of Foreign Policy in ECOWAS* (London: Macmillan, 1994), Chapter 11.

2. UN Secretary-General, *Report of the Secretary-General on Liberia*, UN Security Council document S/26422, 9 September 1993, p. 11.

3. Ibid., p. 4.

4. David Wippman, 'Enforcing the peace: ECOWAS and the Liberian civil war', in Lori F. Damrosch (ed.), *Enforcing Restraint: Collective Intervention in Internal Conflicts* (New York: Council on Foreign Relations, 1993), p. 165; see also W. Ofuatey-Kodjoe, 'Regional organizations and the resolution of internal conflict: the ECOWAS intervention in Liberia', *International Peacekeeping*, 1 (3), 1994, pp. 261–302.

5. *Africa Research Bulletin*, 15 February 1990, p. 9557 (emphasis added). The implicit pejorativeness of this anthropological description was responsible for the tensions that long characterized the relationship among Liberia's socio-economic groups – Gios, Mandingos, Manos, Krahns, Americo-Liberians. See J. Gus Liebenow, *Liberia: The Evolution of Privilege* (Ithaca, NY: Cornell University Press, 1969); Monday Akpan, 'Black imperialism: Americo-Liberian rule over the African peoples of Liberia, 1841–1964', *Canadian Journal of African Studies*, 7 (2), 1973, pp. 217–36; and Wippman, 'Enforcing the peace', pp. 160–5.

6. See Gani Yoroms, *Regional Security, Collective Defence and the Problem of Peace Initiatives in West Africa: The Case of ECOMOG in the Liberian Conflict*, paper presented at the 17th Annual Conference of the Nigerian Society of International Affairs, Centre for Democratic Studies, Abuja, Nigeria, 9–11 December 1991; W. Ofuatey-Kodjoe, 'Regional organizations and the resolution of internal conflict', pp. 268–81; and Jinmi Adisa,

86 *Clement E. Adibe*

'Nigeria in ECOMOG: political undercurrents and the burden of community spirit', *Small Wars and Insurgencies*, 5 (1), 1994, pp. 83–110.

7. See *Newswatch* (Lagos), 14 May 1990; and Osisioma Nwolise, 'The internationalisation of the Liberian crisis and its effects on West Africa', in Margaret Vogt (ed.), *The Liberian Crisis and ECOMOG: A Bold Attempt at Regional Peacekeeping* (Lagos: Gabumo Publishing, 1992), p. 60.

8. See Chike Akabogu, 'ECOWAS takes the initiative', in ibid., p. 73.

9. See Salim Ahmed Salim's interview in *West Africa* (London), 13–19 August 1990; and excerpts of Yoweri Museveni's interview with the British Broadcasting Corporation (BBC) in *Contact: The Official Journal of the Economic Community of West African States*, 2 (3), November 1990, p. 8. One year later, Zimbabwe's President Robert Mugabe further challenged the sacrosanctity of the OAU's non-intervention clause. He argued that 'the "domestic affairs" of a country must mean affairs within a peaceful environment, but where that peaceful environment is completely gone and the people are no longer in a position to exercise their own sovereign authority, ... surely the time would have come for an intervention to occur.' Quoted in Ben Ephson, 'Right to intervene', *West Africa* (London), 4–10 February 1991, p. 141.

10. *Contact*, 2 (3), November 1990, p. 6. The Nigerian proposal was not without precedent in African diplomacy. When conflict broke out in 1980 between Libyan-backed rebel forces and troops loyal to Goukouni Weddeye in Chad, Western diplomats successfully urged Nigeria to take on a 'leadership' role in constituting and deploying an African peacekeeping force in Chad. Nigeria did, and African peacekeepers were deployed in Chad between 1981 and 1982. Without the promised inflow of technical, logistical and financial support, the mission floundered as Libyan-backed rebels overran the positions of OAU peacekeepers and swept through Njadmena to form a new government. For details, see Amadu Sesay, 'The limits of peace-keeping by a regional organization: the OAU peace-keeping force in Chad', *Conflict Quarterly*, Winter 1992, pp. 7–26; and William J. Foltz and Henry Bienen (eds), *Arms and the African: Military Influences on Africa's International Relations* (New Haven, Conn.: Yale University Press, 1985).

11. During its active years, between 1990 and 1994, the SMC added Guinea and Sierra Leone – two of Liberia's immediate neighbours – as *de facto* members.

12. ECOWAS, *Final Report of the ECOWAS Standing Mediation Committee Ministerial Meeting, Freetown, 5–20 July 1990*, ECW/SMC/FM/90/3/Rev.1, 1990, pp. 4–5.

13. Ibid., pp. 6-8.

14. Ibid., p. 11.

15. Ibid., p. 10.

16. Ibid, p. 11 (emphasis added).

17. ECOWAS, *Decision A/DEC.1/8/90* (Lagos: The Economic Community of West African States, 1990). See also *People's Daily Graphic* (Accra), 3 August 1990, pp. 2–3.

18. *Africa News*, 9–13 December 1991, p. 8.

19. Ibrahim Babangida, 'The imperative features of the Nigerian foreign policy and the crisis in Liberia', *Contact*, 2 (3), 1990, p. 14.

20. Quoted in *Africa Research Bulletin*, 15 September 1990, p. 9802.
21. In this regard, see especially G. Idang, *Nigeria: Internal Policy and Foreign Policy* (Ibadan, Nigeria: University of Ibadan Press, 1974); Stellan Lindqvist, *Linkages Between Domestic and Foreign Policy: The Record of Ghana, 1957–1966* (Lund, Sweden: Studentlitteratur Lund, 1974); and W. Ofuatey-Kodjoe, 'Regional organizations and the resolution of internal conflict', pp. 261–302.
22. Dr Obed Asamoah, quoted in the *People's Daily Graphic* (Accra), 23 August 1990, p. 1. See also A. Essuman-Johnson, 'The Liberian refugee problem and Ghana's response to it', *LECIA Bulletin*, 2 (1), March, 1992, pp. 34–40.
23. *The Guardian* (Lagos), 21 August 1990, p. 1.
24. *People's Daily Graphic* (Accra), 21 July 1990, p. 2.
25. ECOWAS, *Decision A/DEC.1/8/90*, Article II, p. 4.
26. On 23 August Togo, the fifth member of the SMC, announced that it would not contribute troops to ECOMOG because of the absence of a ceasefire agreement between ECOWAS and Liberia's warring factions. For details, see *Africa Research Bulletin*, 15 September 1990, p. 9801.
27. For a detailed account of the military operation, see Nkem Agetua, *Operation Liberty: The Story of Major General Joshua Dogonyaro* (Lagos: Hona Communications, 1992); and Segun Aderiye, 'ECOMOG landing', in Vogt (ed.), *The Liberian Crisis and ECOMOG*, pp. 95–122.
28. Segun Aderiye, 'ECOMOG landing', p. 106.
29. *The Guardian* (Lagos), 14 September 1990, p. 1, and 20 September 1990, p. 1; *Sunday Concord* (Lagos), 23 September 1990, p. 7; *The Punch* (Ibadan), 18 October 1990, p. 7; *People's Daily Graphic* (Accra), 11 May 1991, p. 2.
30. For insight into the differing personalities of the two soldiers, see Agetua, *Operation Liberty*, Chapters 5–8; and Jinmi Adisa, 'ECOMOG force commanders', in Vogt (ed.), *The Liberian Crisis and ECOMOG*, pp. 237–70. This created a diplomatic row between Nigeria and Ghana which was quickly resolved to maintain the ECOMOG coalition.
31. Vogt, 'The problems and challenges of peace-making: from peace-keeping to peace enforcement', in Vogt (ed.), *The Liberian Crisis and ECOMOG*, p. 155.
32. Ibid., pp. 155–7; and Jinmi Adisa, 'ECOMOG force commanders', pp. 237–70.
33. *West Africa* (London), 23–29 August 1993, p. 1484.
34. *Report of the Secretary-General on Liberia*, Security Council document S/26422, 9 September 1993, p. 4.
35. Ibid., p. 5, para. 18.
36. *Report of the Secretary-General on Liberia: Addendum*, UN Security Council document S/26422/Add.1, 17 September 1993, p. 2.
37. *Report of the Secretary-General on Liberia*, UN Security Council document S/26422, 9 September 1993, para. 39, p. 10 (emphasis added).
38. Ibid., p. 6, paras 23–4. See also UN Security Council document S/26200. As an exception, Senegal benefited substantially from US financial and logistical support. In 1991 US support for Senegal's participation in ECOMOG included $42 million in debt-forgiveness, $15 million worth of military equipment and $1 million direct cash allocation. This made Senegal the

largest recipient of US aid directly related to the ECOWAS operation in
Liberia. The other recipients of US aid were Côte d'Ivoire, $1 million;
Ghana, Guinea and Sierra Leone, $0.5 million each; and The Gambia, $0.25
million. For details, see Robert Mortimer, 'Senegal's rôle in ECOMOG: the
francophone dimension in the Liberian crisis', *Journal of Modern African
Studies*, 34 (2), 1996, p. 297.

39.   See Clement E. Adibe, *Managing Arms in Peace Processes: Liberia* (Geneva:
      United Nations, 1996), p. 43; John Mackinlay and Abiodun Alao, *Liberia
      1994: ECOMOG and UNOMIL Response to a Complex Emergency* (New
      York: United Nations University, 1995), Occasional Paper No. 1.
40.   See UN Security Council document S/1994/1174, 16 October 1994; and
      S/1995/7, 5 January 1995.
41.   *West Africa* (London), 25–31 December 1995; and 1–7 January 1996,
      p. 1993.
42.   Ibid., 25–31 December 1995; and 1–7 January 1996, p. 1993.
43.   Ibid., 18–24 March 1996, pp. 422–3.
44.   Ibid., 22–28 January 1996, pp. 97–9.
45.   Max Ahmadu Sesay, 'Politics and society in post-war Liberia', *Journal of
      Modern African Studies*, 34 (3), 1996, p. 402. The economic basis of the fre-
      quent fractionalization of Liberia's warring groups is an important element
      in the continuation of the conflict. According to one report, Liberia's
      diamond exports between 1990 and 1994 amounted to $300 million, timber
      earned $53 million and $27 million accrued from the export of rubber.
      These revenues went directly to the leader of whichever faction controlled
      the regions that generated the resources. For details, see James Butty,
      'Bankrolling conflict', *West Africa* (London), 8–14 July 1996, p. 1067
46.   Ibid., 22–28 January 1996, p. 98.
47.   According to Sesay's account, this was made possible by Nigeria's reversal
      of its earlier instruction to 'ECOMOG to remain neutral and to treat the
      matter as an internal affair' (p. 404). The original instruction came in the
      wake of international, particularly American, condemnation of General
      Abacha's regime in the aftermath of the execution of Ken Saro-Wiwa and
      other human rights activists in November 1995. By instructing ECOMOG
      forces to withold action in Liberia in April 1996, General Abacha was
      saying that: 'It is important for the United States to recognise the relevance
      of Nigeria ... at least in the West African subregion' (*Washington Times*,
      30 January 1997).
48.   Max Ahmadu Sesay, 'Politics and society in post-war Liberia', p. 405.
49.   For a theoretical discussion of the impact of personality on foreign policy,
      see Margaret G. Hermann, 'The effects of personal characteristics of politi-
      cal leaders on foreign policy', in Maurice East et al. (eds), *Why Nations Act:
      Theoretical Perspectives for Comparative Foreign Policy Studies*, (Beverly
      Hills, Calif.: Sage Publications, 1978), pp. 49–68; and Olajide Aluko (ed.),
      The Foreign Policies of African States (London: Hodder & Stoughton,
      1977).
50.   S. Byron Tarr, 'The ECOMOG initiative in Liberia: a Liberian perspective',
      Issue: A Journal of Opinion, 21 (1–2), 1993, pp. 79–80.
51.   For a long time, this was one of the major sources of tension between
      Nigeria and Ghana. For Nigeria, regime insecurity (which Rawlings has

now overcome) was the crucial factor. Within the country's ruling military circles, Charles Taylor's revolt and his successful recruitment of a significant number of 'disgruntled' nationals of other ECOWAS states, including Nigeria, was viewed as a forerunner of 'the coming anarchy': a 'carefully orchestrated' plan to 'destabilize' the entire West African subregion. In Lagos, suspicions were rife that Taylor's recruits included some military personnel who had been declared 'wanted persons' in Nigeria because of their alleged role in an unsuccessful coup attempt to topple the government of General Ibrahim Babangida in 1990. For this reason in particular, confirmed reports reaching Lagos of Libyan support in terms of training and equipment quickly struck a raw nerve in government and security circles, and helped to elevate the Liberian crisis as a national security issue *par excellence* for Nigeria.

52. This development is not surprising to critics of regional organizations who have pointed to the danger of partisanship that may arise should regional organizations intervene in local conflicts in which they are familiar with the actors and issues. See S. Neil MacFarlane and Thomas G. Weiss, 'Regional organizations and regional security', *Security Studies*, 2 (1), 1992, pp. 6–37.

53. See Ademola Adeleke, 'The politics and diplomacy of peacekeeping in West Africa: the ECOWAS operation in Liberia', *Journal of Modern African Studies*, 33 (4), 1995, pp. 569–93.

54. Cf. Mancur Olson, *The Logic of Collective Action: Public Goods and the Theory of Groups* (Cambridge, Mass.: Harvard University Press, 1965); Robert Keohane, 'The theory of hegemonic stability and changes in international economic regimes, 1967–1977', in Ole Holsti et al. (eds), *Change in the International System* (Boulder, Colo.: Westview Press, 1980); and David Laitin, *Hegemony and Culture* (Chicago: The University of Chicago Press, 1986); Duncan Snidal, 'The limits of hegemonic stability theory', *International Organization*, 39 (4), 1985, pp. 579–614.

55. See, among others, Gani J. Yoroms, 'ECOMOG and West Africa regional security: a Nigerian perspective', *Issue*, 21 (1–2), 1993, pp. 84–91; Emmanuel Kwezi Aning, *Managing Regional Security in West Africa: ECOWAS, ECOMOG and Liberia* (Copenhagen: Centre for Development Research, February 1994, Working Paper No. 94.2; E. John Inegbedion, 'ECOMOG in comparative perspective', in Shaw and Okolo (eds), *The Political Economy of Foreign Policy in ECOWAS*, Chapter 12.

56. For the francophone dimension of the ECOMOG mission, see Mortimer, 'Senegal's rôle in ECOMOG', pp. 293–306.

57. Author's interview, Geneva, Switzerland, 3 May 1995. The issue of Taylor's integrity arose because his background as a fugitive from American justice has been widely reported by the West African media. Taylor's reputation in West Africa has also suffered significantly from his public perception as a corrupt, power-hungry iconoclast who indulges in cold-blooded murder.

58. See 'Statements by the President of the Security Council', 23 January 1991 (Security Council document S/22133, 23 January 1991; and S/23886, 7 May 1992), which endorsed the ECOWAS Peace Plan. See also Security Council Resolution 788 of 19 November 1992, which globalized the contentious ECOWAS embargo on the delivery of arms 'and ammunition to Liberia's

warring factions. For a useful critique of UN 'endorsement', see Anthony Ofodile, 'Recent development: the legality of ECOWAS intervention in Liberia', *Columbia Journal of Transnational Law*, 32 (2), 1994, pp. 413–16.

59. See James E. Cooper, 'The fate of the United States and Liberia is interwoven: now is the time for healing', *The Liberian Diaspora*, 3 (11), January 1993, pp. 16–8.

60. See Robert O. Keohane and Lisa L. Martin, 'The promise of institutionalist theory', *International Security* 20, Summer 1995, pp. 39–51.

61. W. Ofuatey-Kodjoe, 'Regional organizations and the resolution of internal conflict', p. 295.

62. See Ofodile, 'Recent development', pp. 396–402.

63. Sesay, 'Politics and society in post-war Liberia', p. 407. See also Stephen Riley, 'Intervention in Liberia: too little, too partisan', *The World Today*, 49 (3), 1993, pp. 42–3.

5 Searching for OAS/UN Task-Sharing Opportunities in Central America and Haiti

Joaquín Tacsan[1]

As is true in other parts of the world, the United Nations (UN) is playing an increasing role in Central America and the Caribbean. After 45 years of self-prescribed ostracism, the UN has launched its first peacekeeping operation in the hemisphere, monitored and verified elections, mediated peace negotiations and helped implement peace agreements. Moreover, the role of the UN in El Salvador and Haiti is considered by many as exemplary peacebuilding experience.

This dynamic UN involvement for the past eight years has broken apart the traditional perception of Latin America as an area pertaining to the exclusive competence of the Organization of American States (OAS). As the largest intergovernmental organization of the Americas, the OAS was designed to have, and is perceived in general by member states as having, chief competence over hemispheric matters. Therefore, no inter-American problem or dispute – and thus, no Central American or Caribbean question – could have been taken to the UN without being previously handled by the OAS. This is not the case anymore, as may be suggested by the UN's leading role in bringing peace to El Salvador and Guatemala.

Interestingly, the present decade has also witnessed a renewed optimism toward the OAS. After years of inaction during the past decade, the OAS has been able to achieve some growth, especially in the human rights and democracy fields. The OAS played an active role in monitoring elections in Nicaragua in the context of the UN Observer Mission (ONUVEN) and in helping to disarm and reintegrate the Contras in the framework of the Commission for International Support and Verification (CIAV/OAS). Despite the lack of enforcement mechanisms, the OAS has provided hemispheric leadership in the protection of democracy and human rights, taking the first initiatives to negotiate with Manuel Noriega's dictatorship in Panama and with Raul Cédras' *de facto* regime in Haiti. The antidemocratic

behaviour of these leaders prompted negotiations and decisive con-
demnations. As for its role in human rights, the Inter-American Court of
Human Rights, an organ of the OAS's protection system, rendered a
judgement that resulted in the indictment of high-level Honduran military
officers who in the 1980s had ordered the abduction and killing of
hundreds of university students.

This article focuses on determining the normative and operational capacity
of the OAS in order to examine the possibility of task division and cooperation with the UN. The core consists of an exploration of OAS achievements
in the monitoring and diplomacy arenas and how such achievements can
translate into greater or lesser interorganizational task-sharing.

I submit that, if the UN and the OAS were to share tasks on the basis of
each other's 'appropriate performance' as I define below, monitoring and
diplomacy in the hemisphere would see a clearer division of tasks and
more effective collaboration between the two organizations. In some
cases, the two would work separately. In others, the UN would come to
the subregion on its own with the OAS playing a subsidiary role, very
much in the way that the UN did in 1988 during its first peacekeeping
mission in Central America. There would be occasions in which the OAS
would take the lead, and others in which the regional organization would
call upon the UN to undertake joint action, as they did in Haiti.

LESSONS FROM OAS INVOLVEMENT IN CENTRAL AMERICA AND HAITI

Is regional better?

From 1980 to 1989, when Central American countries were facing a
period of political and military tensions, civil war and foreign intervention,
the OAS played an almost insignificant role in the isthmus. Indeed, con-
tentions by Nicaraguan Sandinistas that the OAS was controlled and manipulated by Washington were enough to thwart any OAS involvement
in the region. The Reagan administration's interventionist policies in
Nicaragua and questionable OAS sponsorship of US intervention in
Guatemala in 1954 and the Dominican Republic in 1965 were sufficient
evidence for Nicaraguans that the OAS was not an impartial actor.

Inaction in Central America caused the OAS to lose credibility in Latin
America as a whole. Failure in Central America built upon the Falklands
Islands incident to undermine hemispheric confidence on the organization.
In fact, the OAS's marginal role in the war between England and

Argentina was perhaps the first palpable case of the OAS's disability. Latin Americans painfully had to see how Washington, the main engine of hemispheric solidarity, bluntly supported the British, taking sides with the 'external' power and 'betraying' the most sacrosanct principles of Pan-Americanism: collective defence, solidarity and sovereignty.

A marginal role in the Falklands War and the lack of activity in Central America seriously affected the OAS. Despite the organization's growing human rights regime and some technical assistance functions, it was clear that the OAS had failed to accomplish its main purpose: the maintenance of peace and security in the region. OAS deficiencies constituted fertile ground for scepticism, and in the hemisphere, some even challenged the need for a regional organization, favouring *ad hoc* regional mechanisms and arrangements.

Increasing distrust around the OAS coincided with greater optimism about the UN. In fact, hopes for a new world order were placed in the UN, but only during the first years of the post-Cold War era. Today, excitement for the UN has fallen back almost to Cold War levels and the need for task-sharing with regional and non-governmental organizations (NGOs) has become desirable. There is a greater need for an OAS that could handle crucial peacemaking and peacebuilding tasks in the Americas and that is capable of effective task-sharing with the UN.

Fortunately, in contrast to what occurred a few years ago, the OAS apparently has been salvaged by a new sense of direction. The OAS is providing leadership in favour of formal democracy in the Americas, observing elections and monitoring human rights observance, condemning coups and, generally speaking, helping to restore democratic order in Peru, Guatemala and Haiti. New organizational goals, norms and procedures seem to have helped to revitalize a once declining institution.

This new scenario once again stimulates debate over the traditional regional/universal dichotomy. On the one hand, regionalists may argue, as John Burton did more than twenty years ago on conflict resolution, that 'the necessary first step of breaking up and uncovering issues is far more likely to take place in regional discussion than at a centralized forum comprising one hundred nations.'[2] On the other hand, advocates of universalism point out that neighbours are not always impartial and that they normally lack adequate material and personnel resources to properly handle intra-member conflicts. 'Extraneous actors', universalists say, like the UN, can easily achieve impartiality and attain greater credibility in resolving local conflicts.

Regionalists would reply that members of regional organizations are more likely to understand the factual background of disputes and share the applicable norms and procedures. Furthermore, as Joseph Nye observed about regional settings, 'talking is more productive and certainly easier, the greater the general feeling of sympathy and friendship among the participants.'[3] The regional/universal debate can never be resolved. Indeed, neither side will be able to provide the necessary empirical evidence to sustain their arguments, and both sides are plagued with relativism, because none of their generalizations is free from exceptions. These exceptions are too many to sustain any important pattern. For example, those who assert that regional is better at resolving conflicts must explain why wars in El Salvador and Guatemala were so successfully mediated by the UN. Likewise, arguments in favour of the UN will have to underestimate the long-standing tradition of OAS successful appeasement of tensions in Central America.

The Western Hemisphere is perhaps the last place for pondering a hypothesis favouring one of the sides of the traditional regional/universal debate. In the past fifty years, UN diplomacy and monitoring in the region have been small-scale and recent, especially when compared with those of the OAS. The UN had electoral observation and verification roles in Nicaragua and very active mediation, electoral observation and peace-building tasks in El Salvador. Success in El Salvador led to a strong UN involvement in peacemaking in Guatemala and peacebuilding in Haiti. The rest of the UN's involvement in Central America only dates back to the implementation of the Esquipulas Accords in 1988. The diplomatic experience of the UN in Nicaragua, El Salvador, Guatemala and Haiti is not enough to draw the kind of empirical data that is required to support either a universalist or a regionalist position.

From an OAS vantage, it is also difficult to obtain a good empirical case for regionalists. Despite its long history of dealing with hemispheric affairs, the work of the OAS does not show any steady story of success. On the contrary, as was indicated earlier, the OAS has until recently been considered a decaying institution and none of its current work can be considered decisive enough to determine probable OAS advantages over the world organization.

Thus, as far as the Western Hemisphere is concerned, the regional/universal debate is inconclusive. There are, however, more chances for us to find areas of possible collaboration, primarily in the face of the constant and dramatic changes in the international context. The increasing needs for peacemaking and peacebuilding, the growing complexity of issues and conflicts, and the intractability of new local and global problems, are some of the reasons for urgent regional/universal cooperation. This is perhaps the most compelling argument against the traditional regional versus universal perspective. The new debate must look more into the means to accomplish mutual cooperation and assistance rather than competition between regional and universal organizations. Collaboration may grow as far as each organization is allowed to do what it has been doing satisfactorily in the past forty or fifty years.[4]

Based on this premise, some ask 'who does best or better?' We are more interested in 'who performs what appropriately?'. In what areas of work is the organization showing appropriate management of the complexity of the issues that are dealt with and of member states' interdependence in matters falling within the diplomacy and monitoring arenas? I understand diplomacy as the organization's use of political persuasion, mediation and enforcement with the purpose of maintaining peace and security. Monitoring refers to observation, verification and investigation of particular member activities.

To trace the basic appropriate performance within a regional organization we must look at its management of certain situations threatening peace, stability and security. Organizations that 'perform appropriately' are able to redefine means and mechanisms when necessary, innovate approaches and foster members' consensus around certain principles, norms and procedures. Appropriate performers are also good learners; members and staff are ready to internalize innovative normative and operational knowledge and apply such knowledge to decision-making styles. We now consider appropriate performance by the OAS both in the normative and the operational fields.

From normativism to norm creation

The OAS is an ideal setting for both normativism and norm creation. The term 'normativism' is used here to depict excessive production of norms that are not usefully applied for the purposes created. These norms remain in a mythic condition because they only exist on paper and not as operational law. In contrast, norm creation is the learning process by which a body of consensual norms is created by members to resolve practical needs and fit new institutional goals, even if such innovation may imply a redefinition of other principles, norms and procedures. Most recently, norm creation has prevailed over normativism, although this has not usually been the case. It is important to explain both processes of normativism and norm creation in some detail.

Normativism
The Pan-American conferences, which started in 1926 at the Conference of Panama and culminated with the creation of the OAS in 1949, produced a myriad of conventions and treaties. They ranged from the establishment

of unions and confederations to promotion of hemispheric solidarity and
defence alliances to peaceful settlement procedures.[5]

These agreements produced a rich normative base for collective under-
takings, particularly to avoid conflicts among members and to defend them
from foreign interventions that would threaten the territorial integrity and
sovereignty of member states. The text of Article 1 of the 1948
Confederation Treaty is very illustrative in this regard:

> *Article 1.* The high contracting parties unite, ally, and confederate to
> defend the sovereignty and independence of all and every one of them;
> to maintain the territorial integrity of their respective territories, and
> secure full dominion on such lands; and not to consent to offenses or
> wrongdoings against any one of them. To this effect, they will assist
> each other with their terrestrial and maritime forces, and any other
> means available.

Collective defence and security is certainly one of the areas that has received special attention in Latin America. Its major limitation, however, is
a strong bias against foreign invaders so that no collective initiative was
conceived of to defend one member from another. Thus, collective
defence could not be undertaken against any Latin American country.
Interestingly, however, most wars in Central and South America occurred
between the very same countries.

To avoid or terminate conflict between member states, neither the
Confederation Treaty of 1948 nor the subsequent agreements until the
mid-1900s ever considered the possibility of using collective peace-
enforcement. To stop violent behaviour and conflict, the Confederation
Treaty prohibited the use of force by members, consecrated the principle
of non-intervention and relied heavily on the so-called peaceful means for
the settlement of disputes.

This original emphasis on peaceful settlement may somewhat explain
the centrality of diplomacy and the subsidiarity of enforcement in the
present OAS. The lack of enforcement mechanisms to deal with members'
hostility with one another and the long-standing efforts of Latin
Americans to create the perfect peace system provoked a hemispheric attitude towards the complete regulation of continental affairs that has lasted
until the present. In fact, between 1920 and 1940, the American states produced more than 12 formal treaties on arbitration, mediation and conciliation of disputes, none of which was actually applied, except for the
peaceful mechanisms deployed for the dispute between Haiti and the
Dominican Republic in 1937.

With the exception of the Inter-American Peace Committee, an informal instrument that was established in 1940 to provide mediation and good offices, all other mechanisms and treaties created by the American states were never used. The same pattern was repeated once again years later with regard to one of the main components of the Inter-American System, namely the 1949 American Treaty on Pacific Settlement of Disputes (Bogotá Pact) – one of the mostly acclaimed instruments for conflict resolution that has never been applied to any inter-American dispute. The prolific treaty creation process that preceded the OAS, and even included some of the organization's major pillars, was indeed excessive normativism with little use and application to hemispheric reality.

At least two basic reasons explain why OAS members have been so reluctant in using the Bogotá Pact. First, although the pact is widely considered one of the most complete pieces of legislation on peaceful settlement, it is precisely its highly sophisticated and formalistic approach that makes it so impractical. Second, the pact lacks an enforcement provision that would make the parties comply with any settlement arrived at under the pact.[6]

Norm creation

The lack of enforcement mechanisms within the Bogotá Pact may have led many OAS members to frequently invoke the Inter-American Treaty of Reciprocal Assistance (the Rio Treaty). Signed in Rio de Janeiro in 1947, the Rio Treaty provides for collective defence, not only from foreign attacks but also from any action or threat posed by one member against another. At the heart of the Rio Treaty is Article 3:

> *Article 3.* The High Contracting Parties agree that an armed attack by any one state against an American State will be considered an attack against all American States. Thus, each one of the said Contracting Parties commits itself to help and confront the attack, in application of the imminent collective and individual self-defense recognized in Article 51 of the UN Charter.

This provision represented enough guarantee of enforcement for members negotiating in the framework of the Rio Treaty. At the same time, the treaty also provides for peaceful settlement mechanisms as a complement to the right of self-defence, making it the perfect replacement for a formalistic Bogotá Pact. Applications of the treaty include the 1949 and 1955 Nicaragua/Costa Rica disputes, the 1957 Honduras/Nicaragua conflict and the 1969 El Salvador/Honduras (Soccer) War.

The Rio Treaty was the most useful and more frequently invoked instrument in inter-American affairs. Before the Rio Treaty was severely damaged for not being applied in the Falklands War and in Nicaragua, a great deal of learning and informal norm development occurred in the OAS. Without such normative development, the OAS would have been destined to disappear.

The demise of the Cold War witnessed a resurgence of norm creation processes in the OAS. The emergence of democracy as the undisputed form of government in almost every corner of the world easily restored one of the traditional discourses within the OAS. Mainly to support US hegemonic interest in the region, democracy had always occupied a place of honour in the organization's purposes. The exclusion of Cuba, the invasion of the Dominican Republic in 1965 and the ousting of Guatemala's Arbenz in 1954 are a few examples of hemispheric rhetorical uses of democracy in the fight against communism. The post-Cold War era, however, shows a different phenomenon. The current promotion of formal democracy is not necessarily a product of Washington's hegemonic interests. The democracy rule rather seems to resemble a unanimous distaste for power concentration in the hands of a few and rejection of the corrupt practices and repressive methods of military dictatorships. Upgraded from a 'Charter purpose' to an organizational goal, the democracy norm has put the OAS once again in the lead. The day the international community intervened in the internal affairs of Haiti to oust a dictatorial regime and restore the elected authorities, the OAS affirmed a new regional norm and started to change the shape of international law.

During the period between 1949 and 1995, four important norm creation trends can be identified in the Inter-American System that, one way or the other, will have an impact in OAS/UN task-sharing possibilities. First, the protection of democracy has been elevated to a regional entitlement. In 1979 the OAS took unprecedented steps to deal with the Somoza dictatorship in Nicaragua and planted a seed of change. Following a meeting of the ministers of foreign relations called by the government of Venezuela to consider the grave events taking place under the Somoza regime, the OAS issued a resolution calling for the replacement of Somoza and for the installation of a democratic and multiparty government that would represent the free will of the Nicaraguan people. This resolution legitimized all efforts to oust Somoza, including the insurrectional activities by the Sandinista revolutionary movement.

OAS absence from conflict in Central America during the past decade did not allow observers to realize that the 1979 resolution would be recreated in the future for other cases and against other dictatorial regimes. In the early 1990s, resolutions condemning the dictatorial regimes of Noriega in Panama, Fujimori in Peru, Serrano Elías in Guatemala and Cédras in Haiti followed the one adopted against Somoza a decade earlier. Peace in Central America came at the very moment at which a full wave of civilian and democratically elected governments were taking hold in the Americas. In fact, the first significant OAS involvement in the Central American peace process was the 1989-90 electoral observation mission to Nicaragua. Confronted with this new task of verifying the election process, the OAS was forced to awaken from ten years of inertia, not without internal trauma. A redefinition of organizational goals and tasks was of the essence, as this was the first time that the OAS would observe an electoral process in one of the member states.

A period of constructive self-criticism and historical changes in the Americas converged in the adoption of several important documents. Foremost, the 1985 Protocol of Cartagena de Indias modified the preamble of the OAS Charter to state that representative democracy is a condition for the stability, peace and development of the region. The protocol further amended Article 2 of the OAS Charter, adding as an essential purpose the organization, promotion and consolidation of representative democracy with due respect for the principle of non-intervention. These additions have been the normative base for more than twenty electoral observer missions that the OAS has organized since 1989.

The other central pillars of the protection of democracy are the Santiago Commitment to Democracy and the Renewal of the Inter-American System and the related OAS General Assembly Resolution 1080 on Representative Democracy. Resolution 1080 establishes an expeditious mechanism to defend democracy, requiring the OAS Secretary-General to convene immediately a meeting of the Permanent Council 'in the event of any ... sudden or irregular interruption of the democratic political institutional process or of the legitimate exercise of power by the democratically elected government in any ... member state.' The Permanent Council shall examine the situation and decide whether to convene an *ad hoc* meeting of ministers of foreign affairs or a special session of the General Assembly, who shall then take all necessary measures, in accordance with the OAS Charter and international law. This process has been invoked three times so far: in Haiti in 1991, in Peru in 1992 and in Guatemala in 1993. The Santiago Declaration displays a fresh goal in a very decisive and innovative manner: the promotion and protection of democracy. The declaration, in my opinion, creates the opportunity for a renewal of the Inter-American System, at least on four grounds:

- The Santiago Declaration rescues an old idea from the Charter's text, that of the promotion of democracy, and upgrades it to principle. That principle has prevailed as the main purpose of the organization, forcing the OAS to make significant internal and bureaucratic changes.
- For the first time in 12 years, member states are all committed to the same goal and US interests coincide with the organizational goal. So far, the hegemon has allowed the OAS to exhaust its initiatives, and it has only used unilateral force when the OAS proves insufficient.
- Even though the protection and promotion of democracy has become one of the international community's aspirations, the OAS has taken the lead when trying to restore democracy. The protection and restoration of democratic regimes is certainly one in which the OAS has demonstrated a great deal of appropriate performance. Recognizing the complexity of the situation, the organization has taken immediate and decisive action every time there is a breakdown of constitutional order within a Latin American country. A great deal of learning can be traced from the OAS resolution against Somoza to the efforts undertaken by the organization to restore President Aristide in Haiti. What started with an isolated resolution in 1979, has grown to become a complex process of early warning and substantive resolutions, mediation missions, OAS/UN cooperation, human rights monitoring mechanisms and electoral observation. Operational growth has been steady and substantively managed by the OAS, which has deployed increasingly larger civilian missions for an extended period of time.
- The UN can rely on the leadership of the OAS to call early attention to any antidemocratic behaviour. Also, when non-democratic regimes in the hemisphere threaten peace and order, both internally and regionally, the OAS can thus provide the normative bases to make UN intervention possible. The normative development of the people's right to democracy seems to have been internalized by OAS state members. However, it is not yet clear whether they are willing to concede such a right to the Cuban people. Fidel Castro, Cuba's strongman, has managed to maintain a dictatorial regime in the country without having to confront a strong reaction from the OAS. In fact, during the most recent 1996 General Assembly in Panama, no members suggested the need to ask for democratic progress in the island, even though they condemned the US for enacting the widely criticized Helms-Burton Act. The OAS cannot meddle in Cuban affairs for the simple reason

that Cuba is not an active member, but it may ask a member state to press for further political openings from Fidel. The case of Cuba is the last stumbling block against the full validation of a learning process around the democracy rule.

There has been a weakening of the sovereignty and non-intervention principles. Sovereignty has always been very sensitive in Latin America, especially in dealings with Washington after the renewed military and economic strength gained by the US after the Second World War. Roosevelt's Good Neighbor Policy was not enough to appease Latin concerns. The question is then 'why would countries so sensitive to the risk of American intervention have promoted institutions which, according to the critics, would serve merely to cloak or even thinly to legitimate American threats to their political independence?' According to Tom Farer, 'the simple answer ... is that they would not and they did not. They devised the institutions of the Inter-American System not to legitimate but rather to *contain* American power.'[7]

Indeed, the OAS Charter, the Rio Treaty and the Bogotá Pact, jointly known as the 'Inter-American System', were designed as a Latin American safeguard against probable US intervention. The central norm of such a complex normative compound is the principle of non-intervention, as enshrined in Article 18 of the Charter:

> *Article 18.* No State or group of States has the right to intervene, directly or indirectly, for any reason whatsoever, in the internal or external matters of any other State. The foregoing principle prohibits not only armed force, but also any other form of interference or attempted threat against the personality of the state or against its political, economic, and cultural elements.

The principle of non-intervention was first developed in the Inter-American System and later became a significant contribution of the OAS to international law. It is also a widely violated principle. The USA has managed to intervene in Guatemala, the Dominican Republic, Nicaragua, Grenada and Panama, sometimes unilaterally and sometimes under the auspices of the OAS. Latin American countries have also intervened in one another's internal affairs.

Moreover, Washington has always found legal arguments for not applying the principle. One of those arguments is that non-intervention does not apply in relation to dictatorial regimes that deny the right to vote and massively violate human rights. Another argument is the need for intervention due to the lack of capacity to stop internal conflicts from spilling into neighbouring countries. These exceptions to non-intervention were considered invalid by the International Court of Justice (ICJ) in the *Nicaragua Case*.[8]

Despite the ICJ's strict interpretation of the principle of non-intervention, the OAS seems to have interpreted the principle as excluding only forcible unilateral intervention, and not as an obstacle for collective action by the organization in matters concerning the survival of a democratic government. The OAS has started to intrude into national affairs of member states and has adopted several resolutions with respect to democracy. Resolutions on the domestic affairs of Nicaragua, Panama, Guatemala, Peru and Haiti are some examples of this kind of involvement. According with OAS practice sovereignty can only be recognized to countries with democratically elected governments.

On different grounds, sovereignty and non-intervention have suffered enormous setbacks in both the regional and the universal contexts, although with greater impact in the former. In the universal context, sovereignty yields in the face of collective interventions on humanitarian bases. Humanitarian concerns may also be used by the OAS to intervene in the internal matters of a member state. However, intervention for the protection of democracy is an established principle in the Western Hemisphere, but it does not seem to be a fully recognized entitlement in the universal context. No one seems to believe that it is legitimate to intervene in Iraq on the simple basis that Saddam Hussein's regime is not democratic. The same could be said for Gaddafi in Libya, the regime in Myanmar and many other leaders and countries in Asia and the Middle East.

In this regard, the OAS is providing renewed leadership on the promotion of democracy, a recent normative development that may soon become fully incorporated as an integral part of modern international law. Since this is a trend that has been taken consciously and consensually by member states, it may in fact be considered to qualify as appropriate performance by the organization. The core aspects of legitimate intervention have been properly narrowed to avoid the misunderstandings of the past. Collective action and protection of democracy are by far the main pillars of the new doctrine. No unilateral intervention, by any means whatsoever, is acceptable. This seems to be the main message of the recent OAS rejection of the Helms-Burton Act for its long-arm extraterritoriality, even over Washington's angry objections at the 1996 General Assembly in Panama.

OAS leadership is a breakthrough in traditional conceptions of sovereignty and non-intervention and also has great impact on the chances for OAS/UN task-sharing as demonstrated by the joint operation that both organizations organized and implemented in Haiti. By recognizing Aristide as the legitimate president and decreeing an economic, financial, commercial and arms embargo on Haiti, the OAS permitted UN involvement in what otherwise would be treated as a purely domestic matter. The OAS initiative to cooperate with the UN came at the precise moment when Cédras openly disregarded the Protocol of Washington of 23 February 1992, which the OAS promoted and patronized. The OAS realized that dialogue could not yield resignation by Cédras and that the type of measures prescribed in Chapter VII of the UN Charter were made necessary.

The Ad Hoc Meeting of Ministers of Foreign Affairs adopted Resolution 4/92 and decided:

> To mandate the Secretary General of the Organization of American States to go to the extreme within the framework of the Charter to seek a peaceful resolution of the Haitian crisis, and, in conjunction with the secretary-general of the United Nations, to explore the possibility and advisability of bringing the Haitian situation to the attention of the United Nations Security Council.

An OAS civilian mission created to restore democracy in Haiti was replaced by the OAS/UN International Civilian Mission in Haiti (MICIVIH), which helped to monitor the human rights situation and elections in Haiti, as soon as Aristide returned to the island. By opening the possibility for UN involvement in Haiti, the OAS allowed for UN-authorized enforcement action through a US military occupation and subsequent UN peacekeeping operation. The UN enforcement action and the military aspects of MICIVIH complemented OAS diplomatic efforts in Haiti.

What has been said above concerning legitimate intervention for democracy unfortunately cannot apply to conflict resolution by the OAS. As much as it is regrettable, no recent progress has been achieved in this area. The OAS can only mediate a conflict when all parties to the dispute have accepted such involvement. No significant changes have been introduced to fill in the gaps left by the Rio Treaty and the Bogotá Pact. No innovations are perceivable in this field as no attempts to devise mechanisms for peacekeeping and peace enforcement have been made.

The fact that the OAS shows little progress in the peace and security area implies that the UN would mainly take charge of such matters. Thus, we see little OAS/UN task-sharing in this area because the UN takes charge in light of the OAS's lack of capacity. However, new hemispheric problems are gaining in complexity. There could be more room for task-sharing. The Haiti crisis is a good example of complexity because the OAS provided leadership in the protection of democracy and basic peacemaking, while the UN was responsible for peacekeeping and peace-enforcement.

Third, a human rights regime has developed. According to Krasner, a regime is a set of principles, norms and procedures that make expectations converge to solve a particular problem.[9] From this perspective, an international regime is an ideal form of international cooperation.

With the Universal Declaration on Human Rights as the foundation, the Americas have an established set of principles, norms and procedures to make member states' expectations converge in and for the protection of human rights. The principles are provided by the 1948 American Declaration on the Rights and Duties of Man. The norms, understood as standards of appropriate behaviour, are detailed in the 1969 American Convention on Human Rights. In addition to these basic instruments, a series of inter-American agreements have been developed on specific aspects for safeguarding human rights: the Inter-American Convention to Prevent and Punish Torture; the Additional Protocol to the American Convention on Human Rights on the Area of Economic, Social and Cultural Rights; the Protocol to the American Convention on Human Rights to Abolish the Death Penalty; and the Inter-American Convention on the Forced Disappearance of Persons.

The procedures are connected by the investigative and fiscal functions of the Inter-American Commission with the judicial and consultative role of the Inter-American Court of Human Rights. Both the commission and the court, however, do not just constitute mechanistic procedural tools. They apply, interpret and clarify a dynamic normative body that guides state behaviour and policy-making. The inter-American human rights regime has been internalized by state members and bureaucracies as a central aspect of the organization's life. In addition to the growing number of cases submitted to the Inter-American Court, human rights protection tasks have been approached by the OAS and the UN with no reference to task-sharing. The UN has for almost a decade been deeply involved in human rights education and protection in Central America. Both internal peace processes in El Salvador and Guatemala started by developing a set of human rights standards that the negotiating parties, the government and the guerrillas are willing to respect *vis-à-vis* each other and the rest of the nation. This process is guided and mediated by the UN Secretary-General's special representative to the negotiations. The United Nations has also established a major human rights component in the supervision, monitoring and peace-building activities of the UN Operation in El Salvador (ONUSAL) and the UN Mission in Guatemala (MINUGUA).

The Inter-American Commission of Human Rights has been invited to investigate specific cases of human rights violations, but the OAS seems to exert little leadership in introducing human rights at the national and local levels. A different approach has been taken in Haiti. The division of labour within MICIVIH gives all military aspects to the UN with human rights observation and protection activities to the OAS. In fact, all civilian tasks have been allocated to the OAS, including election monitoring and the restructuring of the Electoral Tribunal.

The human rights regime in the Western Hemisphere has performed appropriately. Most of the decisions by the Inter-American Court of Human rights have been complied with, totally or partially. They are given a special reverence by a huge network of human rights non-governmental organizations which in turn serve as *epistemic communities*.[10] NGOs, in association with the Inter-American Commission on Human Rights, have been able to prosecute dozens of cases and have forged new attitudes within the hemisphere's governments.

There is a perception in Latin America that the OAS's human rights protection mechanisms are closer and are more accessible than those of the UN. While it makes little difference to go to the UN Human Rights Commission in Geneva or the Inter-American Commission on Human Rights in Washington, the fact that the court is located in Costa Rica and that the OAS system is better known in Latin America seems to work in favour of the regional framework. The human rights field is definitely one area of cooperation in which the OAS can reliably share tasks with the UN.

However, interorganizational cooperation does not stop in the area of human rights protection, it also deals with the eradication of the fundamental sources of human rights violations. Among such sources is Latin America's reliance on the military for crime control and the maintenance of internal order. Designed to wage war and overpower an enemy, the armed forces are less well equipped than civilian police for internal security. Several massacres and human rights violations in Central America and Haiti have occurred at the hands of the military. Counterinsurgency training and ruthless practices make the armed forces the major threat against human rights. To prevent further human rights violations, the military should be confined to their headquarters while civilian police should be given training and equipment. In what could be termed as a peacebuilding goal, both the OAS and the UN could share tasks and work together towards prevention, at the same time as they undertake the traditional investigation of violations and prosecution of human rights violators.

FROM INSTITUTIONAL DISCAPACITY TO OPERATIONAL REHABILITATION

Peacemaking

The OAS stopped peacemaking efforts after being excluded from active participation in most peace negotiations in Central America. After a very hectic agenda during the first three decades of its existence, the OAS suddenly suspended major initiatives in good offices, mediation and conciliation, peacemaking under Chapter VI of the UN Charter. If inter-state tensions have been reduced in the hemisphere, it is not because of the OAS.

Lower inter-state tensions may be due to the necessity to group in regional or subregional blocs to confront emerging global political and economic pressures. The end of several insurrectional wars has brought a national pressure on national leaders to focus on social and economic problems at home rather than security issues. As publicized annually in UNDP's *Human Development Report*, there has been a significant reduction in the average developing country's military spending, from around 5.5 per cent of gross domestic product (GDP) in 1985 to around 3.6 per cent in 1994. And Latin American and Caribbean states lead the way with an aver age expenditure of only 1.6 per cent in 1994.[11] This fact suggests a growing degree of confidence among hemispheric states and less preoccupation about external invasions. The end of the Cold War deprived most insurrectional groups of their principal international sponsors, leaving them with no other choice but to search for peace.

It must also be noted that the peace negotiations in El Salvador and Guatemala were mediated by the UN and not by the regional organization. The OAS also played no role in more recent armed conflicts between Peru and Ecuador. The simple rejection of President Fujimori to accept the participation of the OAS was enough to stop the regional institution from mediating or facilitating dialogue. Although the Rio Protocol already provided for a group of friends to mediate, the OAS could have at least warned Peru and Ecuador earlier about using force, as they ultimately did. No arms embargo was decreed by the OAS and no resolutions were adopted by its organs to condemn the offensive attitude of both countries. No shuttle diplomacy was done by the OAS Secretary-General, and no other forms of diplomatic isolation against the warring parties were taken by member states.

Equally upsetting is the lack of action by the OAS in the Colombian conflict. Although it could be regarded as internal, its pervasiveness harms the possibilities for full-fledged democracy. There cannot be a fully demo-cratic government in Colombia when excessive resources are allocated to maintaining a huge army, and frequent human rights violations and re-stricted freedom of movement are the order of the day.

None of this, however, should serve to diminish the successful peace-making record of the OAS in Central America from 1948 to 1969, nor does it mean that the OAS cannot again work on conflict resolution. Furthermore, informal mechanisms or *ad hoc* groups can perform better than regional organizations with such human and institutional resources as the OAS's. As a regional organization, the OAS has the political standing and institutional capacity to investigate situations that have degenerated into armed conflict and formulate better means for verification and moni-toring of compliance with previously agreed obligations.

There is a point in remembering Contadora, the 1983 *ad hoc* peace ini-tiative for Central America, to support my argument. As an *ad hoc* proce-dure, the group of Contadora lacked investigation and verification capacity. This weakness not only reduced its effectiveness in dealing with specific disputes among the Central American countries, it also greatly delegitimized the group as a suitable mediator and facilitator. Parties to the conflict distrusted Contadora and doubted that the group could verify com-pliance of an eventual agreement, especially in aspects related to a re-gional balance of military power. The fact that no agreement was signed during the Contadora process shows that informal *ad hoc* means do not always work.

Even the Esquipulas agreements, which were negotiated with the leadership of Oscar Arias, President of Costa Rica and 1987 Nobel Peace Laureate, at some point needed the support of international organizations in the areas of compliance verification and disarmament and demobilization of former combatants. Indeed, the UN Operation in Central America (ONUCA) verified compliance and the OAS organized and led the CIAV/OAS mission, which is still in charge of demobilizing and reintegrating the Contras in the northern regions of Nicaragua.

The above-mentioned institutional advantages for conflict resolution over *ad hoc* procedures have not worked in favour of the OAS in the recent past because the warring parties have not asked the OAS to facili-tate or mediate. Moreover, a lack of leadership in this area makes the organization indecisive. To everyone's surprise, the OAS Secretary-General did not insist when he tried unsuccessfully to intervene in the war between Peru and Ecuador. Under the OAS Charter, that war required the OAS to take action when war erupted, even if there was a group of friends established under the Rio Protocol. Furthermore, and this might be more understandable, Secretary-General Gaviria has shown only limited interest in the organization's meddling in the internal affairs of his own country, even if there are sufficient humanitarian reasons to pledge for peace and to facilitate a negotiation process. Despite all this, I still do not think that the OAS's peacemaking is finished.

The end of the regional crisis and of internal armed struggle in Nicaragua, El Salvador and Honduras did not completely eliminate the danger of war in Central America. The OAS would sooner or later have to use its peacemaking capacity, as demonstrated two or three decades ago. Some change in hemispheric law may help, especially in the area of conflict resolution. The OAS must be able to call governments ex officio to the negotiating table within the context of the Inter-American System and to take enforcement measures against states that are reluctant to negotiate and use force. The OAS is allowed, although it would not hurt to state it expressly in a legal instrument, to take measures affecting internal affairs of member states if humanitarian reasons or the protection of democracy so demand such measures.

Intractable internal wars should also be a matter in which the principle of non-intervention must not apply anymore. People die in civil wars, as they do in bilateral conflicts. Although unilateral interventions are outlawed, collective good offices or mediation should be made available and sometimes imposed on states when humanitarian needs are acute. This is the case of Colombia, where there is no justification for allowing civil war to persist indefinitely, and permitting killings to rationalize narco-trafficking and corruption.

As much as reforms are needed in conflict resolution by the OAS, some progress has been achieved in the area of conflict prevention – that is, confidence-building initiatives to prevent inter-state conflicts. This is a significant step forward, especially if seen in the volatile security context of the Americas. Population growth, increased migration to neighbouring states and internal instability could lead to heightened border tensions. As has been recognized elsewhere, a military under extreme duress at home might try to ease pressure by diverting popular attention to historic threats to national sovereignty.

The Regional Conference on Confidence-Building Measures of 1992 adopted a Declaration indicating the following measures for confidence-building:[12]

- gradual adoption of agreements for advance notice of military exercises;

- exchange of information and participation of all member states in the United Nations Register of Conventional Arms and Standardized International reporting on Military Expenditures;
- promotion of development and exchange of information concerning defence policies and doctrines;
- consideration of a consultation process with a view to proceeding towards limitation and control of conventional weapons;
- agreements on invitation of observers to military exercises, visits to military installations, arrangements for observing routine operations and exchange of civilian and military personnel for regular and advanced training;
- development and establishment of communications among civilian and military authorities of neighbouring countries in accordance with their border situation.

As important as these measures are, they should be constantly revised, verified and augmented. They must of course also be implemented. Efforts toward demilitarisation, reduction of military expenditures and transparency in arms acquisitions are fundamental for a better sense of cooperative security in the region.

Another area requiring confidence-building is the possibility for tension and conflict that may arise out the recent entry into force of the UN Convention on the Law of the Sea. Not unique to the Americas, the Convention provides for an Exclusive Economic Zone (EEZ) that is to be measured as a belt of sea as wide as two hundred miles from the base line from which the territorial sea is measured. The many cases of adjacent and frontal states whose EEZs overlap could bring back to life old border problems and nationalistic sentiments which, if not properly managed, could yield many new conflicts that could propel the use of force. Delimitation problems between Nicaragua and Colombia, Venezuela and Colombia, and Peru and Ecuador are a few examples.

A commission within the OAS should collect all relevant scientific data and legal opinions that could be useful to guide countries in their future delimitation efforts. The commission may be active at least in the elaboration of maps, surveys of the natural resources of EEZs and continental shelves and the landscape and geographical characteristics of coasts and continental shelves. The right information may avoid unnecessary misunderstandings and conflicts. To the extent that relations between states are oriented, codified and regulated by explicit commitments and scientific knowledge, and in accordance with mutually accepted parameters, there will be fewer incentives or conditions giving rise to conflict.

Peacebuilding

Peacebuilding operations involve investigation, verification and monitoring, including observation of elections and the demobilization and reintegration of former combatants. So far, UN peacebuilding efforts have normally ended when formal democracy is restored. This has been the case in Cambodia and Haiti, where the UN basically verified compliance with the respective peace agreements and built the necessary institutions and mechanisms for open and competitive elections. In El Salvador, the UN took a more comprehensive approach, dealing with human rights, impunity, the creation of a civilian police, the redistribution of land for the Farabundo Martí National Liberation (FMLN), and reintegration of former combatants.

As of today, the OAS has not demonstrated appropriate performance in this area – at least, what can be drawn from the two basic peacebuilding initiatives of the regional organization: CIAV/OAS in Nicaragua and MICIVIH in Haiti. CIAV/OAS was created in 1989 as part of a division of labour between the OAS and the UN. By the end of 1989 it was clear that disarming the Contras would mean working in two countries. It was expected that one group of Contras would stay in Nicaragua and another in Honduras. The OAS/UN agreement in Tela, Honduras, provided that CIAV/OAS would take care of the Contras in Nicaragua, while CIAV/UN were to handle the Contras in Honduras.

The electoral defeat of the Sandinistas in 1990, and the ascent to power of a coalition involving Contra leaders, encouraged most former Contras to return to Nicaragua. Since no Contras remained in Honduras, CIAV/UN was dismantled.

The challenge of CIAV/OAS was to disarm, demobilize and reintegrate some 22,000 former combatants in the northern and central regions of Nicaragua, following a three-phase plan: Phase I (July–August 1990): Disarmament and Demobilization; Phase II (1990–91): Emergency Aid (food, lodging, basic training, tools); and Phase III (1991–present): Projects for Infrastructure, Housing, Agriculture and Farming. Although phases I and II were fully accomplished, due to its complexity, phase III has not been fully completed. Progress with reintegration has so far been partial for reasons not only attributable to CIAV/OAS. Divergent approaches to the reintegration problem from various quarters of international cooperation and government have made it difficult to move forward during the past four years. The resurgence of organized violence by the North 3-80 group in the Northern province of Quilali and the sporadic operations of groups of former soldiers and Contras also known as 'revueltos' is evidence of uncompleted work by CIAV/OAS. Nonetheless, the six-year experience on a very complex and dynamic problem shows some learning that must be documented and built upon by the OAS.

CIAV/OAS played a fundamental role in favour of former Contras and ex-combatants in general. The Contras in particular have benefited from CIAV/OAS because they were disarmed without having negotiated their demobilization and the OAS helped them. Indeed, the Contras asked for no especial concessions from the Sandinista government or the international community to deliver their weapons and simply relied on what the Esquipulas process and the Chamorro government may have given them. If not for CIAV/OAS, who provided them with land and human support at the time they were needed badly, war would have probably regained intensity and the peace process may have been reversed. Still today, there remains great concern for the demobilized population. Not having found complete acceptance and support from Nicaraguan society and government, they have no choice but to use violence in order to satisfy their needs. The OAS is required to remain in Nicaragua and try to agree with the United Nations Development Programme on a common approach to deal with reintegration and social adaptation of former combatants.

If the UN and OAS Secretaries-General saw each other as rivals in Nicaragua and Honduras in 1989 and divided the CIAV operation, the joint operation in Haiti suggests that it is more effective and less expensive to work together. In fact, MICIVIH was established as a fully integrated human rights observation mission by both the OAS and the UN in February 1993, at the request of President Aristide and as part of the international effort to resolve the Haitian crisis. After being evacuated on security grounds from Haiti in two occasions, MICIVIH resumed activities on 26 October 1994, after Aristide was fully restored in office.

In an unprecedented manner, MICIVIH's Executive Director always reported to the OAS Secretary-General and to the Special Representative for Haiti of the UN Secretary-General. MICIVIH maintained a separated status but had a close working relationship with the United Nations Mission in Haiti (UNMIH), which handled the military and police components.[13] With an orderly and efficacious working style, MICIVIH documented the human rights situation, made recommendations to the Haitian authorities, implemented a civic education programme, helped solve problems such as those relating to arbitrary and illegal detentions, and facilitated medical assistance to victims of human rights abuse and the return of displaced persons. MICIVIH also observed the electoral campaign as a whole and monitored the rights of expression and association of Haitians during this period. Less obvious is the so-called institutional building as both the Haitian judiciary and the electoral tribunal must undergo significant adjustment and reform. However, human rights groups, which received support from MICIVIH, have been active promoting these institutional changes.

Despite the appropriate performance of both the OAS and the UN in Haiti, it is still difficult to understand why the reintegration of ex-combatants was left aside, especially in light of the vast experience the OAS achieved in Nicaragua through CIAV/OAS. Performances that take into account previous experiences are able to build on the basis of practice and innovation as well. This is the essence of appropriate behaviour.

CONCLUSIONS: OAS–UN COOPERATION IN THE NEW MILLENNIUM

Former UN Secretary-General Boutros Boutros-Ghali struggled to equip the UN to manage a growing number of threats to international peace and security. However, inadequate resources and lack of understanding of regional specificities work against effectiveness and, ultimately, against UN legitimacy as a whole. In his *An Agenda for Peace*, Boutros-Ghali stressed the need for cooperation with regional organizations in the management of threats to peace and security. Later, cooperation between the UN and regional arrangements is discussed in his *Supplement to 'An Agenda For Peace'*, which calls for greater task-sharing in peace operations between the UN and regional organizations.[14]

The laudable idea of cooperation between universal and regional organizations has not been clearly spelled out. To achieve further progress toward organizational cooperation we must first find out the areas in which organizations are achieving or could achieve minimum levels of appropriate performance. It seems reasonable to evaluate areas of appropriate performance at the regional level before we determine task-sharing opportunities with the UN.

The OAS and the UN possess opportunities for task-sharing in the area of peacebuilding, the protection of democracy and human rights, and the protection of confidence-building measures among regional member states. All of these areas are intrinsically related and should be looked at integrally, so that each of them is approached with the others in mind. For example, peacebuilding should not lose sight of the need to protect and strengthen democratic rule and human rights. Confidence-building measures should be based on the premise that democratic regimes are the best way to build confidence and peace.

Stronger regional organizations have more opportunities for appropriate performance and task-sharing. Appropriate performance seems to be a dependent variable of decisive leadership from a secretary-general, a clear and consensual normative framework and an institutionalized but flexible procedure. If taken seriously, the OAS may be able to achieve the necessary levels of appropriate performance for a complete range of joint actions with the UN in the Western Hemisphere.

NOTES

1. This article was in draft at the time of Joaquín Tacsan's tragic death in an airplane crash in Nigeria in November 1996. It has been lightly copy-edited only to conform with the publisher's style as requested by the family (Editor).
2. John Burton, *Peace Theory*, cited by J. S. Nye, *Peace in Parts: Integration and Conflict in Regional Organization* (Boston: Little, Brown, 1971), p. 129.
3. Ibid., p. 130.
4. Ronald Scheman, *The Inter-American Dilemma* (New York: Praeger, 1988), p. 179. Advocating for the regionalist side, Scheman arrives, however, at a similar conclusion. His propositions are: (a) the nature of the problems of ordering a global community is of such magnitude that the transition from our current form of nationalist behaviour to international cooperation cannot be made successfully through rigid, centralized approaches; (b) Regional arrangements within a global framework hold considerable potential to make the world development system work with sufficient flexibility and adaptability to satisfy widely divergent values and patterns of living.
5. Latin American countries prolifically signed several treaties in the nineteenth century alone. The Perpetual Confederation and Union Treaty of 1926, the Congress of Lima (1847–48), the Continental Treaty and the Washington Convention of 1865, the II Congress of Lima (1864–65), and the III Congress of Lima (1877–80) and Montevideo (1888–89). See F. V. García Amador, *The Inter-American System* (Washington, DC: General Secretariat of the Organization of American States, 1981).
6. One formalistic obstacle for using the Bogotá Pact is the provision in Article 4 that no settlement procedure can be initiated without having terminated the ongoing procedure. Another is the requirement that all parties involved in the conflict agree to initiate a procedure.
7. Tom J. Farer, *The United States and the Inter-American System* (Washington, DC: The American Society of International Law, 1978), p. 4.
8. International Court of Justice, *Case: Military and Paramilitary Activities in and against Nicaragua*, June 1996.
9. Stephen D. Krasner (ed.), *International Regimes* (Ithaca, NY: Cornell University Press, 1983), p. 1.

10.   See Ernst B. Haas, *When Knowledge is Power: Three Models of Change in International Organizations* (Berkeley: University of California Press, 1990).

11.   United Nations Development Programme, *Human Development Report 1996* (Oxford: Oxford University Press, 1996), p. 212.

12.   *Declaration of Santiago on Confidence- and Security-Building Measures*, November 1995.

13.   See Robert Maguire, Edwige Balutansky, Jacques Fomerand, Larry Minear, William G. O'Neill, Thomas G. Weiss and Sarah Zaidi, *Haiti Held Hostage: International Responses to the Quest for Nationhood* (Providence, RI: Watson Institute, 1996), Occasional Paper No. 23.

14.   Boutros Boutros-Ghali, *An Agenda for Peace 1995* (New York: United Nations, 1995). Contains both reports.

6 On the Front Lines in the Near Abroad: the CIS and the OSCE in Georgia's Civil Wars

S. Neil MacFarlane

As is pointed out by Muthiah Alagappa's framework analysis for this volume, that regional organizations[1] might relieve some of the burden on the United Nations (UN) in the area of conflict management gained new currency after the Cold War. As Boutros Boutros-Ghali pointed out, the goal of such task-sharing was not only to distribute management burdens more effectively by taking advantage of hitherto under-utilized regional capacities, but also to democratize international relations through the devolution of power to regional entities.[2] In addition, some would argue that regional organizations are better prepared than global ones to address specifically regional problems.[3]

However, regional organizations face a number of structural deficiencies, and they may be less capable of impartiality in addressing problems among and within regional states.[4] Notably, power asymmetries at the regional level raise the prospect that regional multilateral organizations may be used by locally dominant states to achieve their own self-interested objectives. There is an element of irony here in that hegemony[5] by some accounts lays the basis for effective cooperation – in that the hegemon is both willing and able to provide the public good of order – but by its very nature is likely to turn the pursuit of order to the hegemon's own advantage.

The record of activity and effectiveness (or inactivity and ineffectiveness) of regional organizations in the post-Cold War era in cases such as the Gulf, Somalia, the former Yugoslavia and Rwanda suggests that much of the initial enthusiasm about regionalism in the security realm was misplaced. This might well lead to a re-emphasis on the exclusive role of global organizations (and notably the UN), but given the latter's difficulties, this seems unpromising.

Alternatively, it raises the possibility of creative combinations of subregional, regional and global organizational activities that maximize the advantages and minimize the disadvantages at each institutional level through a synergistic approach to local problems. Notably, might it not be possible to rely on regional structures, including hegemonic ones, to provide order in the face of rising levels of local conflict and the reluctance of extra-regional actors to commit themselves, and yet to commit broader multilateral mechanisms in an effort to enhance transparency and to situate the hegemon's activities in a shared normative structure and in so doing to temper the hegemonic agenda?

The case at hand, the Republic of Georgia, is a good one to test this possibility. It involves efforts by a regional power with hegemonic aspirations (Russia) to manage – directly in the case of South Ossetia and indirectly via a subregional organization – two civil conflicts. A broader regional organization, the Organization for Security and Cooperation in Europe (OSCE), is active in efforts to temper Russian intervention in the South Ossetia case. The UN is attempting to play a similar role with respect to Abkhazia.

The UN faces a dilemma in task-sharing in Georgia, as elsewhere in the former Soviet space. On the one hand, it is loath to become directly involved in regional conflicts because no consensus on such action is present among the permanent members of the Security Council. Moreover, doing so would only add further burdens to an already stretched peacebuilding apparatus in the UN system. On the other hand, the organization and its members perceive an interest in enhancing peace and stability in the former Soviet space. The combination of these two factors leads to a search for task-sharing with regional organizations. However, the principal regional organization thus far willing and able to undertake such tasks happens to be dominated by a regional hegemon, Russia, which displays little reluctance to manipulate conflict management in pursuit of a self-interested agenda of influence-building and control.[6] Unqualified reliance on the organization consequently jeopardizes another basic norm of the UN – respect for the sovereignty of its members. Life is full of sloppy compromises. In this instance, UN task-sharing must find a middle ground between these inconsistent imperatives.

In this chapter, I examine external efforts at conflict management in Georgia in an effort to assess the extent to which synergy has been achieved. First, to what extent has this blend of external activities been effective in keeping the peace and in producing durable settlements to the conflicts in question? Second, to what extent have the roles of the OSCE and the UN operated to mitigate the impact of the Russian presence? Third, to what extent did the broader international context in which UN task-sharing proceeded affect the nature and effectiveness of task-sharing?

UN deliberations on the Abkhaz question occurred more or less simultaneously with decisions on task-sharing in Haiti and Rwanda. Arguably, this concatenation of crises may have affected UN efforts to deal with each one.

I argue that the combination of regional and global efforts evident in the case has been effective in keeping the peace in a strict sense. Moreover, the presence of international observers has enhanced transparency and to some extent has acculturated Russian forces to international norms regarding peacekeeping. This has resulted in gradual improvement in the performance of the Commonwealth of Independent States (CIS) and Russian forces in the field. However, the Georgian mix has been unsuccessful in producing progress towards political settlements in the two conflicts. Moreover, international efforts have had little restraining effect at a strategic level on Russian efforts to manipulate these conflicts in order to induce Georgian acquiescence in the broader regional agenda of Russia in the Transcaucasus.

This paper begins with a short discussion of task-sharing in the former Soviet region and is followed by a background section dealing with the conflicts. Then I go on to look at the mandates of the OSCE, the CIS and the UN Observer Mission in Georgia (UNOMIG) in the conflicts and their effectiveness in fulfilling them. This leads to a discussion of the efforts of the various organizations to promote a durable peace in Georgia. The next section deals with the extent to which the regional power has pursued a unilateral agenda by multilateral means and the tension between this agenda as the objectives of the international community in the region. The conclusion discusses what the Georgian case tells us about the effectiveness of 'supervised devolution' of responsibility for conflict management and resolution.

SUBCONTRACTING AND THE FORMER SOVIET UNION

The term 'subcontracting' is not really appropriate for peace-related operations of the OSCE and the CIS in the former Soviet space in general or Georgia in particular. The concept implies a decision on the part of one organization to devolve a defined set of responsibilities upon another on the basis of mutual gain. In the case of the former Soviet Union, such activities generally occur on the basis of national (Russia) or regional (OSCE or CIS) decision.

That said, the regional players do recognize to varying degrees the purview of the United Nations and its Charter over their actions. The

OSCE had declared itself to be a Chapter VIII organization and therefore presumably accepts the limitations on its behaviour contained in this section of the Charter.[7] The delineation of responsibility over conflicts in Georgia (with the UN taking the international lead on Abkhazia and the OSCE on South Ossetia) is based on an agreement between the two organizations.

Russia has sought UN approval for CIS actions in Georgia, not least out of a desire to secure external finance for force deployment, and the Commonwealth of Independent States Peacekeeping Force (CISPKF) in Abkhazia operates with the approval of the United Nations Security Council, as established by Resolution 937 of 21 July 1994. There are, however, numerous instances in which such approval has not been sought (for example, the Russian peacekeeping operation in South Ossetia) or has not been granted. And in any event, rather than initiating action, the UN finds itself in the delicate situation of facing requests for international legitimization of decisions taken by others.

From a UN perspective, there are specific advantages in relying on regional organizations for the management of conflict in the former Soviet space. Notably, it is clear that Russian policy-makers are uncomfortable with the idea of a prominent role being granted to external actors in dealing with conflict in the former Soviet space.[8] More recently, this has been extended specifically to the activities of international organizations in the management of conflict. As one group of influential Russian foreign policy commentators and policy-makers put it in May 1996, 'it is definitely not in Russia's interest to see outside mediation and peacekeeping operations on the territory of the former Soviet Union.'[9]

In these circumstances, it is difficult to conceive of substantial UN conflict management activities in the former Soviet space, since they are likely to be opposed by Russia, one of the five permanent members of the Security Council. Other key players, and notably the United States, are reluctant to contemplate such operations, not only given the cost, but also in view of the importance of maintaining good relations with Russia. In consequence, it makes sense for the organization to let others take the lead.

BACKGROUND[10]

Georgia is a country of some 5.4 million people in the Transcaucasian region of the former Soviet Union. Although the Georgian majority constitutes over 70 per cent of the total population, there are numerous ethnically defined and territorially compact minorities in the country. Two of these minorities, the Ossets and the Abkhaz, have been involved in civil conflicts with the central government and the Georgian majority since the early 1990s. The key events are summarized in Table 6.1.

The conflict in South Ossetia

The conflict with South Ossetia began during Georgia's transition to independence in 1989–90. The leadership of the South Ossetian Autonomous Oblast' of the Republic of Georgia, threatened by the overt chauvinism of rising political forces among the Georgian majority, declared its secession from Georgia and desire to unite with the North Ossetian Autonomous Republic of the then Russian Soviet Federated Socialist Republic. The Georgian Supreme Soviet annulled this declaration and abrogated the *oblast's* autonomous status in a climate of growing intimidation and violence in Tskhinvali, South Ossetia's capital. In the face of rising violence, Soviet Interior Ministry forces intervened but did not succeed in curbing the conflict. They were withdrawn as the Soviet Union collapsed. The war continued until June 1992, when a durable ceasefire agreement was obtained through the mediation of Russian President Boris Yeltsin. Estimates of casualties from the war vary, although most agree on around 1,000 dead. The war also produced approximately 110,000 refugees, from both South Ossetia and the rest of Georgia whence many Ossets were evicted.

The ceasefire agreement on South Ossetia envisaged the deployment of a mixed Russian–Georgian–Osset force to police the line of contact. Initially, the force comprised one regiment of Russian forces, and one battalion from each of the parties. By 1995, the Russian complement had shrunk to one battalion, matching the other two. The initiative was Russian; no approval from international organizations (including the CIS) was sought.

In December 1992, an OSCE Mission to Georgia was established in Tbilisi at the invitation of President Eduard Shevardnadze in order to 'promote negotiations on a peaceful political settlement of the conflict'.[11] The ceasefire has been stable since June 1992. A degree of freedom of movement has been established inside South Ossetia and between it and the rest of Georgia. Visits with Osset units of the peacekeeping force suggest low levels of readiness and little sense of threat. Their principal preoccupation seemed to be the prevention of thefts of firewood.[12] A low level of economic exchange between Georgian and Osset settlements in South Ossetia and between South Ossetia and the rest of Georgia has also re-emerged. OSCE monitors in the spring of 1996 judged the situation to be calm and did not anticipate any change.[13] In contrast, there has been

120   S. Neil MacFarlane

Table 6.1   Key events in the Osset and Abkhaz conflicts

South Ossetia

January 1989	Founding of Osset Popular front (*Ademon Nykhas*).
November 1989	Armed confrontation in Tskhinvali begins.
March 1990	Georgia declares sovereignty.
October 1990	Zviad Gamsakhurdia elected chairman of Georgian Parliament.
November 1990	South Osset region Soviet attempts to upgrade region's status to autonomous republic. Decision annulled by Georgian government.
December 1990	Georgia annuls autonomy of South Ossetia. State of emergency declared.
January 1991	Gorbachev calls for Georgian withdrawal from South Ossetia.
December 1991	USSR dissolved.
January 1992	Gamsakhurdia driven out of Tbilisi. Military Council takes power.
March 1992	Shevardnadze returns to Georgia as Chair of Military Council.
June 1992	Renewed Georgian offensive in South Ossetia. Russian–Georgian agreement on regulation of conflict in South Ossetia.
July 1992	Deployment of mixed Georgian–Osset–Russian peacekeeping force in South Ossetia.
December 1992	Deployment of OSCE long-term mission to Georgia.

Abkhazia

July 1989	Anti-government riots in Sukhumi.
May 1990	Mountain Peoples Congress in Sukhumi demands exit of Abkhazia from Georgia.
August 1990	Abkhaz government declares sovereignty.
July 1992	Abkhaz government annuls current constitution, restores 1925 constitution and states intention to secede from Georgia. Decision annulled by Georgian Supreme Soviet.
August 1992	Georgian forces enter Abkhazia. Hostilities begin.
September 1992	Russia mediates ceasefire.
October 1992	Abkhaz offensive against Gagra. Georgian request for UN peacekeeping force. (Repeats request in January 1993.)
May 1993	Special Representative of the Secretary General for Georgia appointed. Second ceasefire agreement, which fails immediately.
July 1993	Third Russian-mediated ceasefire agreement.
August 1993	Security Council authorizes deployment of advance team of a 50-person observer force for Abkhazia to observe ceasefire compliance.
September 1993	Ceasefire collapses. Georgian forces and population driven from Abkhazia. Deployment of UNOMIG suspended.
December 1993	Memorandum of Understanding between Abkhazia and Georgia on cessation of hostilities. Security Council authorizes deployment of full observer force.

Table 6.1 (Continued)

February 1994	Shevardnadze and Yeltsin request UN peacekeeping force.
April 1994	Moscow Agreement on formalization of ceasefire and initiation of political talks. Request for peacekeeping force with Russian contingent. Quadripartite (Abkhaz–Georgian–Russian–UNHCR) agreement on refugee return (never implemented).
May 1994	Abkhaz–Georgian agreement on peacekeeping operation.
June 1994	CIS agrees to provide peacekeeping force.
July 1994	Formal deployment of CISPKF. UN Security Council Resolution 937 recognizes CISPKF decision, expands UNOMIG and extends its mandate.

little movement towards a settlement of the dispute, despite agreement between the parties on a security memorandum in May 1996.

The conflict in Abkhazia

The conclusion of the phase of active hostilities in South Ossetia was closely followed by the beginning of war in Abkhazia in August 1992. After the overthrow of Zviad Gamsakhurdia in a prolonged firefight in central Tbilisi in November 1991 to January 1992, Gamsakhurdia returned to his home region of Mingrelia in western Georgia and mounted a rebellion there. In consequence, the Georgian National Guard and associated paramilitary forces entered Mingrelia to pursue a counter-insurgency. Supporters of Gamsakhurdia were using Abkhazia as a sanctuary from which to resist Georgian forces and also to hide kidnapped Georgian officials, including Deputy Prime Minister Sandro Kavsadze. As a result, the newly arrived Eduard Shevardnadze sought and obtained the approval of the government of the Abkhaz Autonomous Republic for a limited hot pursuit operation into eastern Abkhazia in the Gali Raion.[14]

When Georgian forces entered Abkhazia, they found the road open to the capital, Sukhumi, and moved on in violation of the informal agreement with Abkhaz authorities. As they arrived in Sukhumi, the Abkhaz Parliament was in the process of deciding to bring Abkhazia's 1925 constitution back into force. This constituted a declaration of sovereignty. Georgian forces responded by attacking the Parliament and driving the Abkhaz government out of the city in September. The Abkhaz reconsolidated their position in the northern part of the region and began a counter-offensive, taking Gagra in October 1992 and then advancing to Sukhumi by mid-1993.

At this stage, Russia brokered a ceasefire, agreeing to act as its guarantor and deploying monitors to ensure that its disarmament and encampment provisions were respected by the parties. The United Nations responded to Georgian appeals by deploying a small observer group, UNOMIG, to Abkhazia in the late summer of 1993. The ceasefire failed before the UN mission was fully deployed, and the Abkhaz, benefiting from Russian and North Caucasian assistance, retook the capital in September 1993, ejecting Georgian forces from Abkhazia. Abkhaz forces also drove out the region's Georgian population of some 250,000 people (46 per cent of Abkhazia's population).

The last days of the campaign in Abkhazia also witnessed a revival of the Zviadist rebellion behind Georgian lines in Mingrelia, threatening the complete collapse of the Georgian state. At this stage (in October 1993), Shevardnadze flew to Moscow and agreed that Georgia would join the Commonwealth of Independent States. Russian forces intervened in the conflict in Mingrelia and suppressed it. They also deployed along the Abkhaz–Georgian line of contact in late 1993 to separate the warring parties. In June 1994, the Commonwealth of Independent States, acting on the basis of an agreement between the parties in May, legitimized the deployment as a regional peacekeeping operation based on the consent of the parties. The Security Council in turn accepted this decision in July 1994. Resolution 937 also provided for an expansion of UNOMIG from 40 to 136 observers.

The ceasefire has held since the end of 1993, with the exception of limited exchanges of fire in the Kodori Valley – the only part of Abkhazia that had not been fully evacuated by Georgian forces – in late 1993 and 1994. Violence, however, did not disappear altogether. Limited spontaneous return of refugees to the Gali District in 1995 and in greater number in 1996 was accompanied by repeated instances of terrorism targeting local Abkhaz officials and by substantial violations of human rights in the security zone established by peacekeepers. In the meantime, little progress has been made towards a political settlement allowing refugee return and the restoration of Georgian jurisdiction in Abkhazia. Although the Abkhaz side appears to have abandoned the objective of full independence, their insistence on a confederal relationship with the Republic of Georgia remains a substantial distance from the Georgian advocacy of a federal structure for the country.

MANDATES AND PERFORMANCE

In these two conflicts, primary responsibility for management was devolved to one subregional organization (the CIS in Abkhazia) and to one state (Russia in South Ossetia). In each instance, the activities of the primary actor were supplemented by an international multilateral presence – the UN in Abkhazia through UNOMIG, the activities of the Special Representative of the UN Secretary-General (SRSG, Edward Brunner) and the role of the UNHCR in the negotiation of return for internally displaced persons (IDPs); and the OSCE in South Ossetia in the form of the OSCE mission. Their activities in relation to conflict management and political settlement were embedded in broader roles in Georgia.

In order to assess the effectiveness of these actors, greater precision with regard to their mandates is desirable. The mandate of the peacekeeping force in South Ossetia is the most conservative of the various actors in conflict management in Georgia, involving the suppression of hostilities and then interposition to prevent their resumption.[15] There are no explicit humanitarian or other functions in the mandate, although the activities of the peacekeeping force were accompanied by the establishment of a Joint Control Commission (Russia, South Ossetia, Georgia) to deal with modalities of the ceasefire and by Russian diplomatic efforts to mediate a settlement.

The mandate of the OSCE Mission in Georgia involves the conduct of negotiations with both sides in the conflict in the hope of removing sources of tension in their relationship, maintaining contacts with both officials and the population in the conflict zone, cooperation with local military forces in support of the ceasefire, the gathering of information on the military situation and the investigation of incidents, and cooperation in the creation of the political bases for the achievement of lasting peace.[16]

To these ends, the mission has mounted regular trips by military and civilian personnel to the line of contact to visit peacekeeping units, to monitor their weapons and personnel levels, and to consult with government personnel in South Ossetia and neighbouring regions of Georgia. In addition, members of the mission act as mediators in instances of local disputes that carry some risk of disturbing the ceasefire. The mission also facilitates humanitarian assistance and delivers small amounts of such assistance itself.

The objectives of the mission are to enhance transparency, transfer international norms to the peacekeepers, maintain an early-warning capability through fact-finding, and build confidence among local inhabitants and military and paramilitary forces. With the passage of time, the OSCE mission's role and, indeed, the role of the organization as a whole expanded. The outbreak of hostilities in Abkhazia led to dual OSCE and UN efforts to mediate a settlement, with the UN Secretary-General designating a special representative for Georgia, Ambassador Edward Brunner, and the OSCE doing likewise (Ambassador Gyarmati).[17] The two organizations coordinated their efforts through much of 1993, and eventually agreed that the United Nations should be the lead organization on the matter of Abkhazia, the OSCE retaining status as a participant in the negotiations on political settlement. The OSCE has also taken up a human rights role in cooperation with the United Nations in that region. The OSCE – at the invitation of the Georgian government – has also assumed human rights monitoring responsibilities with respect to minority populations in the rest of Georgia, observed both the 1992 and 1995 elections, and has provided technical assistance to the Georgian government in the areas of constitutional and judicial reform.

The OSCE mission in Georgia has by and large fulfilled expectations, at least as regards the monitoring of the peacekeeping force in South Ossetia, confidence-building between the parties at the local level and the promotion of dialogue between the parties at both official and unofficial levels. By Georgian account, the mission's broader activities have also contributed significantly to the promotion of a stable and democratic transition in the country as a whole. OSCE human rights activities have greatly enhanced transparency in this area and, as such, have probably contributed to an improvement in the position of minorities, as well as in the treatment of people imprisoned for acts of opposition (some would say terrorism) to the current government. They have produced significant progress towards a political settlement of the Osset–Georgian question. Little progress is evident in the negotiations. This cannot, however, be taken as evidence that task-sharing does not work. There is no reason to believe that, had it assumed a direct role, the UN would have done any better, for reasons that are further discussed below.

The relationship between the United Nations and the OSCE in Georgia has been relatively untroubled, although in specific instances there have been the problems that one might expect in interorganizational cooperation. The lack of progress on the Abkhaz front led to an increase in OSCE activity with respect to that conflict in 1995–6, particularly in the area of human rights monitoring. The organization originally intended to open a human rights office in Abkhazia on its own, but after a certain amount of exchange with the UN, it was agreed that such an office be opened by both organizations, with the UN in the lead and the OSCE playing a supporting role. Jealousy over turf has been supplemented by organizational incompatibility in this joint effort. The OSCE is a rather unstructured and *ad hoc* organization. The UN is not. The result is that it has taken more than a year to negotiate the parameters of a joint representation that will probably number fewer than five people.[18] Relations between the missions in the field have also been somewhat strained because the OSCE has received more favourable treatment in the press and is generally perceived in Georgia to be doing a reasonably good job.

Turning to Abkhazia, the original mandate of CISPKF, which has survived more or less intact since, is attached as a protocol to the Moscow Agreement of 14 May 1994 between Georgia and Abkhazia on the ceasefire and separation of forces. The two sides agreed to establish a security zone along the line of contact, in which there would be no armed forces from the two sides. Adjacent to this zone on both sides was a restricted weapons zone, in which artillery, most mortars, tanks and armoured personnel carriers were prohibited. Heavy military equipment originating in the zone was to be stored in designated areas. Georgian forces were to withdraw from the Kodori Valley. Volunteer formations from outside Abkhazia assisting Abkhaz forces were to be disbanded and removed.

CISPKF units were to be deployed to the security zone. The parties agreed that the PKF's principal function was to 'exert its best efforts to maintain the ceasefire and to see that it is scrupulously observed'.[19] It was to supervise the implementation of the agreement with regard to the security zone and the restricted weapons zone. Moreover, in contrast to the South Ossetian case, the CISPKF presence was to 'promote the safe return of refugees and displaced persons, especially to the Gali District'. Rules of engagement were unspecified in the documents establishing the force.[20]

The Security Council's recognition of the CISPKF in July 1994 brought an expansion in the mandate of UNOMIG. The force was expanded in order to 'monitor and verify the implementation by the parties' of the May agreement, 'to observe the operation of the CISPKF', to verify the removal of troops and heavy equipment of the parties from the security zone, to monitor storage areas for heavy equipment withdrawn from the security and restricted weapons zones, to monitor the withdrawal of Georgian troops from the Kodori Valley, to patrol the Kodori Valley, to investigate alleged violations of the May agreement and to assist in the resolution of such incidents, to report to the UN Secretary-General on the implementation of its mandate and related developments, and to 'contribute to conditions conducive to the safe and orderly return of refugees and displaced persons'.[21]

Again, there are at least two dimensions to effectiveness. The first focuses directly on how well the players fulfilled the mandates that guided their action. The second focuses on the extent to which the separate or joint actions of the respective organizations fostered movement towards a political settlement and addressed other recognized needs deriving from the conflict. With regard to the first, one might well argue that the principal objective of the international actors is to prevent renewal of conflict. Conflict has not been renewed. Therefore, they have essentially fulfilled their mandates. In the Abkhaz case, like that of South Ossetia, the interposition of peacekeepers has stabilized ceasefires and has prevented any renewal of conflict.

Moreover, as in South Ossetia, relations between international observers and Russian peacekeepers have on the whole been good. With the exception of UNOMIG difficulties in obtaining access to the coastal areas of the security zone in late 1994, there has been no obvious CISPKF effort to hinder UNOMIG activities. The two bodies often patrol jointly. They consult on mine and other hazards. CISPKF has agreed to provide evacuation assistance to UNOMIG in the event that it is needed.

The problem in assessing the role of CISPKF and UNOMIG in stabilizing the ceasefire is that one cannot know the counter-factual argument. In the case of Abkhazia, the ejection of the Georgians resulted in the establishment of a geographically defined and defensible front line. Georgia was in no position in 1993 and 1994 (and arguably even now) to contest the outcome. In this respect, one might well argue that the ceasefire would have held in any case. Such an inference is supported by the experience of Nagorno Karabakh next door in Azerbaijan, where a ceasefire has held since May 1994 in the absence of any peacekeeping force.

There was at least one organized effort to break the ceasefire and to 'liberate' Abkhazia from the Abkhaz. In 1995, former Defence Minister Tengiz Kitovani and several hundred armed followers moved by bus from Central Georgia towards the ceasefire line, having announced their intention to take Abkhazia back. This was perhaps the most dangerous organized effort to breach the May 1994 agreement. However, he was stopped, not by peacekeeping forces, but by interior ministry personnel of the Republic of Georgia. Kitovani now sits in jail.

It is easy to conceive of how spontaneous incidents along the line of contact could have produced inadvertent escalation in Abkhazia as in South Ossetia. International personnel interposed between the parties do reduce the incidence of such problems, and, particularly in the case of the OSCE in South Ossetia, follow up on them to seek a resolution of the question causing the problem. Moreover, the UN rightly points to evidence that UNOMIG and CISPKF remonstrations with local military authorities have minimized the reintroduction of heavy weapons into the weapons restricted zone.[22]

The matter gets much stickier when one moves to issues of protection. This is a more significant problem in Abkhazia where large-scale spontaneous return of IDPs to the Gali District began in 1995 and met with substantial opposition from Abkhaz authorities.[23] Under the terms of the May 1994 agreement, local law still applies in the security and restricted weapons zones, the local authorities retain responsibility for civil administration including law enforcement, and peacekeepers are not empowered to override local officials in the discharge of their responsibilities in these areas. The problem is that the Abkhaz administration is structurally hostile to Georgian returnees. In addition to the lingering acrimony of the civil war, there is the further problem that if a substantial return of refugees occurs prior to a settlement on the political status of Abkhazia, decisions on status will be determined in large measure by returning Georgians. The Abkhaz constituted less than 20 per cent of the population of the region while the Georgians made up more than 45 per cent. In such circumstances, returnees are likely to be targets of intimidation.

This has been a chronic problem in the area.[24] In March 1995, for example, over one hundred Abkhaz with police identity cards entered the security zone and arrested some two hundred returnees. Twenty, mostly male and of military age, were murdered. Some executions took place in the open and were reportedly observed by CISPKF and UNOMIG personnel. Civilians seeking protection from CIS peacekeepers were unevenly treated. Some received protection; some were turned away; some were turned over to Abkhaz police. This reflected a very narrow interpretation of the humanitarian clause in the mandate cited above. CISPKF personnel responded to questioning on these events by arguing that there was no humanitarian or protection component in their mandate, and that the agreement obliged them to allow properly documented local officials to carry out their responsibilities in the security zone.[25] UNOMIG personnel made no effort to interfere either, although they did provide medical assistance to those injured in the action. Those UNOMIG personnel who assisted civilians during this incident reportedly did so in violation of instructions from UNOMIG command in Sukhumi.

Although the basic functions of peacekeeping in a traditional sense were fulfilled, broader aspects of the mandate, including protection, were not. UNOMIG, composed of unarmed observers, was not in a position to take on the issue of protection seriously.[26] CISPKF was, but did not. The problem from the perspective of the UN – leaving aside the ethical problems of standing aside to watch people be slaughtered – is that the failure to address protection damaged the world organization's credibility. UN credibility was in this instance the hostage of the regional organization with whom they were task-sharing. When the CISPKF did not deliver, much of the egg stuck to UNOMIG's and UNHCR's faces, the two agencies being the only high-profile international presences in the area. The result of the UN's association with a peacekeeping venture that leaves the population at risk has been a serious loss of face in the area concerned.[27] Moreover, to the extent that abuse of the population carries some risk of renewal of conflict as well as further embittering the parties, the failure of CISPKF and UNOMIG to deliver on protection may have further complicated efforts to achieve a settlement.

On a more positive note, however, there is some evidence to suggest that encouragement from UNOMIG, coupled with the Russians' own embarrassment, did slowly improve CISPKF performance in 1995–6. Subsequent to the events just described, CISPKF units began shadowing Abkhaz patrols in the region more closely, perhaps reducing intimidation and violation of local human rights. In this sense, one might argue that the interweaving of UN and regional activity did result in a degree of transfer of international norms.

More generally, Russian performance in the early days of both the Osset and Abkhaz operations was handicapped by a lack of units trained for peacekeeping. In the Abkhaz case, early units were drawn in considerable measure from formations already stationed in Georgia. Their connections to the local population compromised their impartiality. The Russian military has since made considerable efforts to train units for such missions, can draw upon a more substantial complement of experienced personnel[28] and is deploying units from outside the region. The level of professionalism among Russian forces deployed to the region thus has increased. Greater UN and other international support of Russian training efforts might well accelerate this process.

There were a number of other perils associated with the devolution of peacekeeping functions to CIS and Russian peacekeepers in Georgia. Notably, when it went into South Ossetia and Abkhazia, the Russian military did not share international standards concerning rules of engagement and comportment with regard to the civilian population and civilian property. Matters were made worse by the state of logistics in the Russian Army. Shipments of supplies to units in the field were erratic and insufficient. The financial crisis in the Russian military resulted in long periods when peacekeepers were not paid. These factors conduced to problems of corruption. Instances ranged from the small scale (for example, the extortion of money from Georgians seeking to cross into Abkhazia from Georgia via the main bridge across the Inguri controlled by CISPKF[29]) to the grandiose.[30] Evidence of corruption was also evident in the Osset case, where, for example, peacekeepers were extorting protection money from vendors in the Tskhinvali markets.[31] Such activities highlight the practical difficulties of relying on poorly paid and equipped regional forces to implement peacekeeping tasks. However, corruption was in part the result of the disastrous financial and logistical condition of the Russian armed forces. It is, consequently, an open question whether UN willingness to finance Russian peacekeeping might have mitigated the problem.

With regard to the second dimension of effectiveness, the extent to which the players contributed to creating the conditions for a political settlement, the OSCE and the Russians have been somewhat effective in establishing and sustaining a dialogue between the parties in South Ossetia. The OSCE has also had some success in re-establishing unofficial contacts between the two sides through track two dialogue. The stabilization of the situation on the ground has allowed some revival of economic links across the line of contact. However, other than a memorandum agreed between the two on confidence-building measures in 1996, there has been little obvious movement towards a comprehensive solution. In the meantime, there has been little success in efforts to return displaced Georgians and Ossets to their homes.

Likewise, in Abkhazia, there is little evidence of progress on the political front. The SRSG for the Abkhaz conflict is widely criticized in the region for what is perceived to be a dilatory approach to the settlement process. Likewise, the CIS and Russia have had little success in pushing the parties towards an agreement, and, indeed, many in the region believe that Russia has made little real effort in this regard, since Georgian dependence on Russia rests in large part on the failure to normalize the Abkhaz situation. Finally, the UNHCR has failed to deliver in its role as leader of the quadripartite commission on return of IDPs to Abkhazia. Its one substantial effort in this regard (the April 1994 agreement on return) was widely criticized for its failure to address the issue of protection of returnees, and ultimately failed in the face of Abkhaz obstructionism.[32]

HEGEMONY AND CONFLICT MANAGEMENT

Underlying these specific dimensions of cooperative peacebuilding in the region is the broader political question raised at the outset of this paper: to what extent does reliance on regional actors jeopardize impartiality and serve particular state interests at the expense of those of the target state or the international system as a whole? It is worth recalling the nature of the trade-off that the UN faces in task-sharing in such circumstances. On the one hand, reliance on a regional actor reduces pressure on the universal organization and, moreover, increases the likelihood that a substantial effort will be made in the area of conflict management. It is fair to say that, in the Georgian case, had it not been Russia that intervened to stabilize the situation, no one else would have. On the other hand, reliance on a regional organization may further the hegemonic aspirations of dominant powers within that organization. Moreover, regional players may have ties to particular actors in a conflict that make it difficult to dissociate regional institutional responses from the politics of the conflict itself.

Russia has clear hegemonic aspirations in the former Soviet space. Although a wide array of opinions are expressed on Russian policy in the newly independent states in the media and in parliament, a dominant consensus appears to have emerged among foreign policy influentials on the need for active presence and influence in the area.[33] Such views have been widely expressed by official statements,[34] influential statements by independent policy groups,[35] advisers to the president,[36] influential political figures,[37] and the president himself. The hegemonic component of Russian policy in the 'near abroad' is evident in their efforts to restore Russian control over the external borders of the former Soviet Union, to reassume control over the Soviet air defence network, to obtain agreements on the basing of Russian forces in the non-Russian republics and by their obvious sensitivity to external military presences (including multilateral ones) on the soil of the former Soviet Union. To judge from Russian policy on Caspian Sea and Central Asian energy development, it extends beyond the political/security realm and into the economic one. Its sources are diverse, and include the Russian imperial hangover, but more practically the fate of the Russian diaspora, the lack of developed defences along the borders of the Russian Federation proper, concern over Islam and discomfort with the spillover effects of instability in the other republics.

The capacity of a dominant power to manipulate a regional organization depends partially on the latter's institutional strength. The more substantial and embedded the organization, the less likely it is to be a creature of particular dominant states within the region. This case is unpromising. We have seen already how one instance of peacekeeping in Georgia (South Ossetia) ignored the regional organization altogether. It was a Russian response on the basis of an agreement mediated between the parties by Russia. There was no pretence of multilateralism. In the case of Abkhazia, on paper the CIS responded on a regional multilateral basis. However, for reasons amply analysed elsewhere,[38] the CIS was (and is) neither multilateral nor an organization. To the extent that it serves any purpose, it is as an instrument of Russian foreign policy in the former Soviet space. The Georgian example is illustrative. In the Abkhaz case, Russian peacekeepers were deployed late in 1993 by a decision of the Russian government and without the imprimatur of the CIS, which caught up in June 1994 by authorizing the deployment of a regional peacekeeping force. However, not a single soldier from a CIS state other than Russia has ever appeared. Nor have the other states in the CIS contributed financially to the force. In short, the CIS mandate is a transparent fig leaf for Russian action in a neighbouring state.

Russia's first activities in these conflicts in Georgia were not the peace-keeping operations. Russia and Russians have been involved in various capacities in these conflicts since their eruption. It is hard to say whether this involvement has always reflected a conscious and coordinated policy, given the chaotic nature of policy-making in Moscow from 1990 to 1994. However, the involvement of Russia (including peacekeeping) has served to render Georgia dependent on the Russian Federation, and this depend-ence has led to Georgian concessions that are entirely consistent with the evolving hegemonic consensus in Russia on relations with the other former Soviet states.

To take the case of South Ossetia, the insurgency in the region was funded out of Russia, and many of those fighting were Russian citizens from North Ossetia. Although it is more than likely that these people par-ticipated for their own reasons, most of them related to ethnic loyalty, Russia made no attempt to interfere with the passage of volunteers and of matériel across the frontier into Georgia. It also did not pressure the North Ossetian Autonomous Republic of the Russian Federation to limit its in-volvement. Support of or tolerance for Osset initiatives is consistent with the pattern of North Caucasian politics, in which the Ossets have been one of the most reliable allies of Russia in a very difficult region. Another example of this point is the role of Russian federal forces in defending the Osset claim to the Prigorodnyi Raion in 1991–2 against Ingush efforts to reclaim the area for Ingushetia.[39]

In the Abkhaz case, insurgents used Russian military equipment, pre-sumably obtained from Russian bases in Abkhazia, in order to push the Georgians back. When Russia brokered a ceasefire in mid-1993, it took on responsibilities to monitor compliance and guarantee the agreement. The Georgians (albeit slowly) did remove heavy equipment restricted under the agreement from Abkhazia. The implementation of the disarmament was, by contrast, ineffective with respect to the Abkhaz. This created the regional military imbalance that permitted Abkhazia's rapid push to victory in September 1993. The asymmetrical quality of Russian monitor-ing of the Sochi Accord appears to be a clear example of Russian govern-ment partiality in the period leading up to the deployment of the Russian peacekeeping force in late 1993. Large numbers of Russian citizens participated on the Abkhaz side in the final offensive. There was no effort to stop them from entering Abkhazia even though their purpose was known.

The consequence for Georgia was dramatic. Georgian forces were ejected from Abkhazia and faced a serious rebellion in Mingrelia that was being assisted by the Abkhaz. The state was in danger of total collapse. It was at this stage that Shevardnadze went to Moscow to plead for Russian help and caved in on several major components of Russia's agenda in its relations with Georgia. Notably, Georgia signed the CIS Accord and agreed in principle to a military cooperation agreement that would render more or less permanent the Russian military presence in Georgia, as well as guaranteeing substantial Russian influence in Georgia's military. It was only when these objectives were attained that Russia interposed its peace-keepers and provided the military assistance necessary to quell the rebellion in Mingrelia.

The final point to make concerns the role of Russia in negotiations for a political settlement of the two conflicts. Although the reviews of Russian mediation in both the Osset and Abkhaz cases are mixed, Russia has not mounted the kind of pressure on the insurgent parties necessary to push them towards a compromise. Abkhazia is supposed to be under blockade, for example, but Russia has made little effort to enforce it. In both instances, enough gets through to sustain the insurgencies. One is left with the impression that Russia is not looking for a settlement, since a durable solution to the wars would reduce Georgian dependence on Russia.

CONCLUSION

In the case considered here, task-sharing has produced a greater degree of stability than would otherwise have been the case. Russia has taken on peace-related operations that no one else (including the UN) was willing to tackle. Their presence makes a considerable contribution to ensuring that there is no accidental resumption of hostilities. This has allowed a degree of normalization in Georgia. In this sense, the experience of UN task-sharing is positive.

However, judgement is complicated in considerable measure because Russia was to some degree instrumental in causing these conflicts and has used them to enhance its control of the affairs of Georgia and the Transcaucasus. Although the activities of both the UN and the OSCE to mitigate the impact of the Russian presence in Georgia and to promote international norms have had some effect, they have done little to alter this basic fact. From the Russian perspective, task-sharing is a means of re-asserting control while benefiting from the legitimizing effects of involvement by international organizations.

From a policy perspective, this begs the question whether a different approach to task-sharing might not have had more effective results in furthering the objectives of the UN. It is certainly not difficult to identify areas in which improvements could have been made. The deployment of larger numbers of Russian-speaking observers in UNOMIG and the construction of a tighter structure of relations between UNOMIG and CISPKF might well have enhanced the performance of both organizations while assisting in the spread of international practice to Russian forces in the field. Greater attention by UN observers to the issue of protection might have produced better performance of CIS peacekeepers in this area of their mandate. A willingness to finance CISPKF operations in whole or in part could have been used as leverage to secure greater CISPKF compliance with international norms. The Russians were clearly interested in such support. None was forthcoming. Finally, greater international assistance in the training of Russian peacekeepers might well have accelerated their adaptation to international standards.

In short, although this particular case illustrates eloquently the pitfalls of reliance on regional organizations and actors to provide the public good of security, there are methods available to mitigate the negative consequences of such task-sharing and to enhance prospects for realizing its positive effects. Although they were not adequately explored in the Georgian case, the latter experience provides a number of useful lessons to take into account when contemplating future devolutions of tasks related to regional security.

NOTES

1. Following the approach by Muthiah Alagappa, I define regionalism and regional organization to be 'cooperation among governments or non-governmental organizations in three or more geographically proximate and interdependent countries for the pursuit of mutual gain in one or more issue-areas'. Given the focus of this paper, the discussion is limited to inter-governmental organizations and the issue-area of security.

2. Boutros Boutros-Ghali, *An Agenda for Peace*, reprinted in *An Agenda for Peace 1995* (New York: United Nations, 1995), paras 63–4.

3. For a summary of such arguments, see S. N. MacFarlane and T. G. Weiss, 'Regional organizations and regional security', *Security Studies*, 2 (1), Autumn 1992, pp. 10–11.
4. Ibid., p. 11.
5. A situation in which 'a single powerful state controls or dominates the lesser states in the system'. See R. Gilpin, *War and Change in World Politics* (Cambridge: Cambridge University Press, 1981), p. 29.
6. In fact, one might argue that the post-Soviet experience has added a novel dimension to the general concept of conflict management, since in a number of cases, the activity is not limited to conflict prevention, containment and resolution, but also to conflict generation.
7. Notably those contained in Article 53 to the effect that 'no enforcement action shall be taken under regional arrangements or by regional agencies without the authorization of the Security Council', and in Article 54 to the effect that 'the Security Council shall at all times be kept fully informed of the activities undertaken or in contemplation under regional arrangements or by regional agencies for the maintenance of international peace and security'. Article 53 is not relevant to OSCE or CIS activities in the former Soviet space, since they are not enforcement but lie more in the realm of Chapter VI.
8. See the 'Foreign policy concept' and the 'Draft concept of military doctrine', in Foreign Broadcast Information Service (FBIS) USR (Central Eurasia), 93–037: 1–2 (25 March 1993); 'Basic provisions of the military doctrine of the Russian Federation', *Rossiiskie Vesti* (18 November 1993), pp. 1–2. See also S. N. MacFarlane, 'Russian conceptions of Europe', *Post-Soviet Affairs*, 10 (3), July–September 1994, pp. 234–69, for a general overview of evolving Russian views on external involvement in the former Soviet Union.
9. 'Vozroditsya li Soyuz? Tezisy Soveta po Vneshnei i Oboronnoi Politike' (Will the Union be reborn? Theses of the Council on Foreign and Defence Policy], *Nezavisimaya Gazeta* , 23 May 1996.
10. For more substantial background on these conflicts, see S. N. MacFarlane, L. Minear and S. Shenfield, *Armed Conflict in Georgia: A Case Study in Humanitarian Action and Peacekeeping* (Providence, RI: Watson Institute, 1995), Occasional Paper No. 27; S. Goldenberg, *Pride of Small Nations: The Caucasus and Post-Soviet Disorder* (London: Zed Books, 1994), pp. 81–114; and S. Hunter, *The Transcaucasus in Transition: Nation-Building and Conflict* (Washington, DC: CSIS, 1994), pp. 100–41.
11. *OSCE Handbook 1996* (Vienna: OSCE, 1996), p. 21.
12. Interviews near Gori, June 1996.
13. Interviews in Tbilisi and Tskhinvali, June 1996
14. On this point, see S. M. Chervonnaya, *Abkhazia-1992: Post-kommunisticheskaya Vandeya* (Moscow: Mosgorpechat', 1993).
15. According to Russian military sources, Russian troops deploying to the line of contact initially faced some hostile fire. This was suppressed through the use of superior firepower, a process facilitated by the force's rather broad rules of engagement. One Russian military officer characterized the latter in the following form: any violation of the ceasefire would be 'immediately and severely punished'. See P. Baev, *Russia's Peacekeeping in the*

Caucasus, a discussion paper for the Norwegian Institute of International Affairs/Western European Union Conference on 'Peacekeeping in Europe: Assessing UN and Regional Perspectives', Oslo, 17–18 November 1994, mimeograph, p. 14. For more general discussion of Russian peacekeeping, see A. Raevsky and I. N. Vorob'ev, *Russian Approaches to Peacekeeping Operations* (New York: UNIDIR, 1994), Research Paper No. 28; M. Shashenkov, 'Russian peacekeeping in the "near abroad"', *Survival*, 36 (3), Autumn 1994, pp. 46–69; and S. N. MacFarlane and A. Schnabel, 'Russia's approach to peacekeeping', *International Journal*, 50 (2), Spring 1995, pp. 294–324.

16. *SBSE: Missia v Gruzii* (Tbilisi: OSCE, 1994), mimeograph.

17. On this point, see CSCE, *Third Meeting of the Council: Summary of Conclusions* (Stockholm: CSCE, 1992), p. 12.

18. As one OSCE Tbilisi mission member put it in somewhat frustrated terms in May 1996, 'It's so easy to get two people into a car and up to Sukhumi to do some human rights monitoring. But to get the same two people assigned there by two different bureaucracies takes months.' Interviews in Tbilisi, May 1996.

19. *Protocol to the Agreement on a Cease-Fire and Separation of Forces*, mimeograph.

20. At a seminar in Moscow in June 1995, I asked what the rules of engagement for the force might be. Russian officers present evinced a degree of confusion on this point, suggesting a degree of unfamiliarity with the concept. Perhaps the best indicator of the Russian view on this subject was provided by a senior officer in the Ministry of Defence who earlier in the seminar had dismissed the definitional travails of Western scholars attempting to address the distinction between peacebuilding, peacekeeping, peacemaking and so on with the curt comment that it was all 'local war'.

21. This discussion focuses on peacekeeping. In the overall context of task-sharing between universal and regional organizations, it is worth noting that a UN agency (UNHCR) retained primary responsibility in another key sphere – the status and return of internally displaced persons in Georgia. For an extended discussion of UNHCR's role here, see MacFarlane et al., *Armed Conflict in Georgia*, pp. 38–42.

22. *Report of the Secretary-General concerning the Situation in Abkhazia, Georgia*, S/1995/181, 6 March 1995.

23. Interestingly, the problem lay not so much with the local administration in Gali, which recognized the inevitability of return and was seeking means to regularize it. The problem lay with incursions by Abkhaz 'police' from neighbouring districts of Abkhazia, acting presumably on the suspicion of the Abkhaz government that the locals were too soft on the returnees. Interviews in Gali, March 1995.

24. This is noted in much UN documentation on the conflict. See, for example, *Report of the Secretary-General*, 6 March 1995.

25. Interviews with CISPKF staff officers, March 1995.

26. The Secretary-General's report of 6 March 1995 notes quite rightly, if rather lamely, that 'neither UNOMIG's mandate nor its strength enable [*sic*] it to prevent violations of the Agreement or to deter armed group's from entering the security zone. However, UNOMIG's protests, together with the action

taken by the CISPKF, help reduce the number and duration of such violations.' It is of course impossible empirically to determine the validity of
such a claim. Its timing, however, was unfortunate, since it preceded by one
week the most serious incursion of this type.

27. After the incidents of March 1995, both UNOMIG and UNHCR representatives in the Gali District commented on the serious loss of UN prestige resulting from their inaction and expressed concern about the possibility of
civilian attack on UN personnel. Interviews in Gali, March 1995.

28. To take one example, a senior staff officer we interviewed in Gali had
served on peacekeeping missions in Moldova, South Ossetia and Tajikistan
prior to his placement in Abkhazia.

29. This had unfortunate humanitarian consequences. Georgian civilians attempting to bypass the tolls had to pass through mine-infested zones, with
some fatalities.

30. An international aid official in eastern Abkhazia told of an instance where a
departing CISPKF unit commander had removed all of the furniture from a
local school, loaded it into a net suspended from a helicopter and flown off
with it all. Interviews in Gali, March 1995.

31. The UN Office was in 1995 contemplating support of market development
in Tskhinvali as a means of building confidence between the Georgian and
Osset communities, but an informal feasibility study recommended against
proceeding for this reason.

32. The agreement included provision for the screening of potential returnees by
the Abkhaz authorities. This process was extremely slow. By the time the
process was abandoned at the end of 1994, approximately 310 out of a pro-
jected 40,000 displaced persons had returned to the Gali District. Many of
these subsequently left their homes again as a result of the security situation.

33. See MacFarlane, 'Russian conceptions of Europe', pp. 234–69.

34. See *Foreign Policy Concept of the Russian Federation,* FBIS-USR-93-037,
25 March 1993.

35. 'Vozroditsya li Soyuz', *passim.*

36. A. Migranyan, 'Rossiia I Blizhnee Zarubezh'e', Russia and the Near
Abroad, *Nezavisimaya Gazeta,* 12 January 1994, pp. 1, 4.

37. V. P. Lukin, 'Our security predicament', *Foreign Policy,* 88, Fall 1992,
pp. 57–75.

38. See, for example, S. Neil MacFarlane, 'La CEI et la sécurité regionale',
Etudes Internationales, XXVI, 4, décembre 1995, pp. 785–97; Andrei
Zagorsky, 'Die Gemeinschaft Unabhaengiger Staaten: Entwicklungen und
Perspektiven', *Berichte des Bundesinstituts fèr Ostwissenschaftliche und
Internationale Studien,* 50, 1992.

39. The region in question had been transferred from Ingushetia to North
Ossetia when the Ingush were deported to Central Asia during the Second
World War. They were allowed to return in the 1950s, but did not get their
original borders back. In 1991–2, the Ingush population of the area was
cleansed by the Ossets. Federal forces intervened in November 1992 and declared a state of emergency in order to restore order. Since the removal of
the Ingush had already been completed, Russian forces essentially served to
protect the Osset victory. On this incident, see Suzanne Goldenberg, *Pride
of Small Nations,* pp. 200–1.

Part III
Non-governmental Delivery of Services

7 NGO Relief in War Zones: Toward an Analysis of the New Aid Paradigm
Mark Duffield

Relief in war zones provides a metaphor for the post-Cold War era, which is part of its complexity. It signals and reflects some of the most profound historical changes of our time. Although often associated with Africa or the Balkans, the *modus operandi* of war relief also reflects the essence of social change *within* industrialized countries. External humanitarian aid is similarly concerned with the changing role of governments and the increasing importance of subcontracting public functions to private or nongovernmental organizations (NGOs). In many respects, the present international relief system is a projection of the way in which the West is attempting to solve its own internal problems. In both cases, the focus of public policy has shifted from attempting to manage growth and redistribution to trying to contain the effects of poverty and social exclusion.

This structural association between internal and external public policy is to be expected. It would be surprising if Western governments were advocating wildly different scenarios. In both situations, governance is being redefined in more complex ways as the privatization of public and economic life advances. Relief in war zones is also conditioned by the perceived national and regional interests of Western governments. Thus, while there is a structural similarity at policy level, in practice, there is a marked unevenness in application.

The present background to relief in war zones is the growing polarization of the global economy. The existence of a wealth gap between the richest and poorest parts of the world is long-standing. The size of the this gap, however, is widening. Over the last three decades, for example, compared to the poorest fifth of the world's population, the richest fifth has doubled its share of global income from 30 to 61 to 1.[1] At the same time, more than a quarter of the world's population now have incomes lower than in previous decades. In some cases lower than twenty years ago.

This polarization is not a random process but is associated with the regionalization of the global economy. Since the 1980s, its most dynamic

Mark Duffield

elements have been increasingly integrated within North American, West European and East Asian regional systems. This process has recreated an interest in the existence of economic blocs.[2] Of related concern is evidence suggesting that it is those areas which lie outside the main regional configurations where the effects of global polarization are most pronounced: Africa, Latin America and the Caribbean, the Middle East, Eastern Europe and the Commonwealth of Independent States (CIS) countries.[3] Across much of this broad area, average economic indicators have been going backwards as the dynamic regions have continued to grow.

Regional differentiation and increasing polarization has recast the boundaries of 'North' and 'South'. A working hypothesis would now define the North as the main bloc areas, including East Asia, while the South represents those regions lying outside or only partially integrated into these regional systems. This includes parts of Eastern Europe and the CIS countries. As the global economy has concentrated within the dynamic regions, a process of withdrawal from non-bloc areas has begun. Rather than dynamism, many countries are increasingly unstable.[4] Indeed, while there are exceptions, the broad Africa–Eurasia axis subsumes the overwhelming majority of what the UN classifies as complex emergencies.

It is misleading to see economic polarization and impoverishment as a direct cause of instability. While important contributory factors, functional considerations are insufficient explanations on their own. More significantly, the process of regionalization has given rise to differing political or regulatory dynamics. At the risk of over-simplification, the emergence of free market North American, social democratic West European and strong-state East Asian models of regional integration suggest the existence of different 'species' of capitalism.[5] Rather than differences among the main blocs, however, it is between the dynamic and the crisis regions where the key discontinuity lies.

CONTRARY REGIONAL DYNAMICS

That the nature of governance is changing at the national and international levels is widely remarked. While this is true generally, the actual process of governmental change within bloc and non-bloc areas is different. Within the dynamic areas of the global economy the process of competitive state formation has largely come to an end. Indeed, the main emphasis is on redefining sovereignty within the context of new forms of regional economic integration. The process has gone further within the European

Union (EU) where, albeit with hesitation, political unification is developing.

Within the crisis regions beyond the wealth gap, however, the forceful redefinition of political authority is still underway. Indeed, the instability that is associated with this process is the predominant focus of relief in war zones. Rather than new forms of regional integration, the opposite is occurring. Over large parts of Africa, Eastern Europe and the CIS countries, regional fragmentation and political separatism have accelerated.

Either new states have been established or have been redefined as ethnocentric or fundamentalist arrangements. In the forty years prior to 1989, for example, only two new states emerged based on the principle of ethnic seccession – Singapore and Bangladesh. During the early 1990s, ten such states were created, almost all of them in Eastern Europe.[6] The trend toward Islamic fundamentalism in the Middle East and parts of Africa is also part of this process. In some areas, warlord structures have emerged within states. Where the resource base is insufficient for formal state creation, competing warlords have fashioned so-called failed or weak states.[7]

Global regionalization and polarization has given rise to two contrary developments: complex forms of economic and political integration within the main bloc areas, as opposed to ethnocentric or fundamentalist assertion or breakdown outside. Under these circumstances, Western aid policy assumes an added importance. For conventional wisdom this divisive trend is a temporary phase in the process of development and transition toward liberal democracy. If this is wrong, however, and instability represents the emergence of new types of socio-political formation adapted to exist on the margins of the global economy, then the implications are profound. Policy-makers would not even be asking the right questions, let alone providing the answers.

FROM CONVERGENCE TO RELATIVE DEVELOPMENT

Humanitarian assistance has become the West's favoured response to political crisis beyond its borders. Largely through agreements with warring parties, the ability of NGOs to deliver humanitarian aid has grown considerably. It is difficult to discuss relief, however, without mentioning how the concept of development has changed. Through so-called continuum thinking, both are interlinked within the new aid paradigm.

The response of aid agencies to systemic crisis in non-bloc areas has been to redefine earlier developmental goals to accommodate global polarization. Since the 1970s, there has been a move away from modernist ideas premised on eventual social convergence, that is the underdeveloped world eventually approximating the developed. From a contrary perspective, premised on an exploitative link between core (developed) and periphery (underdeveloped), neo-Marxist dependency and world system theories have also gone out of fashion.[8] Rather than a convergence or necessary exploitation, the new paradigm is premised on separate development.

Practical development has been redefined as a multicultural enterprise: on the celebration of diversity and the empowerment of cultural and gender difference.[9] Rather than an absolute quantity, as implied by the now outmoded terms of 'development' and 'underdevelopment', progress has become a relative concept – little more than whatever private aid agencies can actually do. Its NGO proponents have criticized the government-led infrastructural programmes of the 1960s and 1970s. They have been replaced by ideas of local partnership based on empowerment and capacity-building.[10] Budget-conscious donors have been more than willing to accept this social redefinition of the problem. As a consequence, not only has development changed its meaning, contracting of official aid programmes has grown apace.

Compared to the infrastructural programmes of the past, the development projects that emerged during the 1980s provide little more than a basic level of public welfare for targeted groups and communities. Ideally through self-help, they aim to lessen the vulnerability of marginal groups to the rigours of their increasingly precarious existence. Through health, education, agricultural and employment projects NGOs have established what Clark[11] has called 'compensatory programmes' in societies enduring the rigours of structural adjustment, in many cases a prelude to systemic crisis. Earlier notions of social convergence have thus been transmuted into the provision of sustainable welfare safety nets by private agencies.

Ideas of relief and development have become somewhat blurred. Increasingly, development has been reduced to welfare and, indeed, relief. This situation is well reflected in the current debate on the relief to development continuum.[12] Rather than being regarded as separate practices, conventional wisdom now holds that relief should be provided in such a way as to foster people-centred development. Given the decline in overall development funding and the high levels of damage and social disruption in conflict-affected areas, continuum thinking makes little sense in an increasingly polarized world without a relativization of development goals.

EXCLUSION AND INTERNALIZATION

If there is one single factor that points toward separate development and social exclusion at a global level, it is the changing status of the refugee. There has been a steady move away from an international refugee regime focused almost exclusively on the obligations of receiving states and the rights of asylum seekers within them. Increasingly, no one wants to accept refugees, even neighbouring countries within the crisis regions. This has prompted attempts to prevent large-scale population movements crossing international boundaries and, through humanitarian assistance, to support war affected populations within their home countries. Such developments are central to the new aid and security paradigm.

For several decades the total number of people for whom UNHCR is responsible has increased relentlessly. In 1991, for example, the figure stood at around 17 million; by mid-1995 it had risen to 27.4 million. This increase, however, conceals a historic change. From the beginning of the 1990s the number of actual refugees, that is people who have crossed an international boundary and been granted asylum in another state, has been declining. The continued rise in total numbers has been due to UNHCR's involvement with non-refugees. At 12.9 million in 1995, this new category has rapidly grown to become 47 per cent of its total caseload. This non-traditional group roughly divides into internally displaced and war-affected populations within their home countries, people outside of their home country but without asylum status and for whom UNHCR feels concern and returnees to their original countries.[13]

The growing importance of non-refugees to UNHCR graphically illustrates the changed humanitarian and security environment. In less than a decade, attempting to assist such populations, especially the internally displaced and war-affected, has radically transformed the nature of humanitarian assistance.[14] Largely through a series of *ad hoc* Security Council resolutions, a key development has been the ability to provide relief assistance even under war conditions. This has been a major opportunity for NGO expansion. In post-conflict situations a complementary focus on democratization and support for civil society has also emerged. At the same time, barriers aimed at preventing refugees settling not only in the West,[15] but even in countries within the crisis regions have grown.[16] Although the 1951 Refugee Convention is still in force, its provisions are ignored as a new and contrary paradigm takes shape.

Apart from its welfare function, the policy role of relief under war conditions is to help keep conflict-affected populations within their countries of origin. In countries where safe areas have been tried, this has usually been backed by military protection. Where the military is not involved, as in some of the negotiated programmes in Africa, the availability of humanitarian aid itself can discourage population flight.[17] Through the growing influence of continuum thinking, providing relief in war zones has been cast as a first step to recovery and social reconstruction.

SOVEREIGNTY THROUGH PARTNERSHIP

One could describe the Cold War humanitarian system as one in which the external relations between states and the obligations of receiving states toward asylum seekers were the predominant political and moral factors. Since the 1980s, the trend has been increasingly to internalize the effects of political crisis within unstable regions. Whereas the multicultural revision of development demands partnership at the local level, humanitarian aid in war conditions requires partnership at a political level. Indeed, it is this factor that has significantly contributed to the politicization of humanitarian assistance.

The attempt to internalize the effects of political crisis demands a change of attitude toward governments and political authorities within unstable countries. The 1951 Refugee Convention, while detailing the rights of refugees within receiving countries, makes no mention of the sending country. The new paradigm, however, places this rectification at its centre.[18] It is still recognized that indigenous political actors often instigate social disruption. At the same time, however, the notion of state responsibility has been redefined. Within the new paradigm, not only are governments held to account for causing conflict, they must also be encouraged and assisted to normalize the situation.

This duality is the central contradiction within continuum thinking. In practice it can only work if justice is downplayed in favour of the possibility of reconstruction. This possibility, moreover, requires the existence of a benign developmental state. Such contradictions and assumptions clash with the reality of internal war. Moreover, they suggest that, as a general approach to political instability in the crisis regions, the continuum idea is seriously flawed. Such considerations, however, have not prevented aid agencies, desperate for technical solutions, from elevating it to a hegemonic position.

Since the 1980s, political authorities and local actors in refugee-producing countries have approved and been involved in new forms of external intervention by Western aid agencies. New operational tools have emerged in which the subcontracting of welfare and security services has been central. The implications of the emerging paradigm are profound.

By the early 1990s, it was recognized that the age of absolute sovereignty had passed, that notions based on non-interference in internal affairs were quaint. Sovereignty itself, however, has not disappeared and is still a key element in international relations. Indeed, the new aid paradigm is dependent on its restatement. If political authorities are to be made responsible for preventing population displacement and promoting democracy instead of ethnic exclusivism, then their position has to be recognized. What is striking, however, is the contrast in global dynamics. As new forms of regional integration emerge within the main bloc areas, Western aid policy is to reassert a form of sovereignty within the crisis regions.

One could argue that rather than countering regional fragmentation and political exclusivism, the new paradigm *encourages* these developments. While this might be an indirect consequence, it is not the intention. The bottom line of international policy seems clear. The West is unable or unwilling to take comprehensive responsibility for alleviating impoverishment and instability in crisis regions. The only feasible alternative is to encourage political authorities and local institutions within the countries concerned, which has helped push relief and development policy in a self-help direction. Given the extent of global polarization, whether this is enough on its own is a different question.

Partnership with warring parties or sectarian political entities involves a complex redefinition of sovereignty. While formal sovereignty is upheld, it is reshaped to create the space for an emerging pattern of external involvement. Central to this process is an agreement among all concerned – including the UN's member states – that the West's new operational instruments are essentially non-political. Typically, in a relief situation this involves an agreement between the UN and the warring parties that all humanitarian assistance is neutral and designed only to assist civilians in a non-strategic way.[19] Any aid agency that wishes to be part of such operations must abide by such rules. The non-political prescription also extends to social reconstruction and conflict resolution.

WELFARE SAFETY NETS AND PUBLIC SECTOR DECAY

Recasting development in welfare terms signifies a form of disengagement from crisis regions. It represents a break with the approach to underdevelopment that would have been advocated thirty years ago. At the same time, however, the multicultural ethic of the new paradigm simultaneously provides a new way of re-engaging non-bloc areas. Over the past decade or more, a simultaneous process of disengagement and re-engagement has been taking place.

Regarding the present humanitarian system, the current re-engagement with protracted crises properly began in the 1980s. Associated with the growing presence of NGOs, these initial agency interventions where part of a key organizational innovation. By the mid-1980s, a noticeable change in donor funding policy had occurred, from direct donor assistance to recognized governments in favour of international support for private, nongovernmental sectors.[20] This change reflected the decline in support for large-scale infrastructural programmes in favour of smaller, community-based projects. It also established a form of aid market where none had properly existed.

In part, encouraging NGOs reflected the international predominance of neo-liberal thinking and opposition to the claimed excesses of big government. In relation to relief in war zones, however, it was not the whole story. The growing association between human rights abuse and internal war increasingly led donors to distance themselves from the actions of refugee producing governments. The introduction of NGO-managed relief programmes was an initial step in the move toward new forms of partnership. Ethiopia during the mid-1980s is an example of this type of re-engagement,[21] albeit, at that stage, only on the government side. At the same time, decaying state capacity elsewhere within crisis regions further encouraged the appearance of international welfare safety nets. The result was a growing NGO influence at both policy and operational levels.

The involvement of NGOs in welfare provision would not have been possible without a growth of subcontracting. In its basic form, this involves donor governments contracting out their aid programmes to NGO implementers. It has been called 'public service contracting' by some commentators.[22] Within this subcontracting relation, lines of funding and accountability usually reside between donors and the concerned NGOs. While not universal, strong national ties are common. Other than attempting to provide some form of registration, host governments are often absent from such contractual relationships.

The degree to which individual NGOs are dependent upon donor funding can vary. The relationship, however, is pervasive and of growing importance. Within large emergency programmes, owing to the relatively high cost of transport and commodity procurement, donor funding is critical. Even established international NGOs that regard themselves as having an independent development capacity by virtue of public support, generally find themselves relying on donor funding in complex emergencies.

Although there is no necessary causal relationship, international NGO presence has tended to expand as indigenous public provision has contracted. The growth of donor/NGO subcontracting, for example, has been especially marked in regions characterized by internal war, political exclusivism and public sector decay. In such areas, NGOs have increasingly taken responsibility for welfare. In places like Angola, where the recognized government has largely deserted the public sector, NGOs have become the main service providers.[23]

In the mid 1980s, the Horn of Africa was one of the first regions in which international donor/NGO welfare safety nets developed. Despite their uneven and fragmentary character, by the end of the decade they had become an established feature in many other parts of the continent. Until the end of the 1980s, however, conflict was a limiting factor in the spread of the aid market. It was not until new forms of partnership with warring parties were forged with the end of the Cold War that further expansion was possible. In Eastern Europe and Eurasia, for example, welfare safety nets have expanded from the outset as parts of wider UN or regional systems.

NEGOTIATED ACCESS AND ONGOING CONFLICT

Prior to the end of the 1980s, warring parties usually attempted to deny humanitarian assistance to areas controlled by opponents. They were able to pursue a strategy of humanitarian denial largely as a result of the importance previously attached to traditional notions of non-interference in internal matters. As a result, during the Cold War non-government areas in internal wars were out of bounds for most aid agencies. NGOs tended to operate on the side of the recognized government.[24] During this time, relief programmes often took the form of dealing with the symptoms of counter-insurgency and humanitarian denial, of supporting displaced people outside the war zone or as refugees beyond recognized borders.

Within the new paradigm, negotiated access has become the principal means of expanding welfare safety nets in internal wars. In its most basic form, negotiated access involves gaining the consent of warring parties for the movement and delivery of humanitarian aid to civilian populations. Negotiated access is not particularly new. This type of approach has a long pedigree in the field of diplomacy and crisis management.[25] Negotiation was also part of more limited relief operations during the Cold War. What is new is that attempting to secure the consent of warring parties has become the principal means of establishing internationally mandated relief operations that cover all sides in an ongoing conflict.

Negotiated access has supplied a post-Cold War framework within which integrated multisectoral humanitarian programmes have been created. While remaining operationally problematic, it has legitimized cross-border or cross-line type programmes that were previously out of bounds for most aid agencies. An early example of this approach was the UN's Operation Lifeline Sudan (OLS) in 1989. Variants have emerged in places such as Angola (1990), Ethiopia (1990), Kurdistan (1991), Bosnia (1992) and Rwanda (1994).

Where consent is forthcoming, negotiated access has greatly expanded the scope of humanitarian operations. NGOs are now able to work in situations which, less than a decade ago, would have been unthinkable. The enlargement of the sphere of UN and NGO activity, however, is not the only factor of significance. Based on consent, negotiated humanitarian programmes are vulnerable to obstruction and interference by warring parties. The repeated humiliation of the UN in Bosnia, or the frequent obstruction of OLS by the Sudanese government, are examples of this general problem. Nevertheless, negotiated access has great historic and political importance.

During the Cold War, although UN intervention was relatively uncommon, when it did take place it was on the basis of an agreed ceasefire or clear peacekeeping arrangements.[26] UN agencies did not attempt to operate in the context of an ongoing conflict. The *ad hoc* UN resolutions that have made negotiated access possible, however, send a different signal. The new paradigm, while not condoning conflict, now appears to accept that political instability is an unfortunate reality in the South. Unable to prevent internal war, the West has resigned itself to finding ways of working within ongoing crises and managing their symptoms.

INTEGRATED PROGRAMMES AND UN/NGO SUBCONTRACTING

Negotiated access provided the framework for expansion of the aid market in war zones. One of the first operational innovations within this framework was the UN-led integrated relief programme. These have been characterized by an expansion of UN/NGO subcontracting and, in a some places, military protection. The international capacity to respond to complex emergencies, however, has continued to expand. Subcontracting has become more complex. There has been an increase in the role of regional bodies discharging UN responsibilities. This can be seen as a form of political subcontracting. At the same time, the growing use of military and government assets in non-protection roles, for example logistic and engineering capabilities, has extended service delivery into areas beyond the capacity of most welfare NGOs.

Although details differ reflecting the existence of a shared paradigm, integrated programmes in places like Angola, southern Sudan and Bosnia, for example, share a similar basic structure.[27] The move to improve integration has also been encouraged by parallel organizational developments. In the wake of the Gulf War, for example, the UN's Department of Humanitarian Affairs (DHA) was formed to rationalize and enhance agency coordination and funding. Corresponding aims also underpinned the formation of the EU's European Community Humanitarian Office (ECHO) in 1992. Many donor governments have also recently become operational in the humanitarian field. The trend toward more coordination and integration is reflected in the UN Secretary General's 1992 *An Agenda for Peace*.[28]

In practice, the extent of coordination is often minimal. In theory, however, integrated or comprehensive programming operates at several levels. An elementary organizational model for complex emergencies is as follows. On a day-to-day basis, relief operations are usually managed by a UN lead agency with the other UN specialist agencies playing their traditional roles in an integrated division of labour – WFP/food aid, UNHCR/ refugees and displaced persons, UN Children's Fund (UNICEF)/child health, etc. In addition to any specialist function, the lead agency plays a coordinating role. Either on its own, or with the assistance of DHA, it also helps to secure access through negotiation with the warring parties. In Bosnia the lead agency was UNHCR, in South Sudan it is UNICEF, while in Angola DHA plays this role.

Within a complex emergency, NGOs usually operate on the basis of a written agreement with the UN lead agency. In order to work within a mandated system, NGOs have to become affiliated bodies. This often involves accepting notions of neutrality and security guidelines agreed by the lead agency with the warring parties. For the southern Sudan, these are known as 'Letters of Understanding'. In return, the movement of NGOs and relief supplies in and out of the war zone is facilitated by the UN through agreed logistical corridors and modes of transport.

The development of this type of comprehensive programme has meant that earlier donor/NGO safety nets have expanded. At the same time, UN/NGO subcontracting arrangements have also grown. The end of the Cold War has given the UN a new role. At the same time, it has exposed the weak operational capacity within most of its specialist agencies. UNHCR, for example, has been unable to take direct responsibility for its growing case load.[29] As in Bosnia, this vacuum has largely been filled by NGO subcontractors.[30]

An added consideration in relation to UN integrated programmes is the significance of major powers or regional arrangements for NGO contractors. For example, USAID and ECHO are able to mobilize resources on a scale that exceeds most donor governments. Through their NGO clients this can give such donors a significant leverage within UN integrated programmes. OLS in the South of the Sudan is a case in point. At the same time, in other operations, major donors can play a more independent and operational role. The engineering activities of ECHO in Bosnia is one example. Together with UN/NGO subcontracting, such developments reflect a growing organizational complexity of relief work in war zones.

CONFLICT, SECURITY AND PROTECTION

Working in ongoing conflict has pushed security issues to the fore. During the Cold War, internal conflicts had an organizational cohesion that seems lacking today. Opposition movements usually had defined command structures, clear nationalist or socialist platforms and often held liberated base areas,[31] a situation that superpower rivalry tended to support. Today conflicts are often more fluid. Political ideologies are either less in evidence or take an exclusive ethnic or fundamentalist character. The ending of superpower confrontation has also seen a decline in the significance of borders. The recent military maps of South Sudan, Angola, Bosnia or Afghanistan have often taken on a leopard spot pattern as political movements have become more fragmented. As a consequence, providing humanitarian aid is more dangerous and often represents the acceptance of situations of high and continuous risk.

The security of aid personnel and relief supplies in negotiated access programmes has been tackled in two main ways. The first and most common, is what can be called non-military security.

Non-military security

In situations of continuous risk, security planning has become a relative rather than an absolute exercise. In integrated programmes where military protection is not provided, it is common to find civilian (sometimes ex-military) security personnel tasked with assessing the changing nature of risks. South Sudan is an example where such advisers are employed by the United Nations. Agencies are regularly briefed on security matters and evacuation procedures. Through an agreed gradation of response, agency staff are routinely withdrawn and returned to the field according to the security situation. Aid workers and relief supplies consequently ebb and flow with the level of violence, a movement which graphically illustrates the extent to which aid has been incorporated into the rhythm of internal conflict, a situation perhaps unique in the history of warfare.

Military security

The military protection of humanitarian aid is associated with relief operations such as Kurdistan (1991), Bosnia (1992–5), Somalia (1992–5) and Rwanda (1994). It is also linked to the central tenant of the new paradigm – that is, to avert large-scale population movements crossing international boundaries by securing the distribution of humanitarian relief within war-affected countries. In compliance with partnership requirements that such interventions be non-political, military humanitarianism avoids direct involvement in the internal affairs of the affected country. The *ad hoc* UN resolutions that have framed military humanitarianism have therefore commonly focused on the protection of agency personnel and relief supplies rather than pacification activities. At most, military protection has frequently involved some form of so-called safe area policy.

The new paradigm, geared to working in unresolved political crises, has radically changed the nature of peacekeeping. It has given rise to a much broader range of peacekeeping activities. The British Army, for example, has developed an approach termed 'wider peacekeeping'.[32] Consent is central to wider peacekeeping and distinguishes it from enforcement. While vital for protection operations, consent in modern internal wars is no longer a given. It is a variable factor and in some circumstances may only be partial. Securing consent is often a long-term process. The idea of variable consent is a refinement of the concept of negotiated access. Wider peacekeeping and helping secure and maintain humanitarian access, hinges upon the management of consent.

In organizational terms, military protection is best understood as an optional appendage to an integrated and negotiated relief programme. In the case of Bosnia, for example, UNHCR as lead agency negotiated access on behalf of the aid agencies working under its umbrella. Appropriate protection for convoys was then agreed with the military on the basis of the arrangement reached by UNHCR with the warring parties. It is worth emphasizing the optional nature of military protection because numerous

integrated relief programmes, such as Sudan and Angola, are not protected. Indeed, within the crisis regions, non-protected relief programmes
would seem to predominate.

REGIONAL AND JOINT OPERATIONS

While the UN is the single most important body in addressing the issue of
relief in war zones, it does not have a monopoly on the necessary skills
and functions – for example, the ability to deliver relief, apply sanctions or
field military personnel. Under Chapter VIII of the UN Charter, regional
arrangements are able to assume UN responsibilities. Less clear under the
Charter but usually under some form of UN mandate, there has also been a
growth of strong-state interventions. Since the beginning of the 1990s and
especially since 1994, these types of operations have become increasingly
common.

Some commentators have seen this development as resulting from
'strategic over-reach' on the part of the UN.[33] The world organization is
now unable to respond in equal measure following the marked growth in
conflict-related demands. In these circumstances it has, perforce, conceded
the lead to others. While welfare-related activities are often involved, this
situation can be seen as a form of political subcontracting.

Although increasingly common, the basis for such operations remains
largely *ad hoc* and, in some cases, a UN mandate has been sought *post
facto*. The 1991 EU arms embargo on Serbia and ceasefire monitoring in
Slovenia and Bosnia are examples. In the same year, the Nigerian-led intervention in Liberia took place under the umbrella of the Economic
Community of West African States (ECOWAS). In 1994 Russian troops
were deployed in Georgia to end the civil war. At the same time there was
an Organization for Security and Cooperation in Europe (OSCE) agreement for the CIS to intervene in Nagorno-Karabakh. In the same year,
French troops interceded in Rwanda and the US-led invasion of Haiti reversed an earlier military coup. The North Atlantic Treaty Organization
(NATO)-led Implementation Force (IFOR) in Bosnia was also an example
of the trend.

One interesting feature of regional or strong-state operations is the
degree of force. While most operate within some form of UN mandate, the
prescriptions of the new paradigm are weakened. One often encounters a
more overt and robust use of military power. In some cases this has
blurred the distinction between humanitarian intervention and regional
policing. The NATO involvement in Bosnia, for example, has distanced

itself from humanitarian operations in favour of supporting the political process established at Dayton. Some of these operations, however, have also provided opportunities for NGOs to expand their activities. In the case of Bosnia, for example, during the war the majority of NGOs based their activities in Croatia. This was despite UNHCR's role in negotiating access. Following the Dayton peace agreement, most have now left Croatia and established themselves in Bosnia.

SERVICE PACKAGES AND NON-WELFARE SUBCONTRACTING

The involvement of the military in relief operations has begun to expand beyond that of providing protection. The effect of conflict and the systemic crisis within non-bloc areas has led to the erosion and collapse of vital infrastructure. Indeed, such is the extent of global polarization that in many complex emergencies the local facilities necessary to mount a large-scale relief operation no longer exist. Aid subcontracting has increasingly involved NGOs, but in many emergencies the skills and resources required now go beyond the welfare services that most provide, for example aircraft logistics, air-drops, large-scale commodity handling, engineering repairs, civilian policing, judicial structures and so on.

Since 1992, DHA has been coordinating attempts to encourage donor governments to make available non-offensive military and civilian assets in the form of service packages, or self-contained operational units that bring together specific strategic skills or resources. UNHCR has been particularly active in developing the service-package approach. The agency's poor showing in the aftermath of the Gulf War first prompted a need to increase strategic capacity. The Sarajevo airlift, however, is held to be the turning point.[34] This indicated that governments were willing to second skilled personnel and military equipment to UNHCR. Some twenty nations provided components that variously supported the airlift through the Geneva-based air cell, the air hub at Zagreb and the logistical, transport and liaison facilities at Sarajevo. With the assets provided, UNHCR was able to give the necessary vertical coordination. UNHCR subsequently employed the service-package approach in Rwanda in 1994 to cover logistics, sanitation, civil engineering and security services.

The military and civilian assets of governments are an important constituent of service packages. Intergovernmental organizations (IGOs) and the larger NGOs, however, can also act as service providers. Standby agreements with governments or agencies regarding service provision are seen by UNHCR as central to improving emergency preparedness. Service packages also illustrate an important feature of the new paradigm: the more complex relief operations become, the greater the spread of international responsibility. At the same time, they illustrate the manner in which military assets are being separated from protection duties. The potential for Western military involvement is therefore widening.

In relation to NGOs, service packages can be seen as a development of public service contracting. At the same time, however, they have allowed new players to compete for contracts. In the logistics field, for example, in both Bosnia and Rwanda one has seen the emergence of private non-profit organizations providing niche services. In Southern Sudan, USAID has taken the service-package trend even further. Reflecting an earlier stance in the North, it has called for the logistics component of the OLS operation to be handed over to private contractors. In many respects, regarding some services NGOs can claim no major advantage over private contractors.

RELIEF EXPENDITURE AND THE AID MARKET

The development of the new operational tools sketched above has important cost implications. For the past couple of decades, relief expenditures have been increasing. Indeed, since the beginning of the 1990s, this trend has been marked and reflects the spread of protracted crises and internal wars in non-bloc areas. At around $3.2 billion in 1993, since the mid-1980s there has been a sixfold increase in emergency spending.[35] This figure, however, is an underestimate. For example, it excludes food aid and the cost of military peacekeeping. These military costs have multiplied since the beginning of the 1990s. By 1994, total peacekeeping expenditure was estimated to be in the region of $3.2 billion per year and rising.[36] The early part of the 1990s had consumed around a third of all UN peacekeeping costs since 1948. If one allows for food aid and other ancillary costs, even excluding Rwanda in 1994, the West could on average be spending around $10 billion annually on emergencies in the crisis regions.

The upward trend in relief expenditure is occurring at a time when overall development funding is stagnating and declining. This contrast is exaggerated in many complex emergencies where relief funding is the only significant form of external aid. This would caution against being dazzled by rising humanitarian expenditure. In practice, as the crisis regions are re-engaged through humanitarian intervention, the overall bill to the West is probably declining. It is also tempting to interpret rising expenditure as a direct indication of increasing humanitarian need. This would seem logical. The emergence of an aid market, however, again urges caution.

Apart from being of poor quality, the nature of reporting in complex emergencies means that there is usually no direct empirical link between expenditure and need.[37] Food aid requirements, for example, can be estimated one year and deliveries made the next. The two figures rarely are reconciled. Even in large integrated programmes, the extent and nature of need is often intuitive rather than proven. A good example is the alleged continuum from relief to development within the OLS operation. This concept has achieved a quasi-religious status among UN agencies and NGOs. A recent review, however, concluded that no agency had produced any evidence to prove that emergency conditions had passed in the Sudan. Nor, for that matter, had anyone analysed the actually existing development process being pursued by the government.[38] The evidence that did exist not only indicated the continuation of emergency conditions, but that the strategies pursued by the warring parties were as destabilizing as before.

Growing relief expenditure, apart from reflecting an unknown quantity of need, is also symptomatic of increasing numbers of NGOs and fierce competition for funding. In other words, an unidentified proportion of increasing relief expenditure arises from the privatization of aid. There are several factors involved. Increasing relief expenditure is partly related to the rising fixed costs within the system with hundreds of subcontractors delivering similar products in an often disorganized and competitive fashion. Moreover, agencies often grow quickly in emergency situations and new ones emerge. Competition for funding becomes increasingly interdependent with the need to maintain core staff and essential infrastructure.

As mentioned, relief is one of the few areas of the aid market that is currently expanding. Not only does the new paradigm reassert sovereignty, it also offers political authorities new forms of partnership. Many regimes and local political actors have lost little time in reorganizing to incorporate the new pattern of aid provision. Even during the Cold War, recognized governments were experimenting with new ways of aid diversion. In Africa, this included exploiting tacit agency support for government counter-insurgency strategies.[39] It also involved the manipulation of exchange rates, diversion of relief commodities and the integration of parallel economic activities within officially controlled aid programmes.[40] The new aid paradigm has allowed this integration to develop further. For example, the partnership suggested by negotiated access has often given warring parties an influence over the assessment and delivery process.[41]

OPPORTUNITIES, LIMITS AND DANGERS

As the West adapts to the new aid paradigm, the former roles of governments and the founding mandates of UN agencies are dissolving and
changing. While far from perfect, the involvement of states at least gave
the previous humanitarian regime a statutory aspect. The privatization of
aid has changed this situation. The current debate among NGOs concerning voluntary codes of conduct and professional standards is symptomatic
of the move toward a more flexible and selective system. This situation
presents dangers and opportunities. Regarding the latter, the current interest in humanitarian issues between and within agencies suggests that improvement is possible. Moreover, new operational tools have given
agencies unprecedented access to war-affected populations. At the same
time, in broadening responsibility by including new players the emerging
aid paradigm has reconfirmed the principle of collective responsibility, a
helpful antidote to isolationism.

The key issue is defining the real opportunities and limits within the
new system. A sober appraisal would suggest that, at best, both directly and
through the political protection that it can offer, humanitarian intervention
can help stabilize a crisis situation. For the people who benefit, this is
justification enough. Even achieving this limited outcome, however, as
opposed to compounding and entrenching problems, demands effort. Rather
than superficial functional prescriptions, more serious analysis of social and
political structures is required. At the same time, without a greater harmon-
ization of agendas among the key humanitarian players stabilization is undermined. Stabilization, however, is time limited. Lacking a wider political
and economic settlement – something with more meat than the continuum –
humanitarian aid, even at its best, quickly reaches the limits of the system.

The fundamental danger within the new paradigm is that it is adapted to
manage the symptoms of global polarization and exclusion. The fusion of
development and security concerns, together with the proliferation of new
operational tools, means that Western governments now have the ideological and practical means for selective intervention in a divided world.
Rather than stabilization pending a comprehensive settlement, humanitarian aid becomes a necessary ingredient of political containment. The adaptations sketched in this paper already contain the seeds of a futuristic
nightmare: a world in which a vast and glittering wealth gap separates the
core and crisis regions, in which dynamic areas are securely ringfenced
while those conflagrations within the seething hinterland that threaten core
interests are policed by mobile and technologically replete humo-cops. At
the same time, dynamic regions continue to grow but are deeply divided.

Here the image of outside chaos with its message that it could be worse is one of the few palliatives that weak politicians can offer an insecure and fractious populace.

Nobody wants such an outcome. Exactly how fanciful this scenario is, however, is a moot point. The need for humanitarian assistance is symptomatic of increasing global polarization and the erosion of life-chances on a huge scale. In terms of their numbers and the people whom they now employ, NGOs have been winners. The growing requirement for international welfare assistance should itself be a powerful argument in support of a global new deal. Somehow, however, in the search for technical fixes, this argument has been lost. A first step would be for NGOs, if they are still able, to place the greater good before income and position within the humanitarian marketplace. To coin a phrase, however, this may be one more market that cannot be bucked.

NOTES

1. UNDP, *Human Development Report 1996* (New York: Oxford University Press for the United Nations Development Programme, 1996).
2. L. Thurow, *Head to Head: The Coming Economic Battle Among Japan, Europe and America* (New York: William Morrow, 1992).
3. UNDP, *Human Development Report 1996*, p. 2.
4. S. Sideri, 'Restructuring the post-Cold War world economy: perspectives and prognosis', *Development and Change*, 24 (1), 1993, pp. 7–27.
5. P. Hirst and G. Thompson, *Globalization in Question* (Cambridge: Polity Press, 1996).
6. A. D. Smith, 'The ethnic sources of nationalism', *Survival*, 35 (1), 1993, pp. 48–62.
7. W. Reno, 'Reinvention of an African patrimonial state: Charles Taylor's Liberia', *Third World Quarterly*, 16 (1), 1995, pp. 109–20.
8. F. J. Schuurman, 'Introduction: development theory in the 1990s', in F. J. Schuurman (ed.) *Beyond the Impasse* (London: Zed Books, 1993), pp. 1–48.
9. M. Duffield, 'Symphony of the damned: racial discourse, complex political emergencies and humanitarian aid', *Disasters*, 20 (3), 1996, pp. 173–93.
10. R. Poulton and M. Harris, *Putting People First: Voluntary Organizations and Third World Organizations* (London: Macmillan, 1988).
11. J. Clark, *Democratizing Development: The Role of Voluntary Organizations* (London: Earthscan,1991).
12. M. Buchanan-Smith and S. Maxwell, 'Linking relief and development: an introduction and overview', *Institute of Development Studies Bulletin*, 25 (4), 1994, pp. 2–16.

13. UNHCR, *The State of the World's Refugees 1995: In Search of Solutions* (Oxford: Oxford University Press for the United Nations High Commission for Refugees, 1995), p. 20.

14. M. Duffield, 'Complex emergencies and the crisis of Developmentalism', *Institute of Development Studies Bulletin: Linking Relief and Development*, 25 October 1994, pp. 37–45.

15. A. Shacknove, *Asylum-Seekers in Affluent States*, paper presented at the Conference on 'People of Concern' (Geneva: United Nations High Commissioner for Refugees, 21–4 November 1996).

16. O. B. Jones, 'Africa hardens heart on asylum', *The Guardian*, 15 May 1996, p. 11.

17. A. Karim, M. Duffield, S. Jaspars, A. Benini, J. Macrae, M. Bradbury, D. Johnson and G. Larbi, *Operation Lifeline Sudan (OLS): A Review* (Geneva: Department of Humanitarian Affairs, 1996).

18. UNHCR, *The State of the World's Refugees 1995*, p. 43.

19. M. Duffield, *Complex Political Emergencies: An Exploratory Report for UNICEF with Reference to Angola and Bosnia* (New York: United Nations Children's Fund, March 1994).

20. Clark, *Democratizing Development*.

21. M. Duffield and J. Prendergast, *Without Troops or Tanks: Humanitarian Intervention in Eritrea and Ethiopia* (Trenton, NJ: Africa World Press/Red Sea Press, 1994).

22. D. C. Korten, *Getting to the 21st Century: Voluntary Action and the Global Agenda* (West Hartford, Conn.: Kumarian Press, 1990).

23. Duffield, *Complex Political Emergencies*.

24. D. Keen and K. Wilson, 'Engaging with violence: a reassessment of the role of relief in wartime', in J. Macrae and A. Zwi (eds), *War and Hunger: Rethinking International Responses to Complex Emergencies* (London: Zed Books, 1994), pp. 209–22.

25. E. Voutira and S. A. Whishaw Brown, *Conflict Resolution: A Review of Some Non-Government Practices – A Cautionary Tale* (Oxford: Refugee Studies Programme, Queen Elizabeth House, Oxford University, 1995).

26. M. Goulding, 'The evolution of United Nations Peacekeeping', *International Affairs*, 69 (3), 1993, pp. 451–64.

27. Duffield, *Complex Political Emergencies*.

28. B. Boutros-Ghali, *An Agenda For Peace: Preventive Diplomacy, Peacemaking and Peace-Keeping, June 1992*, in *An Agenda for Peace: 1995* (New York: United Nations, 1995), pp. 39–72.

29. D. Keen, *Rationing the Right to Life: The Crisis in Refugee Relief* (Oxford: Refugee Studies Programme, 1993).

30. Duffield, *Complex Political Emergencies*.

31. F. Jean, (ed.), *Life, Death and Aid: The Médecins Sans Frontières Report on World Crisis Intervention* (London: Routledge, 1993).

32. H. Slim, 'Military humanitarianism and the new peacekeeping: an agenda for peace?', *Institute of Development Studies Bulletin*, 27 (3), 1996, pp. 64–72.

33. T. G. Weiss, 'Humanitarian action in war zones: recent experience and future research', in J. Neederven (ed.), *World Orders in the Making: Humanitarian Intervention and Beyond* (London: Macmillan, forthcoming).

34. UNHCR, *Concept Paper: Humanitarian Emergencies and Refugees – Informal Consultation on Service Packages* (Geneva: United Nations High Commissioner for Refugees, April 1995), p. 1. See also T. G. Weiss and A. Pasic, 'Reinventing UNHCR: enterprising humanitarians in the former Yugoslavia, 1991–1995', *Global Governance*, 3 (1), 1997, pp. 41–57.

35. IFRCS, *World Disasters Report: 1995* (Geneva: International Federation of Red Cross and Red Crescent Societies, 1995).

36. L. Elliot, 'The poor on hire for global policing', *The Guardian*, 28 May 1994, p. 12.

37. Karim et al., *Operation Lifeline Sudan*; M. Duffield, H. Young, J. Ryle and I. Henderson, *Sudan Emergency Operations Consortium (SEOC): A Review* (London: CAFOD, 1995); Duffield, *Complex Political Emergencies*.

38. Karim et al., *Operation Lifeline Sudan*.

39. Keen and Wilson, 'Engaging with violence'.

40. Duffield, *Complex Political Emergencies*.

41. Duffield et al., *Sudan Emergency Operations*.

8 Democratization from the Outside In: NGOs and International Efforts to Promote Open Elections
Vikram K. Chand

Until recently, the monitoring of elections in a sovereign country by outside actors was extremely rare. The United Nations (UN) had significant experience in conducting plebiscites and elections in dependent territories but did not monitor an election in a formally independent country until 1989 when it reluctantly became involved in the Nicaraguan electoral process. At the regional level, the Organization of American States (OAS) occasionally sent small delegations to witness elections in member states, but these missions were too brief to permit any real observation of the processes, and failed to criticize fraud.[1] Since the 1980s election-monitoring has become increasingly common in transitional elections from authoritarian to democratic rule. Non-governmental organizations (NGOs), domestic and international, were the first to become involved in election-monitoring in the 1980s followed by international and regional organizations like the UN, the OAS and the Organization for Security and Cooperation in Europe (OSCE) in the 1990s. Election-monitors played a crucial role in transitional elections held in the Philippines (1986), Chile (1989), Panama (1989), Nicaragua (1990) and Haiti (1990). In addition, elections began to form a crucial element of UN 'peacebuilding' strategies in countries torn apart by civil strife such as Namibia (1989), Cambodia (1993) and El Salvador (1994). By the middle of the 1990s, international election-monitoring had thus become widely accepted and fairly universal standards established for defining the term 'free and fair' elections.

This paper probes the factors propelling the growth of international and NGO election-monitoring efforts in recent years, and assesses their scope, contribution and limits. It explores the implications of international election monitoring for the changing nature of sovereignty, the development of domestic civil and political society (or what Robert Putnam calls 'social capital')[2] and new patterns of interaction among NGOs, regional

160

organizations and the UN. The paper then looks at these questions through the lens of a specific case study, the Mexican presidential elections of 1994, which were without doubt the most 'watched' elections in Mexican history. It concludes with an assessment of the importance of international election-monitoring for the development of an international political rights regime in the 1990s.

EXPLAINING INTERNATIONAL EFFORTS TO PROMOTE DEMOCRACY IN THE 1980s AND 1990s

The expansion of international election-monitoring activities in the 1980s and 1990s was a direct reflection of the growing support for democracy world-wide. In 1991, for instance, the OAS convention at Santiago declared that member states were required to maintain democratic forms of governance consistent with its charter. Shortly thereafter, the OAS approved the Washington Protocol under which any suspension of democracy in a member state would automatically trigger a meeting of the OAS Permanent Council followed by a meeting of the Hemisphere's foreign ministers or the OAS General Assembly in order to take appropriate measures to restore democracy. In December 1991, the UN General Assembly passed a resolution by an overwhelming majority of 134 to 4 calling on the Secretary-General to establish an office to coordinate requests for electoral assistance by member states, leading to the creation of an Electoral Assistance Unit in the Department of Political Affairs (DPA); in its first year of operation, the unit responded to requests for assistance from some twenty countries.[3] Meanwhile, the Conference on Security and Cooperation in Europe (CSCE) declared at Copenhagen in June 1990 that free elections constituted an 'inalienable' human right. The 1990 Paris charter also called on CSCE members to 'strengthen democracy as the only system of government within our nations', and mandated the creation of a new Office for Free Elections to oversee elections in CSCE states.[4]

The growing support for democracy, particularly free elections, was the product of five factors. First, the global wave of democratization that began in the 1970s and continued through the 1990s radically transformed the make-up of the world's main international organizations. In the last quarter of the twentieth century, more than forty countries have switched from authoritarian to democratic forms of governance. The new predominance of democratic states within intergovernmental organizations (IGOs) inevitably encouraged them to become more active in the promotion of democracy. At the same time, new democracies were also often weak and vulnerable to attempts to roll back democracy in their countries. Placing international organizations decisively on the side of democracy thus represented a form of insurance against a potential regression to authoritarianism, and a deterrent to anyone contemplating an attack on fragile democratic institutions.

Second, the United States was generally supportive of attempts to strengthen the commitment of IGOs to democracy. American leaders such as Anthony Lake defined the promotion of democracy as the new central thread uniting the different strands of American foreign policy in the post-Cold War era.[5] The end of the Cold War freed Washington from having to support dictators as an alternative to the greater evil of global communism, produced an abrupt cut-off of Soviet aid to several authoritarian client states, and was perceived as a major ideological triumph in favour of capitalism and democracy.[6] American officials and academics also advanced a powerful national security rationale: democracies were inherently more peaceable that dictatorships and, based on the historical record, extremely unlikely to go to war with one another, therefore the US should support democracy as a way of underwriting its own security. The reasons why the Kantian democratic peace hypothesis, recaptured by Michael Doyle's 1983 article,[7] was absorbed by American policy-makers so quickly lie beyond the scope of this paper, but there is no question that it provided a powerful motive undergirding much of US democracy-promotion efforts around the world.

Third, domestic changes, particularly the strengthening of civil and political society, made it easier for regime opponents to garner international support for democracy. Both the Inter-American Human Rights Commission (IAHRC) of the OAS and the UN Centre for Human Rights have a experienced a sharp escalation in the number of complaints relating to violations of political rights. This reflects a secular increase in the capacity of dissidents to take their case to the international community. The growing capacity of domestic actors to appeal directly to international fora activates international guarantees for democracy, creates a tradition of international jurisprudence that forms the basis of future appeals, and nudges the existing political rights regime towards enforcement.

Fourth, changes in the global normative climate have contributed powerfully to the growing involvement of IGOs and NGOs in democracy-promotion efforts. Democracy is now perceived to be the only legitimate form of government. To some extent this is clearly the product of the demise of the Soviet Union and the mushrooming of democracies around the world. A more neglected factor in the shift of global norms is the role of the Catholic Church. In the wake of the Second Vatican Council (1959–65), it abandoned historical support for authoritarian governments, such as Salazar's Portugal, not to speak of Mussolini's Italy, in favour of a new theological stance favouring human rights and democracy. Vatican II stressed the importance of social change in the Church's mission, the right to judge 'sinful' political and social structures in the light of the Gospel, lay engagement, more emphasis on collegiality rather than hierarchy and the significance of individual rights.[8]

The election of John Paul II as Pope in 1979 intensified the Church's support for democracy world-wide. In his first papal encyclical, the new Pope, who had experienced the rigours of communist rule firsthand as Cardinal of Poland, not only condemned human rights violations but declared that the Church was 'the guardian' of freedom, which in turn was the basis of God-given human dignity. Given the centralization of the Catholic Church, theological changes at the apex quickly spread to the lower rungs of the organization, thereby conditioning the normative preferences of Catholics and strengthening democratic impulses around the world. Papal visits to several countries (Mexico, 1979, 1990; Poland, 1979; Brazil, 1980; Philippines, 1981; Argentina, 1982; Guatemala, Nicaragua and El Salvador, 1983; Korea, 1984; Chile, 1987, and Paraguay, 1988) served as a catalyst for galvanizing supporters of democracy in them.[9] The Church, with its organizational resources, institutional credibility and international scope thus emerged as a formidable opponent to authoritarian regimes. It is therefore no accident that Catholic countries dominated the ranks of democratizing countries in the 1970s and 1980s. Major shifts within the Church strengthened global democratic norms directly with a powerful global actor coming out in support of democracy, and indirectly by contributing to democratization in a host of countries.

Fifth, the rise of election-monitoring by outside actors to defend democracy reflects the erosion of traditional state sovereignty. Rising economic interdependence made states more porous to outside influences including pressures to democratize. The trend towards regional economic integration was an important factor influencing democratic development in Spain, Portugal and Greece in the case of the European Economic Community (EEC), and Mexico in the case of the North American Free Trade Agreement (NAFTA). The collapse of the Soviet Union removed an important obstacle to American (and international) efforts to promote democracy abroad, and opened the door to the revival of moralism in American foreign policy. Meanwhile, states themselves have undergone a profound mutation in recent years. The spread of urbanization, communications, education and economic development has produced what James Rosenau regards as a global improvement in civic skills,[10] constraining government and heightening domestic pressures for democratization. Furthermore, the rising importance of subnational loyalties, whether ethnic, regional or religious, poses a new challenge to state dominance of society.

WHY ELECTION-MONITORING?

Election-monitoring involves a gamut of activities. These include the passive observation of electoral processes, pressure for changes in the electoral environment, verification of voter registration lists, balloting and the count, mediation between the government and opposition, the provision of technical assistance and, in the most extreme cases, the actual administration of elections by outsiders.

Election observation serves five distinct functions. First, the presence of observers improves the credibility of the election process by deterring fraud. This encourages opposition parties to participate rather than boycott the process and invariably boosts voter turnout as well. Incumbent governments who expect to win often have a strong incentive to invite international observers to give their victory credibility in the eyes of public opinion. For example, Daniel Ortega clearly expected the Sandinistas to win the February 1990 elections in Nicaragua, and took a gamble by inviting the UN, OAS and the Council of Freely-Elected Heads of Government chaired by Jimmy Carter to observe the elections.

Second, observers play an important role in providing technical assistance to improve electoral processes world-wide. Such assistance has ranged from training poll-watchers, helping to design an appropriate sample for parallel vote tabulations including quick-counts, and financing the purchase of logistical equipment. In Nicaragua, for example, the UN designed a quick-count based on a stratified sample of 8 to 10 per cent of the vote that showed Violeta Chamorro with a 16 point lead over Ortega.[11]

Third, observers can play an important role in mediating disputes, and bridging the chasm of distrust among rival political contenders. In El Salvador, for example, the patient mediation of both UN Secretary-General Jávier Perez de Cuéllar and his representative Alvaro de Soto kept the peace talks between the government and the Farabundo Martí National Liberation Front (FMLN) alive, eventually resulting in a series of breakthrough agreements.[12] In Nicaragua, Carter helped broker a series of agreements between the Sandinistas and the opposition that allowed for the participation of Miskito Indians in the political process, the adoption of a code of civility among all political parties and the release of much-needed foreign funds for the National Opposition Union (UNO).[13] The mediation of Carter, the UN's Elliot Richardson and OAS Secretary-General João Baena Soares helped facilitate a smooth transition from Sandinista hands to UNO in the crucial hours after the 1990 elections.[14] In the Dominican Republic, a tense standoff between the government and the opposition, which questioned the results of the 1990 elections, was successfully defused by deft diplomacy by Carter's delegation.[15]

Fourth, observers play an important role in opening up the electoral process by bringing problems out into the open and pressuring for their rectification. In Namibia, the UN, which possessed the right to veto South Africa's conduct of the elections, successfully pressured the South African Administrator-General (AG) to revise the electoral law to permit voting by secret ballot, counting in the major regional centres rather than in a single fraud-prone national centre and full access to voting stations by South-West African People's Organization (SWAPO) representatives.[16] UN pressure also forced the AG to abandon plans to subject Namibia's new Constituent Assembly to South African control by making its decisions subject to veto by the AG and judicial review by South African courts.[17] In Nicaragua, Guyana, Suriname, Paraguay, Chile and Mexico, outside observers succeeded variously in pressuring governments to strengthen the independence of election commissions, improve the quality of the voter registration list or draw up a new one altogether, give the opposition greater access to polling stations on election day and permit quick-counts.

Finally, outside organizations have been called on to administer the electoral process or supervise it usually as part of a wider peacebuilding strategy. In Cambodia, the UN organized and conducted the 1993 electoral process from start to finish,[18] while in Namibia it meticulously supervised an election organized by the South African government. In Bosnia, the OSCE organized elections for a tripartite presidency, a federal parliament and regional parliaments in September 1996, but it was forced to postpone municipal elections due to a host of difficulties including voter intimidation, the reluctance of refugees to return to localities where they once lived and widespread tampering with voter registration records.

SYNERGY IN ELECTION-MONITORING?

Most analyses have neglected the dynamic interaction between the different sets of actors involved in election-monitoring. Yet, the patterns of interaction, task-sharing and specialization may turn out to be decisive in explaining the difference between the success and failure of a mission. From a purely functionalist point of view, the UN has major advantages over other organizations in organizing elections in areas that have experienced serious internal strife and where authority has broken down. The UN has more experience in peacebuilding missions, greater organizational, financial and technical resources, and is capable of mobilizing a higher level of consensus among the major powers through such mechanisms as the 'friends of the Secretary-General' than most regional organizations or NGOs. The Cambodia operation, for example, cost about US $1.5 billion, involved 15,000 troops and 7,000 civilians, and lasted 18 months. In Namibia, the UN deployed 4,650 soldiers, 1,700 police monitors and 1,600 election supervisors at a cost of about $367 million. In El Salvador, a much smaller country, the UN fielded a mission of some 1,500 personnel at its height; with no fixed departure date, it cost just over $100 million.

In addition, such peacebuilding missions require delicate cooperation between the mission's military and electoral wings. In both Cambodia and Namibia, UN election officials relied on military assistance to prevent voter intimidation, protect UN installations and provide logistical support. To the extent that the military wing was unable fully to demobilize the former antagonists and decommission their weapons before the elections, its presence was all the more necessary to deter armed interference with the process. In fact, demobilization prior to the elections was mostly a failure in Nicaragua and Cambodia, and only a partial success in Namibia and El Salvador. Yet, even in major peacebuilding missions, the UN can benefit from the presence of NGOs and even regional organizations. In Namibia, pressure from the Organization of African Unity and the Non-Aligned Movement (NAM) on the Secretary-General strengthened the UN's resolve in the face of unreasonable demands by the AG. NGOs also added to the chorus of support for the UN in Namibia. In El Salvador, the UN mission (ONUSAL) depended on NGOs for assistance in implementing programmes, and for reliable information.

In countries where an existing government remains in power and where the UN plays only a monitoring rather than organizing role, the actors are likely to be more evenly matched. For example, the UN Observer Mission to Verify the Electoral Process in Nicaragua (ONUVEN) collaborated closely with the OAS and Carter. In fact, the UN was by no means the dominant player. The OAS covered far more polling stations on election day (70 per cent) than the UN, and Carter played a much greater role in mediating disputes than Elliot Richardson or Baena Soares.

As relatively small groups with limited resources, NGOs are driven to create specialized niches based on comparative advantage. The

International Human Rights Law Group is particularly good at analysing election laws, the International Foundation for Election Systems at providing electoral equipment and technical support. The Council of Freely-Elected Heads of Government led by Jimmy Carter has played a crucial role in democratic transitions throughout Latin America and the Caribbean. The prestige of its members, institutional credibility, media visibility and access to high-placed decision-makers put it in an unusual position among NGOs to exert pressure for electoral reforms, mediate disputes among contending parties, influence the thinking of US government officials and shape public opinion. Sometimes, however, a country can be deluged with too many inexperienced observers, leading to clashing accounts, partisan behaviour, a failure to coordinate with others and confusion.

Political factors can also influence the cast of characters in election-monitoring activities. During the Cold War, Washington marginalized the UN from Latin American affairs in favour of the OAS, which was more susceptible to US control.[19] In the wake of the end of the Cold War, however, a growing *rapprochement* between the UN and the OAS has taken place.[20] Both organizations collaborated closely in the 1990 Nicaraguan and Haitian elections. Eventually, however, the UN came to dominate the resolution of the Haitian crisis. The need to tighten the OAS embargo against the Haitian military junta required an expanded UN role, which also signalled that the international community was serious about its intent to restore democracy. Key OAS members such as Brazil, Mexico, and Chile also opposed sending military forces to Haiti,[21] fearing to undermine the principle of non-intervention and distort the purposes of the OAS. The US was thus left with little choice but to seek UN approval for the use of armed force in Haiti through the Multinational Force (MNF).

THE DILEMMA OF SOVEREIGNTY

Election-monitoring by outsiders goes to the heart of the debate about the changing nature of sovereignty, more so than humanitarian assistance.[22] The latter occurs in the context of political and economic breakdown and can be rationalized as a temporary expedient to deal with an emergency. More or less the same can be said of elections organized by international organizations as part of a peacebuilding strategy. In the case of elections monitored by outsiders in functioning states, however, it is difficult to avoid the debate about the implications for sovereignty. The debate stems partly from the conflicting imperatives of the UN and OAS Charters, which establish free elections as a universal human right but also proscribe interference in the internal matters of states.[23]

Proponents of a 'right to democratic governance' make several arguments to justify election-monitoring in sovereign states.[24] First, the concept of sovereignty is itself subject to change in response to new domestic and international conditions. Simply saying that election-monitoring interferes with sovereignty evades the question of what sovereignty is and how it may have changed over time. Second, election-monitoring enhances the domestic legitimacy of the government and strengthens the state and its capacity for 'sovereignty'. Third, true sovereignty resides with 'the people', not the state, and to the extent that international election-monitors seek to empower 'the people' their activities are consistent with sovereignty. Finally, states are not free agents but subject to limitations stemming from natural rights that their citizens possess as moral beings, as well as legal obligations voluntarily contracted by states under several international covenants on human rights including free elections.

Many governments are now willing to allow international observers, not necessarily because they agree with these arguments, but because they find it a politically convenient way to gain credibility, placate the opposition and avoid a deterioration of relations with the international community and the United States. Still, election-monitoring by outsiders can frequently become a target of suspicion and outright hostility. Some of this concern is grounded in a healthy scepticism of Western motives based on bitter experiences with colonialism and US interventionism to 'save democracy'.[25]

Experience suggests that there are several ways to defuse these concerns. First, in the case of peacebuilding missions, it may be helpful to create a mechanism consisting of the main political forces in the country formally vested with sovereignty. The UN in Cambodia, for example, set up a Supreme National Council (SNC) consisting of the major Cambodian factions chaired by Prince Sihanouk.[26] Technically, the UN derived its authority from the SNC. The UN made a concerted effort to consult with the SNC and empowered it with several important tasks. Second, international actors must obtain the consent of all major political parties and the government before observing an election, and do so in a strictly impartial fashion. The Council of Freely-Elected Heads of Government, for example, has an iron rule that it will never formally observe an election if the major players do not welcome it. Third, international actors need to make sure that their work is not used by states as pretexts for intervention, though this 'exter-

nality' may be difficult to avoid. In Panama, Carter's denunciation of
fraud in 1989 was used by Bush to justify the invasion of the country, although Carter himself was opposed to armed intervention.[27] Finally, the
US and other countries should forego any attempt to promote democracy
that involves the unilateral use of force or run the risk of a serious backlash against international efforts to promote democracy.

Multilateral force to enforce the results of an internationally monitored
election has been sanctioned only in Haiti. The UN also continued to recognize the deposed Aristide as the legitimate ruler of Haiti, thus modifying
the 'effective control' standard for UN recognition in favour of one based
on democratic legitimacy.[28] The shaky legal pretext for such action by the
Security Council was that the Haitian military junta posed a threat to regional peace. The UN action in Haiti sets a political (but not legal) precedent for the use of multilateral force to protect democracy, strengthening
the enforcement capacity of the international political rights regime. The
decision to intervene in Haiti was the result of a constellation of factors
that will not easily come together again including Haiti's strategic weakness as a small and dependent country, the state of prolonged chaos in a
country off the United States and the consequent threat of a mass exodus
of Haitian boat-people, Aristide's democratic legitimacy and doggedness,
the international isolation of the Haitian military regime and China's decision not to veto the use of force by the Security Council.

BUILDING INSTITUTIONS

De Tocqueville's *Democracy in America* identified a strong civil and
political society as the basis of a healthy democracy.[29] Strong societal institutions including civic associations, religious institutions, a free press,
political parties and an independent judiciary help counterbalance state
power, provide a context for developing civic skills, encourage norms of
reciprocity and trust, articulate societal interests and create peaceful channels for the resolution of conflicts that might otherwise result in violence.
Election-monitors can play a crucial role in developing institutions in
several ways. Mediation by outside actors can foster trust among rival
parties by providing guarantees, clearing up misperceptions, relaying information back and forth and resolving key issues. Pressure from outside
actors can encourage governments to develop new institutions necessary
for a fair election to take place, such as an independent election commission, an accurate voter registration list, a human rights ombudsman, an
opening of the official media, transparency in the management of party

finances and so forth. Technical and financial assistance to domestic civic associations by international groups can play a major role in developing election-monitoring groups that can provide a nucleus for the formation of an organized civil society. Finally, internationally observed elections in which all major political parties accept the results represents by itself a democratic breakthrough because it provides for the peaceful transfer of power through the ballot box rather than force.

In the case of peacebuilding missions, the presence of neutral actors such as the UN can represent a 'time-out' from conflict, thereby providing a window of opportunity to reactivate civil society, construct democratic institutions and revive the economy. In Cambodia, the UN presence produced a highly successful election under very difficult conditions with a turnout of 90 per cent, the development of a relatively free press, the growth of several human rights NGOs and new foreign aid commitments.[30] At the same time, the UN was unable to purge the police force of human rights violators, persuade the factions to demobilize and ensure a neutral electoral environment because of the failure of both the Khmer Rouge and the Hun Sen government to collaborate fully with the world organization. The result is that the outlook for Cambodia remains very uncertain.

The effects of UN missions in El Salvador and in Haiti on the development of local institutions have also been quite mixed. In El Salvador, ONUSAL successfully presided over the demobilization of the FMLN, the cessation of the civil war, the creation of a new civilian police force, the installation of a human rights ombudsman and the removal of several top army officials for major human rights violations after investigation by a UN-sponsored commission. Unlike Cambodia, the 1994 Salvadoran elections were organized by the regime, which resisted international advice and conducted a very flawed election.[31] In Haiti, the international community was successful in dislodging the military junta, reforming the police, demobilizing the army and establishing order. Yet, the subsequent parliamentary elections in June 1995 conducted by the Aristide government were, according to one experienced observer, 'the most disastrous technically' he had ever witnessed.[32]

What explains the varying success of the UN in creating institutions for democracy? First, the ability of the UN to create institutions depends vitally on the cooperation of the parties to the conflict. If the parties fail to cooperate or renege on prior agreements, the chances will diminish accordingly. Such cooperation is likely to be more forthcoming if the international community possesses both the will and leverage to maintain pressure for the parties to work towards a solution. Second, developing democratic institutions in countries that lack a democratic tradition is a time-consuming process that may not be achievable in the short-term horizons of most UN and other missions. There is a long and distinguished literature on the 'prerequisites' for democracy that should sound a cautionary note about efforts to transplant democracy to inhospitable conditions overnight.[33] Still, it is possible to err on the side of too much pessimism. Growing interdependence may have quickened the timeframe for the development of democracy in part because of heightened outside involvement. Nor should one be over-deterministic about the prospects for democracy. India has had a highly successful democracy for almost fifty years, despite not meeting one of the usual key prerequisites for democracy: a medium or high level of per capita income. The results in Cambodia, Haiti and El Salvador are mixed; they are not an unqualified failure. The development of international regimes to protect democracy where it is in danger, liberalized trading arrangements to expand economic activity, higher outlays of foreign aid specifically tied to the development of democratic institutions and making respect for human rights a condition for receiving official loans and participating in multilateral institutions can go a long way in improving the prospects for democracy, despite unfavourable domestic conditions.

ELECTION-MONITORING: THE MEXICAN CASE

The Mexican case is interesting for several reasons. First, it represents an opportunity to study the interaction between the UN, several international NGOs, and Mexican civic groups in the task of election-monitoring. Second, resistance to outside interference has been unusually strong in Mexico, making it a good test-case for the erosion of traditional sovereignty norms in the Western Hemisphere. Third, the UN mandate in Mexico was not to observe the 1994 elections but to train and finance domestic observers. Mexico thus represents an excellent case study of the impact of international actors on the development of local civil society and the thickening of social capital.

The main international actors in the 1994 electoral process were the United Nations Electoral Assistance Programme (UNEAP), the National Endowment for Democracy (NED), established by the US Congress in 1983 as an autonomous body to support democratization initiatives around the world, the National Democratic Institute (NDI), which conducts international outreach for the US Democratic Party, and the Council of Freely-Elected Heads of Government. The presence of international observers, euphemistically designated 'foreign visitors' so as not to offend nationalist sensibilities, reflected the low credibility of Mexican elections in the wake of widespread allegations of fraud in the 1988 presidential elections won by Carlos Salinas, the candidate of the official Institutional Revolutionary Party (PRI) party, which has governed Mexico uninterruptedly since 1929 in various guises. The PRI's credibility problem had an important international dimension as well. The decision of the Salinas administration to adopt an export-oriented model based on increasing integration with the United States made it inevitable that the Mexican electoral process would be subjected to more international scrutiny than usual. Indeed, the lack of clean elections in Mexico quickly became a significant issue in Washington debates on the ratification of NAFTA.[34] Growing interdependence also encouraged the emergence of transnational coalitions to improve the human rights climate in Mexico, involving both Mexican and foreign NGOs. Finally, the global spread of democracy meant that the Mexican political system looked increasingly like an authoritarian anachronism in much the same category as such unpopular regimes as Burma, China, Cuba, Vietnam and Indonesia. Thus, the situation was unlike the past, when Mexico's softer and inclusionary form of authoritarian rule had contrasted favourably with the gross human rights violations of the bureaucratic-authoritarian regimes in the southern cone.[35]

The role of UNEAP

The UN Electoral Assistance Programme was formally invited by the Mexican government to provide technical and financial assistance to Mexico's domestic election-monitoring organizations, which the government recognized were a crucial ingredient of a credible election.[36] The government could have financed the domestic observer groups directly but this would have been seen as a transparent attempt to coopt them and had the opposite effect of undermining credibility. The government also hoped that the involvement of UNEAP in training and financing domestic observer groups would make them more professional and objective. The government was particularly worried about the Civic Alliance (AC), an umbrella group of independent NGOs that the government felt was biased towards the leftist Democratic Revolutionary Party (PRD). AC had quickly emerged as the country's most credible election-monitoring group. The government hoped that UNEAP would finance a variety of domestic observer groups from across the political spectrum to ensure that no one civic organization acquired a monopoly on judging the elections, especially not AC. Indeed, while UNEAP channelled $1.5 million to AC, or three-quarters of AC's budget for 1994, the UN agreed to spend roughly

$2.2 million to fund the observation efforts of more than a dozen other groups, including the mammoth National Teacher's Union (SNTE) with powerful ties to the PRI.

Relations between AC and UNEAP were often tense. AC bitterly resented UNEAP's determination to finance election-monitoring groups linked to the government, which AC saw as hopelessly biased, and rival claimants on UNEAP funds, and hinted of a relationship of complicity between the Mexican government and the United Nations. UNEAP felt it was necessary to fund a variety of different observer groups to ensure that it was not viewed as biased towards AC, which had already received about 41 per cent of UNEAP's budget. UNEAP also clashed with AC over the latter's spending priorities, expense estimates and observation methodology. More important, UNEAP was concerned that the left-oriented AC suffered from a tendency to equate a PRI defeat with a victory for democracy. AC's leadership chafed at UNEAP's perceived 'interference', but its heavy reliance on UNEAP funds prevented an open rupture between them.

UNEAP's mission in Mexico represents a highly successful and cost-effective intervention by outsiders to promote the development of local civil society and social capital. Without UNEAP and international financial and logistical support, AC would have been unable to mount a countrywide observation effort. Yet, that UNEAP's mission was so effective also testifies to the pre-existing strength of Mexican civil society. Fair elections had already become a major societal issue, thus providing a reservoir of public support for AC. Its seven founding groups were all closely identified with highly respected figures who served as political entrepreneurs by harnessing growing domestic and international concern for transparent elections to facilitate growth. AC itself was organized as an umbrella group knitting together some 450 NGOs in a dense and reciprocal network. This loose structure gave AC considerable range and flexibility, while cohesion was assured by the prestige of its leadership, overlapping membership among its constituent organizations and a clearly defined goal. UNEAP's mission thus took place in a societal context where a relatively small injection of funds could have a large payoff. Had Mexican civil society not been as developed, it is unlikely that UNEAP's mission would have been as successful. It is always easier to add to an existing stock of social capital than to attempt to create it from scratch as in war-torn countries like Cambodia.

The UN and international NGOs

The Mexican government hoped that the presence of UNEAP would act as a check on other international actors, if only by drawing attention away from them. The government also reasoned that UNEAP as an official international body capable of functioning only at the behest of member states and within strictly defined limits would be easier to control than other international actors. On the ground, however, an almost symbiotic relationship developed between UNEAP and the cluster of foreign NGOs. The Council of Freely-Elected Heads of Government and NDI were in a position to openly criticize the Mexican electoral process, which UNEAP as an official international organization with the limited mandate of aiding domestic election observer groups was unable to do.

Yet, UNEAP had the necessary technical and financial resources to facilitate the growth of a cluster of domestic election-monitoring organizations, and the leverage to demand a high degree of professionalism and neutrality from them. In a few crucial instances, NGOs contributed functionally to UNEAP's own objectives. By improving the design of AC's quick-count, NDI helped AC allay UNEAP concerns about methodology. NGOs also acted as channels of communication between UNEAP and AC by relaying mutual concerns back and forth, and clarifying misunderstandings. There was therefore little institutional rivalry between UNEAP and NGOs, and the pattern of cooperation that developed in Mexico between them may constitute a model of future interaction.

The role of international NGOs

AC also received small grants from external NGOs including $150,000 from NED and $50,000 from NDI.[37] The fact that AC was supported by NED, with its bipartisan US Congressional support and distinguished board of directors, set AC apart from other domestic observer groups by giving it a fund of international legitimacy, particularly among US opinion-makers. AC's ability to influence international opinion may in turn have worked to enhance its bargaining power *vis-à-vis* the Mexican government. However, Civic Alliance leaders fretted about the dangers of accepting US Congressional support through the NED, which could lead to AC being tarred as an instrument of US interventionism. NED's decision to award its prestigious 1995 Democracy Award to Sergio Aguayo, one of the founding members of AC, represented a public endorsement of AC's work by the international community.

NDI's involvement in designing the quick-count conducted by AC in the wake of the closing of the polls significantly improved both its technical soundness and believability. NDI also supported regional forums on AC electoral observation efforts in the cities of San Luis Potosí, Guadalajara and Veracruz which brought together some 200 local civic leaders in each city, the national coordinators of AC, and international civic leaders from Chile, Paraguay and the Philippines. In addition, NDI sponsored an AC seminar in Mexico City to train election observers and brought together 120 community leaders from all Mexico's 31 states and the Federal District.[38] These conferences played an important role winning over regional elites for AC's electoral monitoring efforts and facilitated its development as a nationwide organization.

Another important international player in the 1994 Mexican elections was the Council of Freely-Elected Heads of Government led by Jimmy Carter. The government's attitude towards the Council was mixed. On the one hand, the government was reluctant to invite the Council to observe the process formally because this could signal a breakdown of the Mexican electoral system and potentially reduce the regime's control over the process. On the other hand, senior government officials knew that the presence of an objective international observer group might give credibility to the election results if the PRD refused to accept the results, a highly likely outcome. The PRD failed to support the 1993 electoral reforms and split over whether to approve a further round of reforms in 1994. The other main opposition party, the centre-right PAN, had voted for both reform initiatives, giving them at least some credibility.

The reforms continued the overhaul of the voter registration list begun in 1990, introduced a new tamper-proof photo identity card for voters, enhanced the autonomy of the Federal Election Institute (IFE) and allowed international observers for the first time. Government officials were concerned that without the presence of international observers such as the Council, the PRD would be able to discredit even a clean election given the culture of distrust surrounding the conduct of Mexican elections and plunge the country into a political crisis. The Council could potentially play a crucial role in the regime's strategy of legitimizing the elections because of its ability to influence public opinion in the Western Hemisphere and the Clinton administration.

For the Council, the main risk in observing the electoral process was that its presence could be used to legitimize an unfair election. However, not to become involved would have meant giving up the chance to influence the process at all. In view of these competing considerations, the Council's approach was low-key. It sent two international delegations (in September 1993 and June 1994) to report on Mexico's electoral reforms, fielded only a small observer mission on election day, and chose not to bring Carter to Mexico at all. The government's decision to permit international observers came far too late, less than three months short of the elections, for the Council to mount a full-fledged observation mission.

The Council had always been concerned that the government would eventually decide to invite international observers in order to bolster the credibility of the elections but not give them enough time to do a serious job. In effect, there was the danger that the government would pull the wool over the eyes of the international observers by using them to improve confidence in a process that could not be properly observed because of time constraints. President Carter himself was unwilling to go to Mexico without a formal invitation from all political parties and the Mexican government. Of all the three major political parties, only the PRD was willing to consider inviting Carter. There was also the danger that in a country like Mexico, Carter would become an issue himself. He had historically observed elections and also played a mediating role. Mexican political actors, although separated by a wide chasm of distrust, were simply unwilling to turn to an ex-US President to sort out their differences. What was possible in Nicaragua was impossible in Mexico, and the Council had to adjust its strategy accordingly.

The Council of Freely-Elected Heads of Government made a useful contribution to the democratization of the electoral process. First, by inviting Mexican civic leaders like Sergio Aguayo to participate in missions in Haiti, Guyana and Paraguay, the Council sensitized them to the role of international and domestic observers in promoting fair elections and helped develop a relationship between the Council and the leaders of Mexico's emerging election-monitoring groups. Second, by holding meetings with Mexican government officials on electoral issues, the Council was able to bring the weight of international public opinion to bear directly on decision-makers. Mexican leaders knew that their actions were under direct international scrutiny. Third, the Council issued two detailed reports on the Mexican electoral process that were widely circulated among government officials, academics and NGOs throughout the Hemisphere.

These reports in effect helped internationalize some of the more arcane but critically important issues of electoral reform. For example, the Council in September 1993 conducted the first study ever of voting patterns in the General Council of IFE and concluded that the supposedly independent magistrate Councillors had supported the PRI on all important decisions that came before the Council in an 11-month period between October 1990 and September 1991. The report thus undercut the government's assertion that the magistrate Councillors were objective, gave opposition parties more ammunition in their bid to reform IFE and ensured that international public opinion would not take IFE seriously unless its governing structure was reformed to allow full independence for the magistrate Councillors. Fourth, the Council's intimate knowledge of the pre-electoral environment and close ties with major Mexican political leaders meant it was the only international actor able to offer an assessment of the entire electoral process leading up to election day and beyond. Finally, the Council as the first international actor to become involved in Mexican elections helped pave the way for the government's eventual decision to allow international observers, thereby contributing to an important opening of the Mexican electoral system that few could have predicted.

On election day, 21 August 1994, the Council in conjunction with NDI and the International Republican Institute fielded 80 observers in all 31 states and the Federal District. The largest international delegation was sent by Global Exchange, an NGO that fielded 105 representatives. Overall, 943 individuals were officially accredited as international observers representing 283 organizations from around the world; the majority came from the United States (68 per cent) followed by Canada (7.6 per cent) and Argentina (3 per cent).[39] International observers probably exerted a psychological influence on the election far out of proportion to their numbers. Their mere presence, which was widely reported in the media, may have helped convince ordinary Mexicans that the elections would be clean, thus contributing to the extraordinarily high rate of turnout among voters. The fact that most observers agreed that the irregularities characterizing the elections had not affected the overall results of the presidential race, and that there was no identifiable pattern to them that might indicate fraud, contributed to the credibility of Zedillo's victory and Mexican elections generally.[40]

According to post-election surveys, about 61 per cent of those asked thought that the elections were clean while 24 per cent did not and 15 per cent did not know. In addition, 64 per cent felt that the IFE had performed very well. This contrasted sharply with pre-election polls taken in June 1994 when 35–45 per cent of those surveyed expected fraud while 65 per cent expected violence.[41] In fact, one of the most impressive features of the elections was the almost complete lack of violence during and after the elections. The presence of international observers, by improving the credibility of election results, almost certainly helped reduce the risk of violence.[42] An attempt by the PRD to protest what it claimed was a fraudulent election without presenting much evidence fizzled out for lack of public support.

THE LIMITS OF ELECTION-MONITORING

International actors in Mexico thus played an important role in supporting domestic observer groups financially, morally and technically. But they

Vikram K. Chand

also exerted an independent effect on the electoral process by nudging the regime further down the path of reform, acting as a psychological deterrent to election fraud, and bolstering the credibility of the final results, thereby reducing the risk of violence.

A contrary view is that international observers may have unwittingly abetted fraud by legitimizing it. The possibility that election observers may legitimize fraud is a danger intrinsic to the task of election-monitoring, and it applies equally to domestic and international election observers. This can occur if observers fail to detect fraud and pronounce the election 'clean', or maliciously ignore evidence of fraud. Neither of these two eventualities came to pass in 1994 in Mexico. The domestic network of observers covered virtually all areas of the country. The quick-count ruled out any chance of fraud at the counting stage. And only PRI-linked observer groups possessed any incentive to cover up evidence of fraud, assuming this was possible, while AC and most international observers had every incentive to expose it.

More problematic is a situation where the official party profits from its huge advantages in terms of financial resources and media access during a campaign, but otherwise holds a clean election. Here the risk is that observers may end up pronouncing an election fair on the basis of results that, although obtained through impeccable voting, may reflect unfair campaign conditions. There is no question that the PRI as a state party enjoyed massive advantages over its rivals, particularly with regard to media access and financial reserves. It is, however, virtually impossible to demonstrate the effects of such advantages on the election outcome. Also, both domestic and international observer groups throughout the campaign strongly criticized the government for allowing such inequities between political parties. AC conducted several studies of the electronic media to track coverage of the presidential race. Pressure by domestic and international observer groups, and opposition parties, in turn contributed to the first serious discussion about campaign and political party finance issues in Mexico. The government's unprecedented decision to permit a televised debate between the three main presidential candidates had an important effect on the race by enhancing the public perception that the opposition could win. Without the presence of observer groups, there would have been less pressure on the government to address these questions.

Finally, experience from other countries, where the government has enjoyed vast advantages over its rivals, suggest that entrenched regimes can lose elections even if the playing field is highly uneven provided the voter registration list, the balloting and the count are conducive to a clean election. More than one dictator has overestimated the advantages of incumbency, called an election to legitimize his authority on extremely short notice, invited international observers to make the election acceptable to the global community and then proceeded to lose in a landslide victory to the hastily organized opposition. 'Stunning' elections like these have occurred in India in 1977, the Philippines in 1986, Poland in 1989 and a host of other countries.[43] Opposition parties can therefore overcome the advantages of state parties if the election itself is clean, which in turn may depend partly on the presence of international observers. The fact the PAN has won gubernatorial elections in four states and several cities, despite highly unequal campaign conditions, is further evidence in this direction.

International observers focus on elections. Elections go to the heart of democracy but obviously democracy involves something more than just elections. Merely holding a clean election will not necessarily resolve such maladies as the maldistribution of income, weak institutions or deep ethnic cleavages. Elections may simply be a form of 'skin-deep' or 'easy' democratization. Yet, clean elections over time can contribute to the growth of institutions such as political parties and civic associations, give the poor a voice in the political system, punish corruption at the ballot box and facilitate the development of rules to deal with conflict. Amartya Sen has shown how competitive political environments can provide an early warning system to prevent famine, while the accountability intrinsic to democracy may induce policy-makers to correct misguided policies before it is too late.[44] The 'skin-deep' criticism is thus exaggerated and misleading.

CONCLUSION

The dramatic growth of election-monitoring since the mid-1980s is intimately tied to fundamental changes in the structure of both domestic and international politics. That election-monitoring has become so widespread in so short a period of time, despite the fact that it so often runs afoul of a state-centric notion of sovereignty, testifies to the depth of these changes. The growth of election-monitoring has major implications for building democratic institutions. Election-monitoring not only facilitates reasonably fair elections but the development of basic democratic institutions and habits as well. The crucial role of NGOs in international monitoring has contributed to greater pluralism in global society, and produced a web of largely cooperative ties based on niche specialization between IGOs and NGOs. Finally, election-monitoring is nothing more than a way of enforcing the political rights enshrined in major international covenants. As external election-monitoring becomes more widely accepted and practised, the effective scope of these rights will expand accordingly.

Election-monitoring has thus become the central element of a rapidly developing international regime to preserve and extend democracy. The United Nations should continue to develop and intensify the patterns of collaboration with international and indigenous NGOs documented in the Mexican and other cases. A better international division of labour between the UN and NGOs would foster democracy.

NOTES

1. R. A. Pastor, 'Elections, monitoring', in Seymour Martin Lipset (ed.), *Encyclopedia of Democracy* (Washington, DC: Congressional Quarterly, 1995), p. 409.
2. R. D. Putnam, *Making Democracy Work: Civic Traditions in Modern Italy*, (Princeton, NJ: Princeton University Press, 1993), especially Chapter 6.
3. Ibid.
4. T. M. Franck, 'The emerging right to democratic governance', *American Journal of International Law*, 86 (1), 1992, pp. 66–8.
5. A. Lake, 'The enlargement of democracy' in *From Containment to Enlargement*, US Department of State Dispatch, 3 (39), 27 September 1993, pp. 658–64.
6. See F. Fukuyama, *The End of History and the Last Man* (New York: Avon Books, 1992).
7. M. W. Doyle, 'Kant, liberal legacies, and foreign affairs', *Philosophy and Public Affairs*, 12 (3 and 4), Summer and Fall 1983, pp. 205–35 and 323–53. Doyle was not the first to point out the connection between peace and democracy. Earlier works on the topic are D. Babst, 'A force for peace', *Industrial Research*, April 1972, pp. 55–8; and R. J. Rummel, *Understanding War and Conflict* (Los Angeles: Sage, 1975–81). Doyle's article provoked far greater interest in the topic.
8. D. H. Levine, 'Religion and politics, politics and religion: an introduction', in Daniel H. Levine (ed.), *Churches and Politics in Latin America* (Beverly Hills, Calif.: Sage, 1979; see also, S. P. Huntington, *The Third Wave: Democratization in the Late Twentieth Century* (Norman: University of Oklahoma Press, 1989), p. 78.
9. Ibid., p. 83.
10. J. N. Rosenau, 'Sovereignty in a turbulent world', in G. Lyons and M. Mastanduno (eds), *Beyond Westphalia: State Sovereignty and International Intervention* (Baltimore, Md.: Johns Hopkins University Press, 1995), pp. 204–9.
11. The Council of Freely-Elected Heads of Government, *Observing Nicaragua's Elections, 1989–1990* (Atlanta, Ga.: The Carter Center of Emory University, 1990), pp. 25–6.

12. C. Eguizábal, 'Las Naciones Unidas y la consolidación de la paz en Centroamérica', in O. Pellicer (ed.), *La Seguridad Internacional en América Latina y el Caribe* (Mexico City: Instituto Matías Romero de Estudios Diplomáticos, 1995, pp. 119–27.

13. The Council of Freely-Elected Heads of Government, *Observing Nicaragua's Elections, 1989–1990*, pp. 16–21.

14. Ibid., pp. 25–33.

15. J. McCoy, L. Garber, and R. Pastor, 'Pollwatching and peacemaking', in L. Diamond and M. F. Plattner (eds), *The Global Resurgence of Democracy* (Baltimore, Md.: Johns Hopkins University Press, 1993), p. 181.

16. National Democratic Institute, *Nation Building: The UN and Namibia*, (Washington, DC: National Democratic Institute), 1990, pp. 26–34; see also L. Cliffe, *The Transition to Independence in Namibia* (Boulder Colo.: Lynne Rienner, 1994), especially Chapters 4, 6–8.

17. National Democratic Institute, *Nation Building: The UN and Namibia*, pp. 35–6.

18. See M. W. Doyle, *UN Peacekeeping in Cambodia: UNTAC's Civil Mandate* (Boulder, Colo.: Lynne Rienner, 1995).

19. On the relationship between the OAS and the UN in Latin America, see R. Greene, 'El Debate ONU–OEA: nuevas competencias en el ambito de la paz y la seguridad internacional', in O. Pellicer (ed.), *Las Naciones Unidas: Visión de México* (Mexico City: Fondo de Cultura Economica, 1994), pp. 72–102; and S. N. MacFarlane and T. G. Weiss, 'The United Nations, regional organizations, and human security: building theory in Central America', *Security Studies*, 2 (1), Autumn 1992, pp. 6–37.

20. A. K. Henrikson, 'The growth of regional organizations and the role of the United Nations', in L. Fawcett and A. Hurrell (eds), *Regionalism in World Politics* (Oxford: Oxford University Press, 1995), pp. 142–7.

21. R. A. Pastor, *Whirlpool: U.S. Foreign Policy toward Latin America and the Caribbean* (Princeton, NJ: Princeton University Press, 1992), p. 282.

22. On the implications of humanitarian assistance for sovereignty, see T. G. Weiss and J. Chopra, 'Sovereignty under siege: from intervention to humanitarian space', in Lyons and Mastanduno (eds), *Beyond Westphalia*, pp. 87–114.

23. R. Pastor, 'Elections, monitoring', p. 409.

24. See, for example, Franck, 'The emerging right to democratic governance'. See also, G. H. Fox, 'The right to participation in international law', *Yale Journal of International Law*, 17 (539), 1992, pp. 539–607; and F. Tesón, 'Changing perceptions of domestic jurisdiction and intervention', in T. J. Farer (ed.), *Beyond Sovereignty: Collectively Defending Democracy in the Americas* (Baltimore, Md.: Johns Hopkins University Press, 1996), pp. 29–51.

25. For a sceptical view of Western efforts to promote human rights in Asia, see B. Kausikan, 'Asia's different standard', *Foreign Policy*, 92, Fall 1993, pp. 24–51.

26. Doyle, *UN Peacekeeping in Cambodia*, p. 84.

27. See National Democratic Institute and International Republican Institute for International Affairs, *The May 9, 1989 Panamanian Elections* (Washington, DC: NDI/IRI, 1990).

28.   For a discussion of UN recognition practices and an argument in favour of democratic legitimacy as the standard for recognition see, G. H. Fox, 'Multinational election monitoring: advancing international law on the high wire', *Fordham International Law Journal*, 18 (5), May 1995, pp. 1658–67.

29.   A. de Tocqueville, *Democracy in America*, ed. J. P. Mayer (Garden City, NY: Anchor Books, 1969), Vol. 1, Part I, pp. 62–84; Part II, pp. 174–95 and 262–311.

30.   Doyle, *UN Peacekeeping in Cambodia*, pp. 32–4, 40–58.

31.   Eguizábal, 'Las Naciones Unidas y la consolidación de la paz en Centroamérica', pp. 128–37.

32.   R. Pastor, in the Council of Freely-Elected Heads of Government, *Mission to Haiti #3: Elections for Parliament and Municipalities* (Atlanta, Ga.: The Carter Center of Emory University, 1995), p. 19. See also, Robert Maguire et al., *Haiti Held Hostage: International Responses to the Quest for Nationhood 1986–1996* (Providence, RI: Watson Institute, 1996), Occasional Paper No. 23.

33.   See, for example, R. Dahl, *Polyarchy: Participation and Opposition* (New Haven, Conn.: Yale University Press, 1971); S. M. Lipset, *Political Man: The Social Bases of Politics* (New York: Doubleday, 1960); see also, Z. Arat, 'Democracy and economic development: modernization theory revisited', *Comparative Politics*, 21, October 1988, pp. 21–37.

34.   R. A. Pastor, *Integration with Mexico: Options for U.S. Policy* (New York: Twentieth Century Fund, 1993), especially pp. 27–8 and 65–7.

35.   See Huntington, *The Third Wave*. See also L. Diamond, J. Linz and S. M. Lipset (eds), *Politics in Developing Countries: Comparing Experiences with Democracy* (Boulder, Colo.: Lynne Rienner, 1990) and Diamond and Plattner (eds), *The Global Resurgence of Democracy*.

36.   See Unidad de Asistencia Electoral, *Posibilidades de Apoyo a Organizaciones No Gubernamentales de Observadores Electorales en Mexico* (Mexico City: UN Mission, 23 May 1994).

37.   The ground for classifying NED and NDI as NGOs lies in their autonomy from Congress, and the executive in the case of NED and from the Democratic Party in the case of NDI. Likewise, the Council of Freely-Elected Heads of Government was created as a private initiative by former President Carter, and operates independently of any government.

38.   *Briefing Paper for the National Democratic Institute for International Affairs and the International Republican Institute's Joint International Delegation to the 1994 Mexican Elections*, August 1994, p. 14.

39.   Instituto Federal Electoral, *Informe Sobre Observadores y Visitantes Extranjeros* (Mexico City: Instituto Federal Electoral, 1994).

40.   For the view of international observers (including this author) on the 1994 elections, see the Council of Freely-Elected Heads of Government, *The August 21, 1994 Mexican National Elections: Fourth Report* (Atlanta, Ga.: The Carter Center of Emory University, November 1994). On the views of Mexico's most important domestic observer group, the Civic Alliance, see Alianza Civica, *La Calidad de la Jornada Electoral del 21 de Agosto de 1994: Informe de Alianza Civica Observación '94*, (Mexico City: 19 September 1994). For the views of other domestic and international

groups, see Instituto Federal Electoral, *Proyecto de Informe a la Camara de Diputados*, Addenda 21, 22 and 23 (Mexico City: Instituto Federal Electoral, 1994).

41.   J. McCoy, 'On the Mexican elections', *Hemisphere*, Fall 1994, p. 28.
42.   For examples from other countries on the possible functions of international observers, see J. McCoy, L. Garber and R. Pastor, 'Pollwatching and peace-keeping', *Journal of Democracy*, 2 (4), Fall 1994, pp. 102–14.
43.   See Huntington, *The Third Wave*, pp. 175–80.
44.   A. Sen, 'Freedoms and needs', *The New Republic*, 10 and 17 January 1994, pp. 31–8.

9 NGOs and Development Assistance: a Change in Mind-set?

Ian Smillie

This essay asks five basic questions about non-governmental organizations (NGOs) working in development and emergency situations. The first has to do with the basic usefulness of the term 'nongovernmental organization'. Many have struggled with the appropriateness – or otherwise – of this expression, creating many new terms in the process. None has caught on. Even the distinction between organizations working primarily as service providers and those whose role is primarily in advocacy does not work very well. Oxfam, for example, works in development and in emergencies, and has been a fierce advocate over the years for specific political action in such places as South Africa, Cambodia and Rwanda. It might well be asked if an organization that receives more than half its funding from government sources – as many northern NGOs today do – can actually be considered a 'non'-governmental organization. The same question, of course, could be asked about 'private' universities and some of the largest 'private' sector firms. Could Boeing survive without government contracts? Is it less part of the private sector than, say, the Sony Corporation because of this 'dependency'? For convenience, therefore, the term 'NGO' will be used throughout this chapter, although it will refer mainly to the larger organizations working primarily in development.

The other questions relate to the comparative advantage of NGOs, the constraints to greater NGO involvement in UN programmes, the thorny issue of accountability and the place of NGOs in civil society. This chapter seeks to address these questions through a discussion of the much-used (and abused) expression 'transparency', examining three basic problems faced by most NGOs, and by the organizations that support and work with them: the real cost of doing business; the enduring problem of evaluation and quality control; and accountability. The basic argument is that a change in thinking on these fundamental issues is required, and that rather than simply mimicking other official development agencies, the UN system could help make NGOs a more stable and effective part of the global development assistance effort in the years to come.

As for the present, NGOs are in a period of fundamental transition regarding their roles in the delivery of development assistance, and this offers the United Nations system opportunities as well as problems. The transition emerges from several developments since the end of the Cold War:

- dramatic cutbacks in official development assistance (ODA), combined with growing taxpayer demand for greater effectiveness in the most oft-stated purpose of aid programmes, ending poverty;
- a new willingness on the part of official development agencies to admit that their ability to reach the 'grassroots' with effective and direct poverty alleviation programmes is limited;
- an agreeable 'fit' between NGOs and current enthusiasms for 'civil society', a fit that also helps where NGOs are seen as a means of downsizing and 'privatizing' ODA;
- an awareness that poverty (in poor countries, and in countries with exemplary growth rates) will not be eradicated by trickle-down, market-oriented development alone;
- a growing awareness (possibly) that the effects of Third World poverty – low-level conflict, war, terrorism, the drug trade, refugees, pollution – no longer stop at international frontiers;
- the apparent success of NGOs in tackling both the symptoms and causes of poverty;
- the evolution and growth of 'transnational NGOs' – World Vision, CARE, Oxfam, Save the Children Fund (SCF) and others – some operating like tightly-knit corporations, others as loose but well-connected networks. These organizations are able to move quickly, have capacities and efficiencies that others (including governments) do not, and have demonstrated political (that is, taxpayer) support;
- the growing number, strength and networking capacity of southern NGOs.

Northern NGOs have, in fact, become much larger players in the delivery of official development assistance than is generally appreciated – as much as 30 per cent in Sweden, 29 per cent in Switzerland, 25 per cent in Norway and 14 per cent in the Netherlands.[1] Almost 28 per cent of USAID spending is channelled through northern and southern NGOs combined.[2] Statistics in the South are more than a little patchy, but in many countries there has been a significant swing in official development spending towards NGOs and away from traditional government-led programming.

These trends, which appear to suggest a larger future NGO role in development assistance, are placed in question, however, by a number of factors:

- NGOs may have stretched the private donor base as far as they can with the spate of emergencies in the early 1990s. Governmental retreat from domestic social sectors has placed pressure on domestic charities, heightening fundraising competition. Expectations that international development NGOs can significantly enlarge current levels of financial burden-sharing are probably, therefore, unrealistic. Competition between international NGOs has also increased, weakening the potential for better coordination.
- Northern NGOs may be undermining public support for, and understanding of, long-term development assistance because increased fundraising competition has led many to emphasize emergency work and to use increasingly emotive fundraising approaches.
- Human rights NGOs like Amnesty International and environmental groups such as the Worldwide Fund for Nature (WWF) have begun to transform themselves, incorporating southern units into their ranks and becoming genuinely transnational in the process. This is not yet true of the large development organizations, some of which are becoming surrogates and executing agencies for official development agencies. Something to watch over the next five to ten years will be the extent to which any of them transform themselves, becoming more than simply networks of northerners working in the South.
- While the 'contracting' of NGOs by multilateral and bilateral agencies makes sense up to a point, it can undermine the essence of what makes them attractive and what makes them a genuine alternatives to the public sector. Their priorities in terms of countries and locations within countries, their target groups, their approach and their choice of sectors can all be manipulated with generous contracting terms. The trade-offs between NGO institutional imperatives (survival, visibility, retention of market share) and developmental imperatives could actually be made more invidious by the addition of UN contracting to the mix. Conversely, longer-term contracts worked out on a cooperative planning basis might reduce the negative influence of some institutional demands.
- Uncertainty about the future role of northern NGOs in development work (as opposed to emergencies) is creating tension and confusion.

Some bilaterals and multilaterals are bypassing them in favour of southern NGOs, which welcome this direct approach. Tensions between southern NGOs, and between them and their governments, however, contribute to much more controlling, if not draconian anti-NGO legislation. It also ignores and may undermine increasingly important non-governmental North-South partnerships around key policy-related development issues such as trade, the environment, weapons and human rights. In other words, an overemphasis on service provision could reduce the NGO voice.

• Those bilateral and multilateral institutions that support southern NGOs directly often have ambiguous purposes. Some simply want effective executing agencies, while others want to learn from the experience and reduce costs. Where 'supporting civil society' is concerned, however, there can be serious problems of selectivity and bias, and important questions about whether it is appropriate for governments to 'strengthen' civil society in other countries. Soviet support for the 1984-5 British coal miners' strike and Libyan support in 1996 for Louis Farrakhan's Nation of Islam met with contempt and even legal action in Britain and the United States.

All of these issues, discussed at length in many recent books about NGOs, pose questions for an evolving relationship between UN agencies and NGOs. Should the former simply mimic what other agencies are doing with NGOs? To a certain extent, this is already happening. The UN Development Programme (UNDP), the UN Development Fund for Women (UNIFEM), the UN Children's Fund (UNICEF) and others, some of them relative latecomers to the NGO scene, all have various funds that support NGOs, sometimes on a matching basis. The UN High Commissioner for Refugees (UNHCR), the World Food Programme (WFP) and others also have direct contracts with NGOs, paying them to carry out programmes that would once have been managed by the agencies themselves. The scale of these contracts is in some cases very large, and can represent a significant proportion of the agency's overall budget.

Inevitably, these arrangements produce opportunities and strains. UN agencies have certain advantages over bilateral donors in that they are not supposed to reflect any national bias or interest. Like NGOs, UN agencies are also recipients, and know the negative side of such relationships. But at a technical level, there is no particular reason why a UN agency might handle the NGO connection better than, say, the Swedish Agency for International Development (SIDA), the United States Agency for International Development (USAID) or the European Union (EU). Beyond the basic pros and cons, however, it can be argued that the United Nations system has a greater role to play where NGOs are concerned, than that of grant-maker, contractor and wannabe partner. The changing role of the state, increasingly urgent development needs in the South and less official development assistance suggest that there is a new opportunity for donor agencies, southern governments and NGOs to concede greater ground to one another, and to create partnerships based on development concerns rather than on perceptions of strategic or organizational advantage. This will require a dramatic shift in mind-set, however, especially by governments (donor and recipient), in thinking of NGOs more as a permanent, planned and negotiated part of the landscape, and less as temporary and somewhat troublesome gap-fillers. In this there is a critical role to be played by the UN family of agencies.

In order to start moving towards that role, however, some of the ritualistic cant offered by and about NGOs must be decanted, perhaps into an open drain. For the sake of discussion, this cant has been organized under three basic 'transparencies': the cost of doing business, the quality of work and accountability.

TRANSPARENCY 1: THE COST OF DOING BUSINESS

Almost every recent study of NGOs calls for greater transparency. But greater than what? Greater than the Ford Motor Company? Greater than the Japanese Ministry of Transport? In most countries, NGOs are required by law to file externally audited annual financial statements, and most will make these available to any donor with the slightest passing interest. Generally, however, annual financial statements, whether produced by an NGO in the United States, Britain or Kenya, are not likely to reveal very much detail, just as the Annual Report of the Ford Motor Company reveals little about the chief executive officer's (CEO) benefits package or the inner workings of the Lincoln-Mercury Division.

Standards in financial reporting vary from country to country, from audit firm to audit firm and from NGO to NGO. Donation income, for example, can only be sampled by an auditor. The value ascribed to goods or services-in-kind are notoriously hard to monitor and judge. The portion of expenses allocated to administration, or the division between fundraising and development education, is handled differently from one NGO and one auditor to another. This is not to say that there are no standards. Some NGO codes of conduct deal with such subjects, as do those of some governments. For example, in the United States, commodities are usually valued by USAID according to government guidelines, but beyond that, there are few rules. In 1991, Feed the Children listed its non-government in-kind income at 79 per cent.[3] The following year, however, state and federal regulators began to examine in-kind donations more carefully, and found that Feed the Children had based its calculations on retail rather than wholesale prices. As a result of negative publicity, the organization revised its 1991 figures, reducing the value of in-kind donations from $86.3 million to $61 million. This had the effect of boosting the cost of its fundraising and administration by 30 per cent.[4] The change brought it more into line with guidelines issued by the Association of Evangelical Relief and Development Organizations, guidelines which discourage the use of retail pricing and which recommend discounting when a product is impaired or nearing its expiry date. The guidelines, however, developed to forestall greater government regulation worked in this case only when government action became imminent.

This is probably an extreme case, but virtually all NGOs engage in some sort of number-fudging. The reasons are simple. Charities are supposed to be run on a shoe-string. Administrative costs are supposed to be as close to zero as possible, the lower the better. The American business magazine, *Money*, 'rates' charitable organizations every year, usually against only one criterion: the cost of overheads. In its 1994 ranking of American charities, the International Rescue Committee was what the magazine called 'the winner', because its overheads were only 7.7 per cent. The Mennonite Central Committee and Save the Children–US came next, but the magazine offered no comment on the quality of their work.[5] Its 1996 ranking put the American Red Cross at the top of the 'efficiency' sweepstakes because it 'dedicated an average of 92 per cent of its income to programs over the past three years – a higher percentage than any other group'.[6] This is like saying that the Lada is the best car in the world (or the most efficient) because it is the cheapest.

Another way of getting at the question of financial transparency (which is at least a partial code word for 'administrative costs') is to look at a specific problem involving one UN agency and its NGO partners. While not specifically related to development assistance, a recent study of the funding relationship between NGOs and UNHCR reveals some interesting dilemmas in transparency for both donor and recipient.[7] The study started with a limited focus on UNHCR's growing unwillingness to contribute towards the headquarters overheads of partner NGOs. UNHCR saw 'its relationship with its implementing partners as one of, precisely, partnership, and draws a clear distinction between such partnerships and contractual relationships ... UNHCR [expects] ... suitable agencies ... at least to cover the overhead administrative costs related to the project from their own or other non-UNHCR resources.'[8]

The principle of partnership, however, begins to come apart around the question of which elements of a project the NGO and the institutional donor should support, around the sharing of both the attractive as well as unattractive but necessary costs. The 'principle' assumes that NGOs have unrestricted funds that they can apply to overheads, or to other aspects of projects that are jointly funded with other institutional donors. Some do. Many do not. In fact many of the very largest NGOs have difficulty in balancing the allocation of funds between situations where they can gain financial leverage (as with UN agencies that might provide a 'match' of 50 per cent or even 95 per cent), and situations where there are no opportunities for matching or leveraging but where there are very real needs.

Between 1990 and 1995, most NGOs involved in emergency work conducted major appeals on behalf of Somalia and Rwanda, and there were selective appeals for the Horn of Africa, Cambodia, Angola and Mozambique. Such appeals generate funds which may be used alone, or to co-finance projects with institutional donors. But the money generated from these appeals is both finite and restricted. Many of the NGOs that have enjoyed significant private donor growth over the past few years are currently experiencing a plateau or even a decline, because the emergencies have left the news. This means that less money is available for continuing emergencies, and even less is available for the 'quieter' emergencies that do not make the headlines.

Unrestricted funding has, in fact, been declining in many NGOs for several years. One way that NGOs have increased the reach of both their restricted and their unrestricted funds has been through bilateral and multilateral organizations. Co-financing obviously makes sense as long as there are resources available. The more an institutional donor is willing to provide, the more the NGO can accomplish. When an institutional donor is willing to fund all the programme costs, it gives the NGO a very real boost in terms of its field capacity. But when there is an unrealistic restriction or a moratorium on overheads at headquarters (HQ), as in the case of UNHCR, the institutional donor does five things.

First, it forces the NGO to cut corners on necessary and legitimate HQ administrative costs, such as planning; the recruitment, selection and support of personnel; procurement and shipping; programme monitoring, reporting and evaluation; financial management and reporting; and public relations with governments, other multilateral agencies and the media. Cutting corners is not the same thing as observing efficiencies. All donors expect NGOs to be professional, to move quickly in an emergency, to apply the best talent available to the task at hand, to be effective and to report clearly, often in a prescribed fashion and on time. And yet somehow, this is supposed to be achievable for 5 per cent or 7 per cent or 10 per cent of programme – usually an arbitrary blanket figure, regardless of whether the programme relates to feeding, logistics, health care or water and sanitation. Any cost accountant would quickly demolish the 'principle' on which such calculations are based, and any private sector CEO guilty of such amateurism would quickly find him or herself without work. By refusing to pay any HQ overheads, a funding agency will simply exacerbate an already serious problem, and will add credence to the frequently heard charge that NGOs are little more than amateurs. When donors pay for amateurs, they should not be surprised when they get amateurs.

Second, by using more and more private donor money – virtually the only source of unrestricted funds available – for administration, NGOs run the very serious risk of being charged with false advertising and losing the very basis of their existence. A public attack on Save the Children–US in 1995 criticized the organization's president for saying that 'In general, we use these private funds to leverage other sources of funding, thus achieving a multiplier effect in terms of our private donations.' The article went on to say that the money Save the Children raises from the American public is not used for work overseas, 'Save in fact uses those funds to pay for administering the restricted money it gets from the government.'[9] And, no doubt, from United Nations agencies.

Third, there is an unusual double standard. It could be regarded as unethical for intermediate institutional donors – governments, the European Union (EU), UN agencies – to take overheads from the original funding source, taxpayers, and then to refuse a contribution towards the legitimate costs of organizations that are actually doing the work.

Fourth, it rewards and contributes to the growth of NGOs with unrestricted money, without questioning how they obtain it. Often those with the fewest financial restrictions are those most guilty of overly dramatic, 'starving baby' fundraising tactics. Widely criticized by the development community at large, by UNDP's *Human Development Report* and by most NGO umbrella groups, such fundraising nevertheless continues apace. By encouraging and working with such organizations, UN agencies could, in effect, contribute to 'the pornography of poverty', reversing the development education efforts that NGOs have struggled with for the past three decades.

Fifth, it encourages rivalry for scarce unrestricted donor funds. One of the consequences is the 'unregulated' and 'fiercely competitive aid market' described by Mark Duffield elsewhere in this volume.

NGOs deal with restrictions on overheads, a policy that is not restricted by any means to UNHCR, in a variety of ways. One is by covering as much of their administrative cost as possible through grants and recoverables from their home governments. After that, the colour of the water becomes darker, indeed less transparent. Among the techniques available for muddying the water are the following:

- *The shell game.* By deft manipulation of various institutional donors, an NGO moves the dreaded HQ expense around under a series of institutional funding arrangements. This may mean that the organization never actually raises private donor funds for this unattractive item, or – in some cases – for anything else.
- *Rubber mathematics.* The NGO assigns as much administration to 'programme costs' as possible, and where necessary pushes HQ costs to the field if this is what an institutional donor wants. The media attack on Save the Children–US explained and censured this practice in considerable detail.
- *The $10 donor in Moose Jaw pays.* There is an impression that some NGOs are rolling in money. It is true that many NGOs have grown significantly in the past few years, despite talk of 'compassion fatigue', and despite ODA cutbacks in all but a few of the countries that are members of the Organization for Economic Cooperation and Development (OECD). Most of the growth has, in fact, been associated with the emergencies of the past five years, and so it would appear that NGOs should be even more capable now than in the past, of providing at least a modicum of support to joint endeavours with UNHCR and other agencies. What this would actually mean, were it true, is that the individual donor – the one least able to stomach overheads – is expected to pay the lion's share.[10]

Various options to the current dilemma present themselves. In the case of UN agencies unwilling to consider a fair division of costs, NGOs could consider campaigning to reduce their governments' contributions to the agency in question, in favour of increased contributions to NGOs. In the case of UNHCR, NGOs are, in fact, handling as much as one-third of the organization's deliveries now, with UNHCR acting more or less as an expensive broker. UNHCR could continue to play a coordinating and political role, advising and organizing NGOs. But if funds went straight from governments to NGOs, the administration costs that are now being incurred by a UN organization (with all the allowances, salaries, offices and associated costs), could be transferred instead to less expensive organizations actually working directly with refugees or in development.

A more sensible approach would see UN agencies agree to a simple principle: if an agency were to support 60 per cent of a project, it would support 60 per cent of the entire cost of the project, including 60 per cent of a negotiated figure for HQ overheads. If it were to support 100 per cent of the costs, this would mean 100 per cent of all costs. UN agencies would need support from governments in such a decision because they (like most NGOs) are under considerable and often unrealistic pressure to do a lot more with a lot less.

Administrative recovery rates for partner organizations, both overseas and at headquarters, need to be established for different types of activity. The myth of the tiny overhead is a dangerous time-bomb waiting to explode in the face of NGOs, UN agencies and donor governments. It encourages false accounting and denies the need to do development work effectively and professionally. It could poison the climate for official development assistance as well as emergency aid if it is not addressed properly and soon. USAID has had a negotiated overhead arrangement with NGOs for years, the Negotiated Indirect Cost Rate Agreement (NICRA). It takes time to establish this agreement, but the resulting transparency, harmony and fairness far outweigh the time and expense involved.

A change in mind-set?

The debates around money and financial transparency are mostly not about partnership; they are about leveraging. As long as a donor agency sees a financial opportunity in playing one NGO off against another (and as long as NGOs can gain advantage by undercutting one another), there will be administrative strife. UN agencies could rise above this and take a leadership role in solving some of the problems by establishing a co-financing formula, perhaps like USAID's NICRA. This would probably be more expensive in cash terms than the current *ad hoc* arrangements, but it would mean that partners could be selected on the basis of track record and expertise, rather than on the basis of false claims of financial modesty.

In the end, it would be more effective and more efficient. And it might help to better explain the real cost of doing development work to the taxpayers and small donors who have been fed a misleading public relations line for years. Whatever the formula, UN agencies could take a lead in developing greater openness and transparency in the way donor agencies deal with NGOs.

TRANSPARENCY 2: THE QUALITY OF WORK

NGOs are an expression of people's need for organization, self-improvement and change. Those that extend beyond their own community can reach places that governments and multilateral agencies cannot, dealing directly with the poor. Using participatory techniques, they are often more effective and less expensive than traditional, top-down development efforts. They can be flexible and innovative, and have pioneered new ways of thinking about health, the environment, gender, technology, small enterprise and credit. They have become recognized as an important element of civil society, fostering citizen awareness and participation in development, and as part of a new approach to governmental accountability and transparency.

Despite the size of the NGO community, however, despite its achievements and the support it receives from ordinary people, from governments and from UN agencies, there are serious doubts about this totally untarnished image. In 1982, Judith Tendler examined 75 evaluations of NGO projects. Her findings were sharply critical of what she called 'NGO articles of faith'. Effectiveness in reaching the poor, in participation, in cost-effectiveness and innovation were all open to serious doubt, and were often 'more important as articles of faith than as standards of self-assessment. That participation leads to improvement in people's lives is an article of faith for [NGOs], not a hypothesis that one is interested in testing.'[11]

More recently, increasing NGO allocations – sometimes at the expense of bilateral and multilateral budgets – along with greater demands for transparency, accountability and effectiveness, have combined to place NGOs under greater scrutiny than ever before. Thus, evaluation is becoming increasingly important. Large NGO omnibus evaluations have been carried out by the governments of Norway (1995), Finland (1994), Sweden (1995), Australia (1995) and the United Kingdom (1992 and 1995). The Overseas Development Institute has conducted a series of NGO evaluations and studies: on poverty alleviation, (1989–90); on NGOs, the state and sustainable agricultural development (1993); and on the changing role of NGOs in the provision of relief and rehabilitation assistance (1993–4). More books on NGOs probably appeared during the first half of the 1990s than was the case over the previous two decades.

The results are mixed. The 1995 ODA study found that the majority of projects were successful and that significant benefits were received by the poor, but that there had been little change in the existing social or economic status quo, and that institutional and financial sustainability had not been achieved. The Australian review covered 216 projects and found that 90 per cent had achieved satisfactory or better achievement of objectives, but observed that sustainability, financial viability and the involvement of women in project planning and implementation could be improved.[12] The Swedish study found that

> the overwhelming majority [of projects] either have achieved, or are well on their way to achieving, the stated and immediate objectives for which SIDA's NGO Division provided the funds ... [But] when the projects are judged against more and more of the nine broader criteria against which they were assessed, their aggregate performance rating dropped progressively. Indeed, very few of the projects examined scored consistently high marks in relation to a majority of these broader criteria.[13]

In 1977, John Sommer, writing about American NGO self-evaluation, observed that everyone talks about it, but few do anything about it. At that time, Sommer saw changes, a 'real trend toward more regular evaluation', but much of what he described was taking place as a result of pressure from USAID. Many of the evaluations were being conducted by outsiders, and many failed to get beyond immediate project aims and objectives.[14]

Five years later, Tendler found that little had really changed: an 'emphasis on the number of people trained, the amounts of equipment supplied, etc. with little real attention to processes, sequences of action and impact'. A 1986 USAID study found that NGO 'measurement of project costs and the valuing of benefits need improvement ... Unfortunately, many [NGOs] had not been very effective at documenting and replicating their innovative experiences. Lessons learned by project managers are generally not shared with other [NGOs], host country institutions, and others.'[15]

In 1990, a British study found the same thing: 'For most British development-oriented NGOs evaluation is still very new. The vast majority of projects and programmes funded by British NGOs in developing countries are not subject to any sort of formal evaluation ... The majority of NGOs do not carry out *any* evaluation.'[16] A 1995 ODA review observes that 'Relatively little emphasis ... seems to have been placed by NGOs, at least until very recently, on evaluations which rigorously examine the impact of their projects and which draw out lessons learned. Where 'evaluations have been undertaken, reports on projects frequently consider only whether the project's outputs have been delivered and not the project's overall impact. Very few of these evaluations have been made publicly available.'[17]

Is all this because NGOs actually do bad work, know it and want to
cover up the terrible truth? Hardly. There are many good reasons to
monitor and evaluate. Among them are:

- to see what is being achieved;
- to measure progress against the objectives of the programme;
- to improve monitoring and management;
- to identify strengths and weaknesses in order to strengthen the
  programme;
- to see if the effort was effective;
- to analyse the cost benefit and determine if costs were reasonable;
- to collect information for better planning management;
- to share experience, to help prevent others making similar mistakes or
  to encourage them to use similar methods; and
- to improve effectiveness for greater impact.[18]

These and other common-or-garden reasons for evaluation can be found
in a dozen books about evaluation. What is seldom included, however, is
an explanation for why NGOs actually avoid evaluation so studiously.
Among those provided by NGOs themselves are:

- complexity (social programmes do not lend themselves to measurement – what counts is process and intangibles such as empowerment
  and capacity-building);
- inappropriateness (it is obvious we are doing good work – attempts to
  evaluate could undermine and demoralize the volunteers and workers
  upon whom we depend);
- time (it would take up valuable time from managers who are already
  stretched to the limit); and
- cost (because our overheads are already overstretched, we can't afford
  it. And anyway, it would divert money from important programming).

There is some validity in these points, but not enough to warrant the
overwhelming paucity of public NGO evaluation that has marked the past
three decades. More fundamental reasons quickly surface at any off-the-
record discussion among NGO workers:

- danger (the overheads are actually a lot higher than the organization
  has made out to the funder – see 'Transparency 1' above);
- danger (the NGO 'projectized' certain activities for the funder, but in
  fact they are part of a larger programme and cannot be disaggregated
  for the purposes of evaluation);

- danger (in order to get financial support, the NGO promised the funder more than it could deliver – a problem not unique to NGOs);
- danger (in a highly competitive world, any hint of failure or under-achievement could result in major cuts); and
- fear (a logical consequence of perceived danger).

A change in mind-set?

The first change has been discussed. It is necessary to reach realistic and appropriate estimates of what it costs to carry out a programme, ensuring that this is properly understood by all parties to an agreement, and sharing the burden fairly between the NGO and the funding agency.

A second prerequisite is for donors to de-emphasize the control and verification function of evaluation, and to put learning back on the agenda. If NGO learning is to be encouraged (and if others are to learn from what NGOs learn) funding decisions must be distanced from evaluation. In other words, if a failed project results in financial punishment, the incentives for objective evaluation and learning are effectively reduced to zero. There must be a tolerance for failure. Disciplinarians may have trouble with the idea of appearing to indulge failure, but it does not mean that anything and everything goes. Failure should carry a stigma when mistakes are repeated or suppressed, when available lessons are ignored and basic research is avoided, and when square wheels are continuously reinvented.

Joint evaluations of common programmes are an obvious way of bridging the very large gap that currently exists between donors and NGOs. For example, WFP wanted to evaluate its collaboration with NGOs in Angola at the end of 1996, with a view to finding out what had worked and what had not and to strengthen collaboration in the future. The standard approach of the past would have been for WFP to carry out its own evaluation, using its own staff or consultants. In this case, WFP opened up the terms of reference to embrace NGO concerns, including the question of whether NGOs could or should be complementary 'partners' or simply contractors. The team included three WFP staff, but it also included representatives of NGOs with which WFP had been working closely over the years.

One way of reducing costs and spreading the lessons learned from NGO work might be the development of sectoral evaluations conducted across the geographical and political borders that constrain donors and NGOs, as well as their projects and programmes in the South. Conducted by a neutral third party, such as a United Nations agency or a university or think-tank, such evaluations could serve the learning purpose as well as the verification imperative, informing and teaching donors and NGOs alike.

A third prerequisite is to increase the level of predictability. NGOs seldom know from one day to the next which donors are going to support them, for what reasons and for what period. The problem is especially acute for southern NGOs where the philanthropic base is weak, and where donor agency dependency is higher. Whether recipients of a grant or a contract, NGOs are vulnerable to the predilections of the latest aid manager arriving on the scene, to political considerations and to a wide variety of other donor vagaries. In 1993, USAID pulled out of Pakistan for political reasons, leaving several NGOs – and the detailed contracts that they had signed – high and very dry. In 1996, the Canadian International Development Agency (CIDA) cancelled funding to Partnership Africa-Canada with only a few weeks' notice, creating havoc among many of the African NGOs and umbrella groups for which it had been an important source of income.

To the extent that UN agencies want to work with NGOs, consideration must be given to supporting realistic planning and management coherence. Care must be taken to ensure that NGOs are treated in a professional and consistent manner, and that great fluctuations in demand are avoided. UN agencies themselves experience the problems of on-again, off-again funding. For NGOs it can be costly and even destructive. A larger role for the UN family of agencies in this regard is suggested in the following section.

TRANSPARENCY 3: ACCOUNTABILITY

An oft-repeated, hoary old chestnut posits that NGOs are basically un-accountable, that many are self-appointed do-gooders and that they have rubber-stamp boards of directors. There may be more than a germ of truth in such views, but they do not reveal the entire picture.

To whom are corporations accountable? The first answer will always be 'shareholders'. But the CEO of a private firm is also answerable in one way or another to his or her board of directors, to employees and their union if there is one, to a variety of government regulatory bodies and – if goodwill and customers figure in the product – to the public at large. NGOs (like most institutions) also have multiple accountabilities. They are accountable to their boards and members. This accountability may be weak or strong, as it can be in the private sector. They are accountable to their staff. They are accountable to their donors, both small and large. Failure to please will mean a reduction in income. They are accountable to the media, upon which they rely for much of their publicity. A scandal can be very damaging to image and income. They are accountable – perhaps in most cases more in aim than in deed – to their beneficiaries. They are accountable to their peers, an accountability sometimes expressed in a code of conduct. Such codes exist in the United States, Bangladesh, Kenya, New Zealand and many other countries. And in most countries there is some sort of government regulatory body to which they also owe a degree of accountability.

Singly, these accountabilities are often weak. Taken together, they exert a powerful influence on the behaviour of an NGO. When one of the accountabilities, however, grows out of proportion to others, problems occur. An overactive interest in pleasing the ten-dollar donor can lead an organization to emphasize starving-baby fundraising, possibly weakening real public understanding of broader development issues, muting NGO advocacy and undermining long-term support for substantive change. Overweening desire to please a major institutional donor can undermine the very essence of what makes an organization *non*-governmental. Too often bilateral and multilateral donors behave as though they, above all others, are owed the primary NGO allegiance. Codes of conduct are notoriously non-binding; for instance, a 1994 NGO scandal in Australia caused the government to de mand a much stronger code than had been devised by NGOs themselves. A media scandal, a political *faux pas* or a change in government can lead to the sudden introduction of difficult new legislation. NGOs in Bangladesh, Pakistan, Sierra Leone, Kenya, Bosnia and Malawi have all struggled with new and sometimes not very helpful legislation in recent years.

In 1995, the London-based Commonwealth Foundation issued a publication entitled *Non-Governmental Organisations: Guidelines for Good Policy and Practice*. The product of more than two years of effort, of regional NGO meetings in Asia, Africa and elsewhere and of extensive government consultation, and of a study of NGO codes in a dozen countries, it goes well beyond the standard set of NGO guidelines. Its most important innovation is its guidelines for governments and donor agencies as well as for NGOs. This is an extremely important breakthrough, one endorsed by the Commonwealth Heads of Government Meeting in Auckland in 1995. The ink was barely dry on their endorsement, however, when the rush began to violate both the spirit and the letter of the guidelines. Canada may have been the first, less than two months later, cancelling a whole range of funding mechanisms for Canadian and southern NGOs without a word of warning or consultation.

Transparency and accountability are increasingly demanded of NGOs (and of UN agencies). In many cases, however, the demands are made by withering government aid agencies that have transformed large parts of their own effort into subsidies for the private sector. While greater transparency and accountability in NGOs are undoubtedly required, care must be taken to ensure that the demands are not simply an effort by fading government bureaucracies to retain control through proxies. Ultimately, accountability is a two-way street. If governments expect transparency and accountability, they have to be bound – at least in some measure – by similar principles themselves. Otherwise they should not be surprised by its absence in NGOs. Just as NGO codes require provisions that make them much more binding than they are at present, so do governments and donor agencies need to be held accountable for the way that they behave towards NGOs.

Here, then, is an important and timely opportunity for the United Nations. The challenge is to find a mechanism for carrying the Commonwealth Foundation's Guidelines forward into broader public discussion, and to seek ways to hold governments, NGOs and funding agencies more accountable for their actions and behaviour.

A change in mind-set?

Where a UN agency is basically interested in working with an NGO to deliver services, there are other important considerations. For example, the impact of NGO interventions can be enhanced in different ways:

- *By increasing the size of the organization or its programme, and thus its impact.* In providing major support for the non-formal education programmes of several Bangladeshi NGOs, for example, UNICEF has dramatically increased their impact on children in Bangladesh.
- *Through strategic alliances and strategic funding, and by increasing impact through a process of influence, networking, training and legal or policy reform.* The same support for the non-formal education work of NGOs in Bangladesh is designed in part to, and has succeeded in, influencing the education policies of the government of Bangladesh and other donors. UNDP's modest support for the very large, World Bank-supported Janasaviya Trust Fund in Sri Lanka, gave it a place at the table and a voice when it became obvious to all but the World

Bank that the project had serious problems. UNDP is currently engaged in an exercise to take the lessons learned in Pakistan's Aga Khan Rural Support Programme to other countries in South Asia. In supporting the development of a gender strategy within the American NGO ACCION, UNIFEM was able, indirectly, to improve gender strategies within dozens of southern NGOs and their micro-enterprise work.

- *By osmosis.* Where diffusion and impact are informal and spontaneous, such as the influence UNICEF has had globally on public awareness about the importance of immunization, NGO programmes also are passive beneficiaries.

Much of what NGOs know can be promulgated in another way, by involving them in the planning and evaluation of UN programmes, even where NGOs may not have direct involvement. Thinking the strategy through before embarking on an NGO partnership might help to make the difference between modest leveraging, and something that could make a longer-term institutional difference of lasting significance.

CONCLUSIONS

In a roundabout way, this article has addressed the question of whether NGOs can share some of the UN burden in the years ahead. The answer is a qualified 'yes'. It is qualified in the sense that it is already happening, in some cases on an impressive scale. But it is qualified also in the sense that it is not happening very well, or very consistently. UN agencies are taking advantage of the same opportunities as other multilateral and bilateral organizations, and they are making many of the same mistakes. The UN could, like the others, do better. But it could also do things differently. As a body of global institutions predicated on a rather special idea at the outset of the UN Charter, 'We the peoples', it could use its good offices to sort out some of the serious problems that currently beset an important part of civil society.

Some of these have been discussed at length: demystifying the cost of doing business; turning evaluation into a learning process rather than a tool for verification and control; enhancing the accountability of both NGOs and governments for development results; helping to put new meaning into the almost hackneyed idea of an 'enabling environment' for civil society and for sustainable development. These, more than projects and training programmes, would genuinely contribute to greater NGO capacity. And in the process, they might help to build greater public support for the United Nations.

NOTES

1. *NGOs and Official Donors*, ODI Briefing Note, Overseas Development Institute, London, August 1995.
2. R. Sholes and J. Covey, *Partnerships for Development: USAID and PVO/NGO Relationships*, INTRAC Occasional Papers Series, No. 11, Oxford, 1996.
3. *Voluntary Foreign Aid Programs 1993*, USAID, Washington, DC, 1993.
4. G. Williams, 'More scrutiny for a relief charity', *Chronicle of Philanthropy* (Washington, DC), 5 April 1994.
5. 'The top U.S. charities', *Money*, December 1994.
6. 'Which charities merit your money?', *Money*, November 1996.
7. I. Smillie, *The Cherry Orchard: UNHCR, CARE Canada, and the Low Cost of Assisting Refugees*, CARE Canada, December 1995.
8. EC/1995/SC.2/CRP.27, UNHCR, Geneva, 4 September 1995.
9. M. Maren, 'A different kind of child abuse', *Penthouse*, December 1995. ABC Television News also investigated the story, widening the criticism and the audience.
10. UNHCR did modify its position on overheads for NGOs in 1996 following considerable pressure from two dozen of its largest NGO partners in North America and Europe.
11. J. Tendler, *Turning Private Voluntary Organizations Into Development Agencies: Questions for Evaluation* (Washington, DC: USAID, 1982), p. 129.
12. 'NGO programs effectiveness review', draft, AusAid, Canberra, 1995.
13. R. Riddell, A. Bebbington and L. Peck, *Promoting Development by Proxy: The Development Impact of Government Support to Swedish NGOs* (London: Overseas Development Institute, 1995), pp. ix–x.
14. J. Sommer, *Beyond Charity: U.S. Voluntary Aid for a Changing Third World* (Washington, DC: Overseas Development Council, 1997), p. 80.
15. *Development Effectiveness of Private Voluntary Organisations* (Washington, DC: USAID, 1986), pp. 4–5.
16. R. Riddell, *Judging Success: Evaluating NGO Approaches to Alleviating Poverty in Developing Countries* (London: Overseas Development Institute, 1990), p. 5.
17. M. A. Surr, *Evaluations of NGO Development Projects: Synthesis Report* (London: Overseas Development Administration, 1995), p. 13.
18. Adapted from M. T. Feuerstein, *Partners in Evaluation: Evaluating Development and Community Programmes with Participants* (London: Overseas Development Institute, 1986).

10 NGOs and the Environment: from Knowledge to Action
Sheila Jasanoff

The place of non-governmental organizations (NGOs) in international governance seems nowhere more securely established than in the field of environmental action.[1] Within the United Nations system, NGOs have been recognized as essential contributors to environmental protection for well over a decade. The 1987 report of the World Commission on Environment and Development, *Our Common Future*, urged governments 'to recognise and extend NGOs' right to know, and have access to information on the environment and natural resources; their right to be consulted and to participate in decision-making on activities likely to have a significant effect on the environment; and their right to legal remedies and redress when their health or environment may be seriously affected.'[2] The 1992 United Nations Conference on Environment and Development (UNCED) held in Rio de Janeiro confirmed by numbers alone that NGOs had taken their place beside states and intergovernmental organizations (IGOs), in particular, those of the United Nations (UN) system, as rightful participants in environmental management. The Global Forum for NGOs held concurrently with the official Earth Summit drew representatives from some 7,000 organizations, outnumbering governments present by about one hundred to one.[3] More important, the intense preparatory activity in the non-governmental sector leading up to and through the Rio conference showed that environmental NGOs had developed extensive skills in scientific and technical exchange, policy-making and policy-implementation, which supplemented their more traditional roles in campaigning, activism and ideological consciousness raising.[4]

Although the centrality of NGOs in environmental action cannot be doubted, systematic assessments of their role, especially in relation to other governing institutions, are scarce. In part, the explosive growth of environmental activism over the past few decades confounds analysis. The term 'NGO' can be applied in principle to an enormous range of environmental actors, from tiny, grassroots coalitions of conservationists or pollution victims to mature, well-funded, technically expert, multinational organizations possessing many of the characteristics of state bureaucracies but without their political accountability.[5] Some of these groups coalesced from the start around environmental concerns, while others have incorporated environmental objectives into broader agendas of social development. Some NGOs, like Europe's staid nature conservancies, have been in action for more than a century, with practices shaped by culture, place and history; others, like the daringly entrepreneurial Greenpeace, have won a place at the international policy table after less than a quarter of a century of world-wide environmental advocacy.[6] Major 'non-governmental interest groups'[7] – political parties, labour unions, industries and trade associations – have spun off a host of specialized NGOs and NGO coalitions to deal with the environmental matters that specifically concern them.[8] Scientific societies and committees, including those established under international regimes, constitute still another class of environmental NGOs with strong claims to political neutrality. Together, these groups display a bewildering diversity of form, function, style and expertise, with missions ranging from research to litigation, from lobbying to community education, and from monitoring to natural resource protection. Clearly, environmental NGOs conform to no simple taxonomy;[9] arguably, the only structural feature they have in common is their formal independence from the state.[10]

Function, then, seems more promising than structure as a starting point for teasing apart the possible lines of collaboration between NGOs and IGOs in the environmental domain. At the heart of environmental decision-making is an attempt to connect knowledge about the world (expressed often, but not only, as scientific knowledge) with actions designed to advance particular visions of natural and social well-being. It is this link between knowledge and action that provides environmental NGOs with their primary point of political intervention. The proliferation of such groups in recent years can be seen in large measure as a challenge to the perceived shortcomings of governments and industry in acting on the world's growing repositories of environmental knowledge. How can NGOs most effectively fulfil their appointed role, and how in particular can their work usefully complement or extend that of IGOs?

NGO activity in building, or rebuilding, the knowledge–action link can take three major forms, each of which carries different opportunities for collaboration with IGOs (see Table 10.1 for a summary). First, and perhaps most familiar, is the role of NGOs as critics of accepted frameworks of environmental knowledge and regulatory policy. The NGOs that most visibly serve this function in the international arena have usually established their credibility through technical expertise and apparent lack of

Table 10.1   NGOs in environmental governance

Function	NGO characteristics	Forums	Contributions
Criticism/reframing	Statelike organizations	• International regimes	• Boundary testing • Epistemic change
	Grassroots organizations	• Local controversies • 'Scientific relief'	• Local knowledge • Epistemic change
	All organizations	• Local and global media	• Symbolic politics • Epistemic change
Epistemic networks	All organizations	• Policy implementation	• Bridging interests • Bridging non-state–state–IGO • Bridging science and values
Technology transfer	All organizations	• Policy formulation • Policy implementation	• Aggregation • Adaptation • Interpretation • Translation

economic interest. A less structured but no less significant role is played by the thousands upon thousands of grassroots organizations whose criticism of dominant scientific and policy frameworks is founded on long-standing experiences in resource management and local environmental knowledge.

A second way in which NGOs can influence the transition from knowledge to action is by creating more inclusive 'epistemic networks' around nationally or internationally defined environmental objectives.[11] Environmental policy networks are most often conceived in the literature as the work of like-minded technical and administrative elites.[12] In many areas of environmental protection, however, success is contingent on the willingness of ordinary citizens to accept the validity of official policy framings and to participate in their implementation. NGOs may be able to facilitate such consensual action because of their experience in integrating environmental concerns with other aspects of community life, such as development, rural poverty, rights of indigenous people, women's emancipation or children's welfare. The ability of environmental NGOs to bridge the lay–expert, activist–professional and local–global divides thus emerges as a particularly important resource in their cooperative arrangements with IGOs.

The third route by which NGOs can take part in the construction of effective knowledge–action links is through information dissemination and technology transfer. IGO–NGO collaboration with respect to such activities can help compensate for the lack of capacity in state institutions. NGO involvement in monitoring and enforcement, for example, is widely recognized as essential by students of international environmental regimes.[13] The three forms of NGO activity in constituting the knowledge–action link are discussed in depth below. A theme throughout is participation, which relates to questions about the accountability of environmental NGOs.

CRITICISM AND REFRAMING

Science is one of the pillars on which modern environmentalism was founded; yet, paradoxically, scientific controversy has proved to be one of the most intractable problems confronting environmental policy-makers. Since Rachel Carson's stirring call to action in *Silent Spring*,[14] NGOs have recognized that scientific knowledge is potentially one of their strongest allies – and sometimes an obdurate impediment – in the struggle to protect the environment. On issues as disparate as whaling, oil spills, ocean dumping of chemical or radioactive wastes, the safety of nuclear power, river-valley development or climate change, disputes among environmentalists, industry and frequently the state have centred on different assessments of the probability and magnitude of adverse environmental effects. In such exchanges, NGOs may usefully open up the debate either by questioning prevailing expert opinion or by expanding the available information base with relevant bodies of local knowledge.

Questioning the boundaries

Although science is environmentalism's favourite battleground, decades of research on environmental controversies indicate that clashes over science are often the surface manifestation of deeper political or cultural commitments that predispose actors to downplay some sources of uncertainty about nature and to emphasize others.[15] The framing of environmental problems, in other words, incorporates more basic social and political as well as scientific judgements.[16] In turn, conflicts that are ostensibly about scientific facts turn out on closer inspection to reflect underlying differences in the framing of the problem by opposing interests, including its causes, severity, boundaries, distribution and possible solutions. Standing outside the peripheries of official, usually state-sponsored, knowledge production, NGOs are particularly well-situated to observe the limitations of dominant expert framings, to question unexplained assumptions, to expose tacit value choices and to offer alternative interpretations of ambiguous data.

Scientific experts frequently protect their authority to deal with uncertain science through a sociological mechanism known as 'boundary work'.[17] This is the process by which expert committees assign the vast array of issues lying between the two ideal–typical poles of 'pure science' and 'pure policy' to one or the other side of the science–policy boundary. Issues deemed to be 'scientific' in this process can then resolved by experts without need for full political or legal accountability.[18] Such boundary drawing is virtually indispensable in environmental decision-making, where total paralysis results unless institutional means are found to cope with uncertainty.[19] Yet, continual questioning of established boundaries is equally essential in order to increase transparency of expert decision-making and allow, as needed, for the incorporation of ethical perspectives and new social or scientific knowledge.

Participation in international environmental regimes provides a formal and much needed avenue for policy criticism by NGOs. Stairs and Taylor present a compelling account of productive boundary testing by Greenpeace in the implementation of the London Dumping Convention

(LDC).[20] Scientific groups operating under the LDC must deal with a host of problems that involve judgement and interests along with science: the interpretation of monitoring data, the definition of 'significant' harm, the assessment of comparative risks and the development of multimedia assessment frameworks. To insiders in these groups it becomes almost axiomatic that what they are doing is strictly 'science'. Efforts by Greenpeace and other NGOs to highlight the value-laden character of such determinations have proved effective in removing the blinders of governmental expertise, although it has also produced 'some backlash as the "old guard" have tried to reassert dominance with accusations that the debate has now degenerated because "policy" has been brought into science'.[21] Such defensive boundary work, as noted earlier, is altogether typical in environmental controversies, where challenged experts seek to defend their turf and therewith their right to speak for science. Stairs and Taylor also credit NGO participation under the LDC with highlighting the extent to which predictive models had failed to account for the complexities of marine ecosystems, thereby initiating a 'paradigm shift' from prediction to precaution. This highly consequential move shifted the burden of proof from those who favour caution to those who wish to undertake potentially damaging activity.

It is reasonable to expect sustained policy criticism and reframing such as has occurred in the LDC from those NGOs that most closely resemble governmental agencies in their grasp of resources, technical expertise and political capacity. Greenpeace, for example, is known for specialist skills in the field of marine pollution, as are other large environmental NGOs such as the Worldwide Fund for Nature, Friends of the Earth and the Sierra Club in their respective areas of environmental involvement. The assimilation of NGOs to statelike status increases their influence but may bring with it the same problems of partial vision and ideological excess that befall experts serving states and IGOs. Thus, Stairs and Taylor point to an ethnocentric bias in Greenpeace's opposition to sewage dumping world-wide.[22] This policy, which is appropriate for northern states disposing of industrially contaminated sewage, may be unnecessary as well as unacceptably costly for less industrialized southern states with different economic and pollution problems. Yearley, as argued below, provides another example in connection with the protection of endangered species.[23]

One of the institutional strengths of NGOs is that they can, when needed, pursue their goals outside the relatively inflexible channels of (inter)governmental communication and negotiation. NGOs' skill in manipulating symbols and grabbing media attention has helped move issues up on official policy agendas and tilted public opinion in favour of precautionary environmental action. But the downside of symbolic politics is that it substitutes the short-cut of emotion for the longer but more durable pathway of reason. For example, effective use of the media overcame corporate and governmental resistance when a determined campaign by Greenpeace led to the 1995 decision by Shell, UK to postpone the planned deepwater disposal of the Brent Spar oil storage tanks. Some have seen this as an important victory for the precautionary principle, since the effects on the marine environment could not be precisely known. Others, however, believe that Greenpeace's strategy placed an essentially ideological vision of the purity of the seas ahead of reasoned selection between alternative frameworks of risk perception and risk management – and perhaps weakened the NGO's credibility in the eyes of marine scientists.

Local knowledge

Environmental controversies occur not only through structured confrontations between governmental and non-governmental experts but also when the impartial and authoritative problem-framings offered by science seem to contradict people's lived experience of their environment. Thus, popular distrust of ruling institutions, rooted in historical experience, often gets translated into uncertainty about the government's scientific assessments.[24] Similarly, localized knowledge of nature gained through non-scientific activities such as farming or grazing may come into conflict with assumptions built into generic scientific models.

Scientific studies, in particular, may presume a homogeneity in environmental conditions or people's relationship with nature that is belied by the experience of local residents. Precision in science is often achieved by narrowing or simplifying the field of enquiry, at times with serious loss of accuracy with respect to local conditions. Thompson et al. offer an instructive example in discussing the causes of flooding in the great river basins of northern India. The problem, they say, can be localized at one level in a long, narrow strip of land extending from Kashmir in the west to Assam and Burma in the east. This picture, however, is profoundly misleading, since the 'cause' is not in reality evenly distributed throughout the region:

> The convolutions of the Himalayan landscape, and its underlying geology, render some localities particularly prone to mass wastage and others virtually immune. And some localities are actually subject to mass deposition; that is where the Kathmandu valley came from. Far from the cause being evenly spread, ninety percent of the 'damage' may result from ten percent of the land ... What is needed is a rejection of

homogenizing generalizations and their replacement by a sensitivity for local contexts.[25]

It follows that failure to recognize heterogeneity within the affected territory can lead to highly divergent, and hence controversial, predictions of risk to specific localities – as indeed has happened in India.

Brian Wynne offers a similar example of conflict between scientific homogenization and local heterogeneity in connection with predictions of radiation risks made by British authorities in the wake of the Chernobyl nuclear accident, which deposited heavy but variable quantities of radioactive caesium over parts of Cumbria.[26] In this case, government experts wrongly estimated the likely risk of caesium uptake in the upland grazing environment because their model failed to account for variations in the acidity of the soil in different parts of Britain. Official policies shifted erratically when actual radiation measurements in Cumbrian soil and plants did not conform to predictions issued from London offices. Sheep farmers might perhaps have compensated for the faulty scientific estimates, and resulting policy uncertainty, with adaptive grazing practices, but their knowledge, based on a lifetime of raising sheep on the affected terrain, was not 'scientific' and hence not deemed relevant by the expert policymakers. Such examples make a persuasive case for closer collaboration between local actors and scientists attached to states or IGOs in building a secure knowledge base for environmental action.

Science after disaster

Conflicts between science and local knowledge can occur with special intensity after disasters that disrupt established frames of knowledge and understanding. A telling case arose in December 1984 in the central Indian city of Bhopal, when a runaway chemical reaction at a Union Carbide pesticide plant released a deadly cloud of methyl isocyanate (MIC), killing some 3,500 people and injuring at least 150,000 others. The sheer scale and unexpectedness of the catastrophe paralysed governmental relief efforts and produced unimaginable administrative chaos, compounding the tragedy for survivors.[27] Fortunately for the citizens of Bhopal, NGOs from all over India trooped into the city, bringing vital stores of energy and expertise to supplement the government's limited resources. A number of victims' groups quickly formed and some remained active for many years, at first aggressively pursuing litigation and later campaigning for just compensation and other forms of relief. Without the help of these organizations, both the Indian government and the state of Madhya Pradesh would have been completely overwhelmed, but cooperation between the private and public sectors proved to be anything but straightforward.

A particularly divisive controversy arose around issues of medical diagnosis, monitoring and treatment. NGOs, led by the Medico Friends Circle, spearheaded one set of efforts to document the victims' health, while the Indian Council of Medical Research coordinated the official epidemiological studies. State and non-state investigators parted early on in their strategies for registration as well as treatment. While government officials sought to bound their task by narrowing the definition of potential 'gas victims' (for example, by excluding 'malingerers'), NGOs understandably took a more expansive view, according greater weight to victims' subjective accounts of their condition. Besides reflecting institutional self-interest, the divergent state and non-state medical assessments pointed to fundamental differences between the governmental professionals' mechanistic understanding of disease causation and the more holistic and systemic views of illness espoused by NGOs.[28]

Adherents of different medical world-views clashed sharply over treatment decisions. Physicians associated with NGOs generally accepted the subjective testimony of many victims that they had been helped by treatment with sodium thiosulfate, a recognized antidote to cyanide poisoning;[29] autopsies performed on dead victims appeared to some to provide pathological evidence of cyanide exposure. Yet, after a brief initial consensus, state medical experts vehemently denied the victims' contention, arguing that there were no objective signs of cyanide poisoning. The situation turned ugly when officials decided to enforce their scientific conviction through strong-arm tactics. The police were ordered to break into volunteer clinics, confiscate available stores of thiosulfate and prevent physicians from dispensing the drug.[30] These methods deepened the victims' already considerable distrust of the authorities and erected almost insurmountable barriers against the possibility of a mutually acceptable settlement.

In retrospect, the 'thiosulfate controversy' as it came to be called could only have been avoided through orderly cooperation and accompanying negotiation of epistemic commitments between state experts and local organizers and activists. When disaster struck in Bhopal, very little was known about the toxicological properties of MIC other than the fact that it was extremely irritating and even fatal at very low doses. The human health effects of sublethal doses had never been studied in detail; what little information was available had mostly been produced by Union Carbide and hence was proprietary in nature. Bhopal became in effect a gigantic, if unwitting, natural laboratory where MIC's real impacts on human beings could be studied for the first time. Careful record-keeping and systematic follow-through would have helped to identify and document the reported ill effects, to chart their progress and eventually to resolve the victims' medical and legal claims. But the mix of sympathetic expertise and perceptive local engagement needed to translate medical knowledge to action in the disaster's wake was sadly absent. Instead, the state's professionalized (and far from institutionally coherent) understandings of 'what the medical science said' about MIC clashed unproductively with the victims' equally unsystematic attempts to make scientific sense of their subjective health experiences.

The failure of organized science to take advantage of unorganized local knowledge remains one of the less well comprehended legacies of Bhopal. Although methyl isocyanate may never be implicated again in a tragedy of similar scope, the generic problem for science and medicine disclosed in Bhopal is likely to persist unless better mechanisms are developed to integrate the varied knowledges that constitute the full meaning of disasters.[31] Large-scale releases of toxic substances, in particular, create the preconditions for health, environmental and socio-economic effects that may never have been investigated, or even imagined, in contained, laboratory-based research. As we know from the Chernobyl nuclear plant explosion, the *Exxon Valdez* oil spill, and a multitude of less consequential tragedies, the impacts of such events can cross political boundaries, endure over long periods of time and affect ecosystems as well as human beings. To understand these complex effects in detail requires a combination of observation, recording, interpretation and communication – possibly of several years' duration – that could appropriately be conceptualized as 'scientific relief'. Such sustained monitoring, moreover, is very nearly impossible to carry out without securing the trust and willing participation of affected populations – a task which states or IGOs may be unable to accomplish without support from NGOs. These considerations furnish a strong argument for IGO-NGO collaboration in post-disaster scientific relief. Some possible costs are discussed below.

EPISTEMIC NETWORKS

NGO involvement in the implementation and enforcement of environmental obligations has long been sanctioned under both domestic and international law. Most US environmental legislation, for example, provides for citizen suits against violators in situations where public officials, upon notification, have failed to prosecute offences. Internationally, the status of

NGOs is somewhat less clearly defined and often unofficial, though no less crucial. In a review of major developments in global environmental governance, Peter Sand observes that, while formal supranational regulation could be accounted a failure, convergence toward higher standards of performance was occurring through more decentralized means, such as mutual recognition of national obligations, diffusion and cross-national learning, and the spread of epistemic networks.[32] NGOs have much to contribute to all of these informal processes not only through knowledge creation, as noted above, but also by bridging conceptual and political divides from the local level to the supranational. Their role in protecting wildlife, most particularly through monitoring and enforcement under the Convention on International Trade in Endangered Species of Wild Flora and Fauna (CITES), exemplifies some of the positive and negative aspects of such bridging work.

CITES was signed in March 1973 and went into effect in 1975; by 1995, 131 parties had ratified the convention. The treaty's core consists of a permit system regulating the export, import and re-export of plant and animal species (and products derived from them) that have been listed in one of three appendices, each requiring a different level of protection. The regime depends on reciprocity, with each member state agreeing to recognize the permits issued by any other. Species threatened with extinction, listed in Appendix I ('black list'), and those that could face extinction if trade were not controlled, listed in Appendix II ('grey list'), must be agreed to by a two-thirds vote of the parties. Appendix III, by contrast, consists of species controlled in any member state and notified to the CITES secretariat. There is no international duty to honour or enforce such unilateral restrictions, but it had become standard practice by the late 1980s for member states to include Appendix III lists in the enforcement instructions given to national trade-control authorities.[33] In general, responsibility for enforcing CITES rests with the parties, who are required to develop 'appropriate measures' to discourage illegal trade.

NGO participation in the implementation of CITES has long been seen as one of the regime's strong points, partly compensating for the secretariat's inability to act against reported violations.[34] The treaty specifically provides for NGOs to participate in the meetings of the parties, where they are entitled to express their opinions and lobby for their positions, although they may not vote. They also play a central role in monitoring compliance. The World Conservation Monitoring Unit is responsible for the computerized tracking of trade in endangered species and reporting data to the CITES secretariat. A division of the Worldwide Fund for Nature is also active in monitoring illegal trade. In addition, NGOs in many countries have been involved in gathering data for scientific studies and are officially represented on the panel that gives advice on the down-listing of the elephant.

Even when states are fully committed to implementing CITES, they cannot hope to achieve compliance solely through the vigilance of domestic customs agents, who are rarely equipped to detect forged permits or false assertions by smugglers, let alone to identify actual examples of protected species.[35] Community awareness, rather than top-down command and control, offers greater promise of effectiveness. Here again active collaboration between IGOs and NGOs could promote the desired results.

There are as well some hidden costs in placing heavy reliance on NGOs for species protection. Some strategic choices made by NGOs in their efforts to preserve wildlife, both under CITES and elsewhere, have raised questions about whose values they represent and whether their judgement in setting priorities is consistent with the regime's objectives, let alone with current scientific knowledge. The increasing power of NGOs under CITES is resented by national governments when resulting policies threaten domestic economic or political interests. African countries seeking the downlisting of elephants, for example, have not welcomed NGO support for maintaining the animal's blacklisted status. Nor are alliances between NGOs and state governments guaranteed to be unproblematic. In one controversial episode, the World Wildlife Fund (now Worldwide Fund for Nature) was discovered to have helped the government of Zimbabwe purchase a helicopter to protect the black rhino in spite of the authorities' shoot-to-kill policy against poachers.[36] This, together with the Fund's aid to Kenya in buying assault weapons and helicopter gunships to protect the elephant, underscored the tragic choices involved in protecting species in developing countries. People's lives were worth less, it appeared, than the charismatic megafauna cherished by northern environmentalists and publics. Disturbingly, the Fund seemed willing to support abroad policies of violence that would have seemed abhorrent at home.

A similar controversy about possible blindness to cultural values arose when Greenpeace and the International Fund for Animal Welfare launched a campaign to ban seal culling in Canada in the 1970s and 1980s. Confronted by evidence that seal hunting was important to indigenous people, these international NGOs argued that the use of modern technology, such as guns and snowmobiles, rendered the hunters' activities non-traditional and hence not worthy of protection.[37] As anthropologists and community activists pointed out, this assessment was based on an overly static understanding of 'traditional' culture, which could only be main-

tained in the contemporary world by allowing some room for technologi-
cal adaptation. Ironically, this dispute turned the normative question of
what should count as 'traditional' into a scientific problem and revealed
substantial differences between local and non-local NGOs' interpretations
of the issue.

TECHNOLOGY TRANSFER: A ROLE FOR NGOs

Environmental action often demands the transfer of knowledge, skills,
technology or other material resources from places where they are readily
available to places where they are in relatively short supply. NGOs of all
kinds have demonstrated that they can participate constructively in such
dissemination, although the skills and capabilities of particular organizations constrain their spheres and modalities of influence. Thus, the more
professionalized multinational NGOs – such as Greenpeace, Worldwide
Fund for Nature and Friends of the Earth – have been able to influence the
politics of national and international environmental agenda-setting by
combining information available from official sources with additional information that they themselves have compiled or generated. By contrast,
smaller, community-based NGOs are more likely to stimulate activity at
the local level than to initiate sweeping policy change. These groups are
especially adept at simplifying and, if necessary, translating difficult
technical information for non-expert users, adapting generic emergency
response measures to fit local circumstances and mobilizing direct action
against local polluters or hazardous facilities.

Given the striking discrepancies in environmental knowledge and policy
preparedness around the world, NGOs can make a sizeable difference
simply by publicizing the environmental performance of leading countries
so as to exert pressure on laggard countries.[38] Strategic use of policy comparisons allowed the Natural Resources Defense Council (NRDC), a
leading US environmental organization, to influence the 1990 negotiations
leading to the revision of the Montreal Protocol on ozone depletion. Prior
to the meeting of government officials in London, several of the leading
international environmental groups had held press conferences and distributed informational brochures to the press, the public and officials. NRDC
went a step further by compiling from existing government proposals a
composite set of target reductions for ozone-depleting chemicals incorporating the maximum reduction proposed for each by any government.[39]
Demonstrating actual state support for each target in the proposal allowed
NRDC to avoid the charge of impossibility conventionally levelled against

any effort to tighten up environmental regulation. The skills that NRDC drew on were as much political as technical. Decades of experience in complex regulatory negotiations were brought to bear in repackaging publicly available information into a form calculated to have maximal policy impact.

Indeed, political imagination and experience in moulding public opinion have proved to be at least as important in NGO lobbying efforts as issue-specific technical knowledge. The NGO-led campaign to remove lead from petrol in Europe in the 1980s provides one illustration. In this case, NGOs pointed to the United States, where catalytic converters had been standardly required on motor vehicles since the 1970s, to argue forcefully that the European automobile industry could afford to meet the same requirement without severe economic loss. Greenpeace, in particular, dramatized the point in Britain through a poster campaign that played on one of the Ford Motor Company's favoured slogans ('Ford Gives You More'); turning the message back on the company, the posters argued that a British Ford car gave customers more pollution than its American counterpart.[40]

Examples like these suggest that aggregating information from states and making it freely available is one of the most promising avenues for cooperation between IGOs and NGOs. According to one count, the United Nations currently manages some nine separate programmes designed to provide member nations and other interested parties with information about environmental and industrial hazards.[41] But mere availability of information provides no guarantee that states will have the expertise or inclination to use it effectively. NGOs enjoy some conspicuous advantages over states as users of international databases: they are less hampered by inertia, more dedicated, more focused on pragmatic (and hence attainable) environmental objectives and often more knowledgeable about the issues they have targeted for action. Better access for NGOs accordingly should promote the objectives of information transfer programmes managed by IGOs.

In an age marked by massive accumulations of information and by instantaneous electronic communication, NGOs can be expected to gain in importance as agents of knowledge transfer. Although the amount of environmental information in the public domain keeps growing, it is frequently available in forms that make unmediated use by lay citizens virtually unthinkable. Technical information remains inaccessible in practice unless it is translated into user-friendly forms. It is no surprise, for example, that the right-to-know provisions of the US Superfund law proved most efficacious in those communities where an environmental NGO worked with residents to interpret the data reported under that programme.[42] On the international level, the linguistic competence provided by NGOs can prove to be a critically important asset, given the increasing importance of English as the world's primary medium of technical communication.[43]

LEARNING AND THE POLITICS OF SOVEREIGNTY

In a model of global governance that looks like the circulatory system, NGOs are sometimes thought to function very much like capillaries, carrying out the same mandate as the major blood vessels but on a smaller scale. It seems clear from the foregoing examples that environmental NGOs, both large and small, are especially well suited to performing repeated, on-the-ground, 'micro' functions, such as collecting samples, taking measurements, mobilizing against environmental violators, educating people at the grassroots and providing interim relief. Even these community-based activities, however, may link up with global policy and politics in a variety of ways: by supplementing existing scientific theories about environmental phenomena with local knowledge; by disseminating, and if necessary translating, environmental information from national and international databases; by disclosing systematic patterns of violations and shortfalls that ought to be addressed at the international level; by reframing dominant policy paradigms to take account of social and scientific uncertainty; and, less benignly, by reinforcing specific, culturally conditioned tilts – even pathologies – in environmental regimes (for example, the emphasis on charismatic megafauna in the implementation of CITES). In all these respects, NGOs function proactively as creative policy initiators, not merely as passive agents of principals situated higher up in the political hierarchy.

The analogy with the circulatory system breaks down more completely when one inserts the state into the picture, since, on many issues of environmental management, the interests of NGOs run counter to those of state authorities. With the globalization of environmental politics and knowledge, there is more than a negligible likelihood of IGOs and NGOs lining up on one side of an environmental issue and national governments on the other, so as to create possible arenas of conflict. The cases discussed above provide some insights into how this happens. In their efforts to educate, mobilize or lobby for policy change, NGOs frequently enlist support from IGOs to battle indifference at the national level. Even the collection of supposedly neutral scientific and medical information by NGOs can become a charged affair because it discloses state incapacity, creates obligations (for example, compensation claims) that the state does not wish or does not have the resources to honour, interferes with entrenched economic interests that are in league with the state, or opposes the scientific orthodoxy of state-sponsored expert institutions, as happened in Bhopal in connection with the thiosulfate controversy.

All this suggests that there is room for improvement in the institutional framework for NGO-state-IGO collaboration in the field of environmental action. Waiting for more coherent authority to develop at the supranational level, as Sand emphatically argues, is not a plausible solution.[44] A more promising avenue is to engage the full range of institutional resources – governmental as well as non-governmental and intergovernmental – to increase the prospects for learning and reduce the potential for interorganizational conflict. What are some steps that can be taken in pursuit of this goal?

Decentralized learning

The past two decades of experience with global environmental management have generated extraordinary interest in the theme of learning.[45] This preoccupation reflects in part an awareness that our framing of environmental problems and related understanding of causes and effects are still embryonic and likely to change rapidly with massive new investments in knowledge-creation. In part, as well, the proliferation of international environmental accords and the associated disclosure of deeply divided environmental views and values prompts an interest in learning. The realization has grown in many parts of the world that the prospects for peaceful coexistence may well depend on how effectively human societies learn to manage their environmental interdependence.

As catalysts for environmental learning, NGOs offer an important alternative to the standard top-down model of knowledge-making and knowledge diffusion in the natural sciences. They supplement in crucial ways the more widely acknowledged role of technical and managerial elites in building epistemic communities and fostering international policy coordination.[46] NGOs in principle can gain access to domains of localized experience and understanding, and offer alternative models of environmental health or sustainability that currently remain outside the purview of organized science.[47] They thus constitute a vehicle for scaling knowledge up from the grassroots – a necessary task, in view of the extreme heterogeneity of ecosystems and human–environment linkages.

Knowledge garnered by NGOs, however, will have to pass through processes of validation and standardization, including perhaps translation into mathematical or statistical language, in order to achieve authority

outside their places of origin.[48] This is where IGOs (along with state institutions) may be in a position to offer decisive help. Performance standards
and technical guidance may often have to be developed on an *ad hoc* basis
in response to particular challenges, as in the aftermath of disasters. IGOs
could play an important part in legitimating the scientific activities of
NGOs if they remain alert to some generic problems and have methods of
responding to them. For example – given the importance of institutional
boundary work in building scientific credibility[49] – collaborative arrangements for environmental monitoring could require the creation of an
expert advisory body to guide protocol development, assist in data collection and storage, provide peer review and help in the interpretation and
dissemination of findings. IGOs could also maintain, make available and
periodically revamp relevant databases of experts and expert services such
as organizations of scientists and physicians in the public interest. Finally,
IGO support can partially compensate for the resource shortfalls that contribute to wavering leadership and unreliable performance by most of the
world's smaller and less experienced NGOs.

Beyond sovereignty

The rise and influence of epistemic networks or communities at the sub-
state level has been remarked upon by many observers of international
environmental regimes.[50] For the most part, however, the analysis of epistemic communities has sidestepped the challenge that such actor constella-
tions may pose to state sovereignty. It has been widely assumed that
ecological epistemic communities will include both national bureaucracies
entrusted with environmental responsibilities and NGOs subscribing to a
shared set of values and problem definitions. Experience of NGO activities
to protect the environment paints a less comforting picture. Both expert,
multinational NGOs and NGOs organized at the grassroots level have
encountered at times violent opposition from state authorities. Their
alliances, if any, with chronically weak national environmental agencies
offer insufficient protection.

Strengthening the ties between IGOs and NGOs may enhance the latter
groups' voice and authority, as well as institutional stability and steadiness
of purpose, but it will not solve the problem of conflict between NGOs and
the states in which the great majority of them operate. The reality is that
NGOs, at least in the short run, need states to act upon and legitimate their
knowledges, world-views and preferred policies. Assisted by the fax and
the Internet and relatively unhampered by competing ideological commitments, environmental NGOs have achieved enormous success in building

networks across state boundaries. But these developments reaffirm to varying degrees the proposition that 'all politics is local'. The international spread of India's famed Chipko movement provides an instructive example. Here, pre-eminently, was a local environmental initiative, organized to protect local natural resources, whose commitments seemed to spread throughout the world.[51] The movement generated actions that could be reinterpreted as symbols of global thinking by actors pursuing different political agendas in places far from India; yet, it arose out of characteristically Indian political oppositions and had to succeed in its immediate context in order to achieve wider influence.

If bypassing states is not the answer, then what can IGOs do to encourage cooperation between state authorities and NGOs on environmental issues? Improved communication and formal participation, preferably built into the design of environmental regimes as in the case of CITES, is undoubtedly part of the answer. In such forums, more states may come to appreciate what US environmental regulators, for example, have recently begun to acknowledge: that effective systems of environmental governance require constant recalibration among national policy commitments and emerging local and translocal problem frames. Scientific analysis of environmental risks, according to a 1996 report of the US National Research Council, therefore should be integrated with forms of deliberation that directly engage citizens and NGOs. Top-down analysis, without horizontal deliberation, may end up all too often addressing the wrong problems.

According to one recent analysis of environmental learning, a necessary precondition is 'the absence of irreconcilable political differences among the dominant member countries'.[52] If this were not already a daunting goal, the addition of intractable epistemic conflicts among state and non-state actors makes action that much more difficult.[53] The explosion of environmental science in recent years, and its diffusion to more and more new actors, has if anything exacerbated the intensity of technical conflict. Greater knowledge seems only to reveal previously unsuspected areas of uncertainty, so that increased scientific understanding turns back and undermines science's own authority. The German sociologist Ulrich Beck refers to this self-destructive phenomenon as 'reflexive modernization' in his influential thesis that risk – rather than, say, class or race or family – now functions as the dominant organizing force in contemporary societies.[54] The quest to build Anderson's 'imagined communities'[55] against this backdrop of contestation is a perilous undertaking for environmentalists, who must compete with states and industry lobbies that command substantially greater resources and often deploy them to profoundly different ends. Collaboration with IGOs can help rectify these inequalities and give NGOs structured opportunities to interject their critical, but essential, voices into the emerging discourses of a global civil society.

NOTES

1. See Peter Sand, *Lessons Learned in Global Environmental Governance* (Washington, DC: World Resources Institute, 1990); Kevin Stairs and Peter Taylor, 'Non-governmental organizations and the legal protection of the oceans: a case study', in Andrew Hurrell and Benedict Kingsbury (eds), *The International Politics of the Environment* (Oxford University Press, 1992), pp. 110–41; and Laurence Susskind, *Environmental Diplomacy: Negotiating More Effective Global Agreements* (Oxford: Oxford University Press, 1994).
2. World Commission on Environment and Development, *Our Common Future* (Oxford: Oxford University Press, 1987), p. 328.
3. See Marvin S. Soroos, 'From Stockholm to Rio and beyond: the evolution of global environmental governance', in Norman J. Vig and Michael E. Kraft (eds), *Environmental Policy in the 1990s*, 3rd edn (Washington, DC: Congressional Quarterly Press, 1997).
4. Steven Yearley, *Sociology, Environmentalism, Globalization* (London: Sage, 1996).
5. See Stairs and Taylor, 'Non-governmental organizations'; and Jessica T. Mathews, 'Power shift', *Foreign Affairs*, 76 (1), 1997, pp. 50–66.
6. Andrew Jamison et al., *The Making of the New Environmental Consciousness* (Edinburgh: Edinburgh University Press, 1990).
7. Susskind, *Environmental Diplomacy*, p. 51.
8. Some business interests have created NGOs to serve as fronts to pursue the founders' economic interests on issues such as wetlands and climate change (see, for example, Susskind, *Environmental Diplomacy*, pp. 51–2). Greenpeace has published a list of over fifty such organizations in 'The Greenpeace guide to anti-environmental organizations' in Yearley, *Sociology*, p. 90.
9. Peter Uvin, 'Scaling up the grassroots and scaling down the summit: the relations between Third World nongovernmental organizations and the United Nations', *Third World Quarterly*, 16 (3), 1995, pp. 495–512.
10. Even this independence may be a matter of degree. Autonomy is tempered in states where NGOs receive substantial funding or other supports from the state. In addition, regular participation in formal policy proceedings, such as regulatory hearings, can bring about a convergence of interests and outlook between NGOs and state agencies, with consequent loss of critical capacity.
11. Sand, *Lessons Learned*, p. 29.

12. See Peter M. Haas, *Saving the Mediterranean: The Politics of International Environmental Cooperation* (New York: Columbia University Press, 1990); and Sand, *Lessons Learned*, p. 29.

13. Haas, *Saving the Mediterranean*; Stairs and Taylor, 'Non-governmental organizations'. See also Peter M. Haas, Robert O. Keohand, and Marc A. Levy (eds), *Institutions for the Earth: Sources of Effective International Environmental Protection* (Cambridge, Mass.: MIT Press, 1993); and Susskind, *Environmental Diplomacy*.

14. See Rachel Carson, *Silent Spring* (Boston: Houghton Mifflin, 1962).

15. See Mary Douglas and Aaron Wildavsky, *Risk and Culture* (Berkeley, Calif.: University of California Press, 1982); Sheila Jasanoff, *Risk Management and Political Culture* (New York: Russell Sage Foundation, 1986); and Stairs and Taylor, 'Non-governmental organizations'.

16. See Donald A. Schön and Martin Rein, *Frame Reflection: Toward the Resolution of Intractable Policy Controversies* (New York: Basic Books, 1994); and Sharachchandra Lele and Richard Norgaard, 'Sustainability and the scientist's burden', *Conservation Biology*, 10 (2), 1995, pp. 354–65.

17. See Sheila Jasanoff, *The Fifth Branch: Science Advisers as Policymakers* (Cambridge, Mass.: Harvard University Press, 1990).

18. For example, determinations characterized as 'scientific' through the boundary work of expert committees may be shielded from judicial and political review. Judges as well as policy-makers generally defer to the findings of duly authorized scientific organizations.

19. Jasanoff, *Risk Management* and *The Fifth Branch*.

20. Stairs and Taylor, 'Non-governmental organizations', pp. 117–20.

21. Ibid., p. 118.

22. Ibid., pp. 133–4.

23. Yearley, *Sociology*.

24. See Brian Wynne, *Risk Management and Hazardous Wastes: Implementation and the Dialectics of Credibility* (Berlin: Springer, 1987); and Wynne, 'Misunderstood misunderstandings: social identities and the public uptake of science', in Alan Irwin and Brian Wynne (eds), *Misunderstanding Science?* (Cambridge: Cambridge University Press, 1996).

25. See Michael Thompson, M. Warburton, and T. Hatley *Uncertainty on a Himalayan Scale* (London: Ethnographica, 1986), pp. 46–7.

26. Wynne, 'Misunderstood misunderstandings'.

27. See Ravi S. Rajan, 'Rehabilitation and voluntarism in Bhopal', *Lokayan Bulletin*, 6 (1/2), 1988, pp. 3–31; and C. Sathyamala, 'The medical profession and the Bhopal tragedy', *Lokayan Bulletin*, 6 (1/2), 1988, pp. 33–56; Sheila Jasanoff, *Learning from Disaster: Risk Management After Bhopal* (Philadelphia: University of Pennsylvania Press, 1994).

28. Sathyamala, 'The medical profession'.

29. Ibid.

30. See Michael R. Reich, 'Toxic politics and pollution victims in the Third World', in Jasanoff, *Learning from Disaster*, p. 189.

31. See, for example, Kai Erikson, *Everything in Its Path: Destruction of Community in the Buffalo Creek Flood* (New York: Simon & Schuster, 1976).

32. Sand, *Lessons Learned*.
33. Ibid., p. 29.
34. Susskind, *Environmental Diplomacy*.
35. Donald G. McNeil, Jr, 'Madagascar reptile theft hits rarest of tortoises', *New York Times*, 2 July 1996, p. 61.
36. Yearley, *Sociology*, p. 138.
37. Ibid., p. 137.
38. Stairs and Taylor, 'Non-governmental organizations', p. 129.
39. See Richard E. Benedick, *Ozone Diplomacy; New Directions in Safeguarding the Planet* (Cambridge, Mass.: Harvard University Press, 1991), p. 166.
40. Yearley, *Sociology*, p. 88.
41. See Frank N. Laird, 'Information and disaster prevention', in Jasanoff (ed.), *Learning from Disaster*, pp. 204-24.
42. Susan Hadden, 'Citizen participation in environmental policymaking', in Jasanoff (ed.), *Learning from Disaster*, pp. 91–112.
43. Stair and Taylor, 'Non-governmental organizations'.
44. Sand, *Lessons Learned*.
45. See Dean E. Mann, 'Environmental learning in a decentralized world', *Journal of International Affairs*, 44, 1991, pp. 301–37; Martin Jachtenfuchs and Michael Huber, 'Institutional learning in the European Community: the response to the greenhouse effect', in J. D. Liefferink, P. D. Lave and A. P. J. Nol (eds), *European Integration and Environmental Policy* (London: Belhaven Press, 1993); Haas et al., *Institutions for the Earth*; and Peter M. Haas and Ernst B. Haas, 'Learning to learn: improving international governance', *Global Governance*, 1 (3), 1995, pp. 255–85.
46. Haas, *Saving the Mediterranean*; and Haas and Haas, 'Learning to learn'.
47. Irwin and Wynne, *Misunderstanding Science?*
48. See Bruno Latour, 'Drawing things together', in M. Lynch and S. Woolgar (eds), *Representation in Scientific Practice* (Cambridge, Mass.: MIT Press, 1990); and Theodore M. Porter, *Trust in Numbers: The Pursuit of Objectivity in Science and Public Life* (Princeton, NJ: Princeton University Press, 1995).
49. Jasanoff, *The Fifth Branch*.
50. Sand, *Lessons Learned*; Haas, *Saving the Mediterranean*; Haas et al., *Institutions for the Earth*; and Mathews, 'Power shift'.
51. Luther Gerlach, 'Thinking globally, acting locally', *Evaluation Review*, 15 (1), 1991, pp. 120–48.
52. Haas and Haas, 'Learning to learn', p. 255.
53. Schön and Rein, *Frame Reflection*.
54. See Ulrich Beck, *The Risk Society: Towards a New Modernity* (London: Sage, 1992). This book, which has been described as a sociological manifesto for the German Green movement, sold hundreds of thousands copies when it was first published, showing that it had struck a deeply responsive chord among German citizens.
55. Benedict Anderson, *Imagined Communities*, 2nd edn (London: Verso, 1991).

Part IV
Conclusions

11 UN Task-Sharing: Toward or Away from Global Governance?

Edwin M. Smith and Thomas G. Weiss

This volume's point of departure was an overextended United Nations de-volving responsibilities toward regional arrangements for security func-tions[1] and non-governmental organizations (NGOs) for the delivery of many services. This reflected more than infatuation with a kind of 'privat-ization' of the business of intergovernmental organizations. Rather, it was the realization that in a world with limited resources and more than enough challenges, a better international division of labour was essential. Rather than bleating, as a die-hard member of the UN fan club might, about the inability of the world organization to perform, it seemed more reasonable and practical to examine the dynamics of what could well be enhanced global governance. Within this context, it makes more sense to ask who does what best, or at least better, than to lament the disappearance of a mythical UN system powerful and well-equipped enough to undertake every task. The analytical and policy perspective thus is untidy – there is no straightforward hierarchical arrangement with a devolution from states to the United Nations, and then from the world organization to regional in-stitutions and NGOs. Rather there are pluralistic, or messy, relationships that vary often by task, historical period and geographical area.

The case studies of regional security arrangements and NGOs involved in the delivery of services in a variety of sectors contains much grist for analytical mills. In particular, there are lessons about the advantages and disadvantages of what oftentimes is referred to as a kind of 'subcontract-ing' – in the title to this volume and elsewhere. Although the quotation marks indicate that many legal analysts undoubtedly are averse to the image because of its connotations in contract law, the notion is that the universal United Nations can devolve responsibilities toward institutional units that are 'lower' (or more accurately, 'less universal') on a hierarchy of institutions. This notion of 'subsidiarity' has begun to generate a theor-etical literature.[2] In a rudimentary fashion, it signifies a search to identify institutional comparative advantages at the global level.

Comparing the dynamics in recent UN experience between regional institutions and non-governmental organizations uncovered at least as many dissimilarities as similarities. These reflect more than differences between the subject matter of regional arrangements, the 'high politics' of national security, and that of NGOs, the 'low politics' of delivering economic and social services.[3] There are fundamental structural and constitutional differences distinguishing the relationships between the United Nations and regional security arrangements, on the one hand, and service-providing NGOs, on the other hand. It is worth re-emphasizing here that a 'subcontractor' follows orders from, and is accountable to, the general contractor. This accurately depicts some NGO endeavours *vis-à-vis* the United Nations, but no regional security arrangements subordinate themselves, either formally or practically, to the world organization.

The management and coordination problems resulting from the UN's task-sharing with both sets of organizations provide distinct challenges. While procedural changes may be sufficient to improve UN-NGO task-sharing and performance, they are insufficient to improve coordination and cooperation between the UN and regional institutions. For the former, 'more effective' could be synonymous with 'better global governance'. For the latter, 'more effective' could indicate a move away from enhanced global governance and toward unbridled regional autonomy or even hegemony in determining actions to foster peace and security. This distinction between formal intergovernmental entities and non-governmental groups provides the core of the difference between these two task-sharing paradigms. The differences involve the nature of the actors, the methods of action and the normative objectives to be served through the respective courses of action. They also reflect unresolved conflicts that arose at the UN's founding. Since these original conflicts are obvious in the role of regional arrangements in the arena of peace and security, an exploration of their early manifestations is appropriate in this concluding essay about UN task-sharing.

This chapter examines first the fundamental ambiguities resulting from the four case studies and the framework for analysis about UN task-sharing with regional security arrangements. Next, the four cases regarding UN task-sharing with service-providing NGOs are scrutinized with a view to answering the five key questions from the original framework for analysis. Finally, there are some conclusions about moving beyond UN subcontracting and some suggestions for changes in policy and operations.

REGIONAL SECURITY ARRANGEMENTS AND THE
UNITED NATIONS

Since the beginning of the United Nations, regional institutions have been a recognized part of the international landscape. For almost that long, the relationship has been problematic. The UN Charter contemplates a clear hierarchy, with the world organization holding primacy to authorize the enforcement actions of regional institutions relating to international peace and security. In contrast, powerful regional institutions, while acknowledging the UN's responsibilities, have been far less clear in affirming their adherence to the world organization's primacy in matters involving vital national security interests. In fact, some member states of regional institutions have been adamant in stating that they would follow exclusively the dictates of their own perceptions of vital national security interests.[4]

Long-standing differences have always had a clear potential for discord, but recent trends have in fact increased the risk of confusion and contention in the collective pursuit of international peace and security. Such trends result from the growing recognition of the practical limitations that constrain the United Nations. In an initial burst of optimism occasioned by the expulsion of Iraqi forces from Kuwait, member states and the secretariat as well as policy analysts overestimated the capability and effectiveness of the UN in mounting and managing complex collective responses to conflicts that came to be classed as 'threats to international peace and security'. Somalia and Bosnia confirmed the scope of that misjudgement. As a result, officials of national governments and international organizations, as well as independent observers, have concluded that the United Nations will be required to delegate to regional arrangements and capable member states some of the tasks essential to effective collective security. The last UN Secretary-General wrote in cautious approval of this notion of task-sharing.[5] In light of additional practical experiences, more thorough analysis is in order of the risks and benefits involved in task-sharing.

Muthiah Alagappa's essay provides an overview of the possible parameters for effective collaboration between the UN and regional arrangements when multilateral responses to problems of international peace and security are required. He points out several factors that should be considered in evaluating the decision to delegate implementation efforts. Among these, the capability of the regional actor and its access to adequate resources play critical roles, but they are accompanied by the level of commitment and the acceptability, legitimacy and accountability of that entity by those in the arena of armed conflict. The cases indicate vast differences among regional actors when comparing these variables.

Perhaps more than any other case examined here, Dick Leurdijk's depiction of Operation Joint Endeavor, which was conducted by the Implementation Force (IFOR) of the North Atlantic Treaty Organization (NATO), has illustrated the comparative lack of capability of the UN to undertake coercive action in an ongoing war. NATO's overwhelming capability and its clear determination to separate contending forces in Bosnia provided critical elements of a generally successful involvement. The member states of NATO held vast resources that could be brought to bear. The record of the UN-NATO interaction provides important insights into the prospects and risks in this practice of task delegation; those insights leave large questions about a number of issues.

At the same time, Leurdijk warns against the search for any preconceived template because 'completely new forms of international cooperation [resulted] not on the basis of a blueprint, but in reaction to developments in the field'. In addition to being cautious about generalizing from this 'singular' case to other regions, he is adamant about keeping distinct the lessons from the period when NATO and the UN sought to establish a peace settlement versus the actual implementation of a peace agreement. The notion of 'accountability' is a theme that goes across cases, but the 'dual key' arrangement between the UN and the NATO is one mechanism for oversight that clearly will not be accepted by NATO in the future. The confusion and feebleness of the original European response also calls into question the purported advantages of geographical proximity in making regional arrangements preferable to global ones. In fact, there is even some possibility that a wealth of institutions within a region may provide a 'smorgasbord' of choices for member states that actually facilitates buck-passing instead of decision-making.

Considerations of geographic proximity or political interest have caused other regional actors to act in situations perceived to be threats to international peace and security. Nigeria motivated other member states of the Economic Organization of West African States (ECOWAS) to become involved in Liberia through the ECOWAS Monitoring Group (ECOMOG) in the case examined in this volume by Clement Adibe. Supportive Security Council resolutions granted some initial legitimacy to the activities of ECOMOG, a status that was enhanced by the later establishment of the UNOMIL mission in cooperation with African participants. Unfortunately, ECOMOG became involved in the conflict so extensively that its claim to neutrality was lost and the UNOMIL mission basically remained on the sidelines. Nigeria overestimated its own capability to conduct the operation, it struggled with limited resources and a political crisis at home and came to be seen as serving its regional hegemonic interests, losing its early claim to legitimacy. Interactions between the United Nations and ECOMOG provide sobering grounds for caution before providing a *carte blanche* in delegating peacekeeping functions to regional groups.

In fact, the existence of an out-of-area participant in a 'regional' institution (that is, the United States in Europe) sometimes can be a helpful stimulus to action. Adibe points to three lessons from his case: steering clear from messy regional geopolitics; avoiding parallel command structures; and shunning unconditional support for regional initiatives. The latter two lessons also emerge from other cases and should be taken into account in future task-sharing. As all of the cases involved 'messy geopolitics', the first lesson, if implemented, might suggest that outsiders leave conflicts to burn out rather than intervene.

The record for more traditional diplomatic activities has been more encouraging. Negotiated settlements in Cambodia, Angola and Mozambique offer grounds for optimism when compared to other UN responses to conflicts where there were no agreements among belligerents. Similarly, nearby states have helped to launch and sustain diplomatic processes as well as helped to monitor elections and disarm parties to conflicts in Nicaragua, El Salvador and Haiti, and progress has also been visible more recently in seemingly intractable Guatemala.

In the case presented here by Joaquín Tacsan, Central America's presidents as actors provided unique knowledge of the political and the normative contexts, which consequently had significant benefits for the peace process. This record as well as that of the Organization of American States (OAS) in Haiti illustrate the potential for cooperation among neighbouring states to assist in conflict resolution and multilateral diplomacy. Because of the unusual normative consensus on regional political and cultural issues, member states were able to influence the working parties to consider new modalities for conflict resolution. The needs for special technical capabilities and massive resources are reduced for diplomatic initiatives of this sort. Concerned neighbouring states can lay claim to a legitimacy that derives from shared values, while their commitment to provide support is credible because of the potential direct costs of continued conflict. The potential for regional arrangements in support of dispute settlement may be an arena of comparative advantage.

One of the variables that emerges from all cases but that seems most clearly pertinent here is what might be dubbed 'cultural' explanations for outcomes. States in the Americas share to an unusual degree a long-standing normative consensus about values – and, as Tacsan indicates, the lengthy legal and normative tradition in the Americas is exceptional. It is plausible that neighbouring states were able to exert pressure on belliger-ents to consider modalities for conflict resolution that far away outsiders, including the United Nations, had more difficulty in initiating and sustain-ing in both Central America and Haiti. The fact that states in the region have existed as independent legal entities for almost two centuries also provides a possible explanation for sustained and effective regional action, particularly in comparison with many of the relatively young, weak or failed states in the other cases.

More problematic questions are raised by the Commonwealth of Independent States (CIS) in the civil war in Georgia, as Neil MacFarlane discusses in considerable depth. Russia played a dominant historical role as imperial ruler of Georgia; as principal partner in the CIS, Moscow seeks to preserve its prevalence in the region by managing conflicts. Outside organizations have provided a handful of observers to help improve the transparency of these operations, decreasing somewhat the risk of violation by Russia of international norms related to peacekeeping. However, it is unrealistic to expect that outside monitoring of any type, let alone the minimalist versions used by the UN and the Organization for Security and Cooperation in Europe (OSCE), could limit Russian strategic manipulation of these conflicts. The relative capability of Russia guaran-tees its dominance in the region. Its access to outside resources serves to support that dominance, although that may give some leverage to the UN as a potential source of funds. As the former imperial power and auto-cratic ruler of all of the 'near abroad', the legitimacy of Russia's role is immediately suspect as reflecting self-interested accumulation of power.

Moscow's insistence on peacekeeping in Georgia has caused grave con-cerns. This hardly is a 'model' for UN task-sharing. Pointing out that no other national or international entity was prepared to become involved or even contribute to financing, MacFarlane stresses the limited leverage over a major power active in its own sphere of influence. Moreover, the timing of the action creates real problems with any notion of 'subcontracting' because Russia as a 'subcontractor' took actions and then sought approval in the form of a Security Council resolution, or 'contract'. At the same time, MacFarlane dismisses calls for unrealistic quick fixes and urges both conceptual and practical efforts to go beyond simplistic conceptions of a division of labour. He 'raises the possibility of creative combinations of subregional, regional and global organizational activities that maximize the advantages and minimize the disadvantages of each level of organiza-tion through a synergistic approach to local problems.'

In relationship to tasks central to the maintenance of international peace and security, each of these cases demonstrates ambiguities and complexities when the United Nations delegates to or ratifies independent initiatives by regional arrangements, *ad hoc* coalitions or powerful individual states. The likelihood of successful and genuine transfers of responsibilities depends not only on the sorts of tasks transferred but also on the modalities available to ensure accountability from the institution acting on behalf of the larger community of states. The purpose of the four case studies was to explore task-sharing practices in order to evaluate the match between possible tasks and the range of designated recipients; some suggestions are found later in this essay.

It is useful to return to the contention stated at the outset of this chapter regarding the problematic structural relationship between the world organization and the original concept and subsequent practices of regional institutions. The officials and diplomats who negotiated the Charter included a role for regional arrangements and agencies. The provisions establishing that role were adopted in spite of many misgivings after many necessary compromises and modifications. The text of the final articles incorporated in the Charter contain ambiguities and contradictions. Beyond those initial difficulties, the evolution of myriad forms of intergovernmental arrangements has placed additional strain on a set of provisions adopted over half a century ago. The case studies demonstrate vast differences between the early conceptions of 'regional institutions' and the current complex and conflicted framework of multilateral interactions and practices.

Many of the doubts and misgivings expressed in the preceding pages of this volume regarding the difficulties of coordination between the United Nations and regional institutions repeat those expressed in San Francisco. At this point, the United Nations must address them by finding workable patterns of collaboration. But those patterns must also be acknowledged by other actors as legitimate efforts to serve broad international interests in addition to narrow or regional and national ones.

Those who drafted the UN Charter provided for the involvement of regional arrangements and agencies in the maintenance of international peace and security.[6] They did not fully foresee the impasse that would arise from the Cold War between what eventually would be dubbed the 'superpowers', the United States and the Soviet Union. They also failed to anticipate the still-born UN military capacities and that regional institutions would offer superior capabilities of the sort necessary for evolving UN operations. However, they did approach the idea of a role for regional institutions in international peace and security with some trepidation. Some expressed concerns about the potential complications posed by the formation of spheres of influence and appropriate definitions for a region. Others focused on preserving options for organization in particular regions rather than providing a general infrastructure for ordering potential relationships between regional and universal organizations. The range of concerns raised among the diplomats in the negotiations foreshadowed the scope of sceptical comments by scholars made more recently, including those spelled out in the cases of this volume.

When finally adopted, the Charter included 'Regional Arrangements' as the title for Charter VIII, but its provisions provided that collective enforcement actions could only be taken by regional arrangements and agencies after prior authorization from the Security Council. In combination with Article 51, they ensured that states within a region could engage in individual or collective self-defence against an 'armed attack' at their own initiative 'until the Security Council has taken measures necessary to maintain international peace and security'. Although adopted by the San Francisco Conference with relatively little fanfare, these articles of the Charter included many unresolved areas of potential confusion and inconsistency.

First, the express protection given the 'inherent' right of 'collective' self-defence established a presumption in favour of autonomous initial local responses in case of an armed attack, but a presumption for external authorization when the Security Council mandated enforcement action in response to a threat to international peace and security. The structure of Chapter VII of the Charter gave responsibility for the identification of threats to the Security Council; delineation of specific acts of 'aggression' was explicitly rejected. As a result, the determination of the existence of an 'armed attack' stands as the primary criterion for justification of initial independent action emancipated from a Security Council blessing. When it is recalled that the customary concept of self-defence permitted action before an attack,[7] the scope of possible action under Article 51 is ambiguous. Very high stakes are involved in concluding that an armed attack has occurred; such a finding would give justification for the most extreme and violent responses. The determination of whether the facts justify the invocation of Article 51 has remained highly controversial.

The affirmation of collective self-defence raises additional questions. The absence of any traditional concept of *collective* self-defence in the customary law tradition makes delineation of its boundaries difficult. Some scholars have asserted that collective defence alliances do not fit within the constraints of Chapter VIII.[8] It is certainly the case that NATO has never held itself out as a 'regional arrangement' under Chapter VIII – in fact, its member states have been careful to specify that it was rather a 'regional organization' and an 'alliance' in order to avoid any connotation of subservience to Security Council decision-making. But the full implications of that argument are unclear. Defensive alliances may escape the requirement of waiting until the Security Council has authorized enforcement action should those states determine that their interests are threatened. Proponents of such a view could cite the actions of the coalition of states that came to the assistance of Kuwait in the 1990–1 Gulf War. They could also cite the actions of NATO in conducting air operations against the Bosnian Serbs in the summer of 1995.

Further, even regional institutions that voluntarily choose to define themselves within the provisions of 'regional arrangements and agencies' of the UN Charter's Chapter VIII find themselves without a clear understanding of the limits of their authority. Although this chapter expressly affirmed the authority of regional arrangements and agencies to 'deal with such matters relating to the maintenance of international peace and security as are appropriate for regional action', there is nothing to indicate which matters are appropriate for such action. The Charter specifies that regional arrangements and agencies may engage in 'enforcement actions when authorized by the Security Council pursuant to its own determination of the existence of a threat and a need to respond'. Chapter VIII indicates that no 'enforcement action' may be undertaken by regional arrangements and agencies without the approval of the Security Council.

Beyond these express terms, however, large areas of uncertainty remain. Although a broad preference for the peaceful resolution of disputes is assumed, there is no framework to guide or limit the actions of regional institutions in matters that have not engaged the Security Council. The provisions of the Charter could be interpreted to permit use of coercive measures by regional institutions against offending target states that have not yet engaged in actual aggression, or threats to the territorial integrity or political independence of other states. Regional balance-of-power configurations remain crucial; such balances remain decisive in the Charter, a fact that is reinforced by the special status accorded the five permanent members. By granting some recognition to regional arrangements and agencies, the Charter may have enhanced their legitimacy even when they engage in actions not specifically authorized by the Security Council.

These ambiguities indicate that the provisions for regional institutions failed to resolve many of the concerns that bedevilled negotiators at both Dumbarton Oaks and San Francisco, and these same problematic issues colour our evaluation of the performance of regional security arrangements analysed in this volume. If the entire system contemplated by the negotiators of the Charter had materialized, perhaps there would have been more practical answers to some of the inherent ambiguities in the present structure. The actual formation of a more effective collective security system may have led to the definition of clearer roles for regional arrangements. However, this possibility was overtaken by Cold War confrontation, as Washington, Moscow and their respective allies formed competitive security alliances that operated wholly outside of the authorization of the Security Council.[9]

The cessation of that bipolar conflict left the world in a much more fluid state, exposing many local sources of antagonism that had been suppressed by the Cold War. Although there was initial optimism about the international capacity to undertake more effective collective responses to security threats, the difficulty of generating effective multilateral responses to various crises quickly constrained that optimism. Recognition by the United Nations of its need for assistance in coping with new crises coincided with the judgement of some regional arrangements that these crises required regional attention; other regional institutions determined that the changes in the circumstances that generated the original reasons for their formation called for reconsideration of their missions. For example, recognition by NATO that its mission had to be adapted to the post-Cold War era led to that organization's willingness to become involved in the crisis in the former Yugoslavia. In light of this and other cases in this volume – ECOWAS in Liberia, the OAS in Central America and Haiti, and the CIS and OSCE in Georgia – many changes in the perceived interests of member states as well as the incentives for involvement in crises allow illuminating comparisons. While there are some similarities in their formal structural links to the United Nations, disparities in their capabilities, ideologies and orientations have led to even more significant differences in the operational problems entailed in the efforts of regional institutions to implement task-sharing with the UN.

The ambiguities in the role of regional arrangements and agencies in the UN structure have generated deeper problems with complex moral implications. The Charter purports to give superior authority to the Security Council. But in the cases in this volume, regional security arrangements sometimes possess greater practical operational capabilities than the council. The Charter's formal hierarchy is maladapted to these practical capabilities. Any reliance by the UN on regional security arrangements implicates normative problems beyond the obvious ambiguities of formal institutional roles. In the arena of international peace and security, inherent questions surround both actors and actions when the UN chooses to delegate tasks.

The emphasis here has been on regional arrangements, but analogous issues arise later in this essay in the discussion of NGO partnerships in humanitarian operations. Although fewer formal problems arise in UN-NGO collaboration, substantial questions arise about similar moral hazards; these question require NGOs to confront important decisions about their core values. These normative issues surrounding UN collaboration with regional security arrangements and NGOs in war zones pose enduring and difficult moral dilemmas in need of greater analysis than a brief treatment here.

Recent extensions of multilateral coercion to interventions by self-interested local actors have raised questions around UN collaboration with regional security arrangements and powerful states. In the cases in this volume, there were instances in which regional arrangements or individual states sought the endorsement of ongoing and proposed actions through resolutions or other formal actions by the Security Council. Each pursuit of an authorization from the UN reflected an effort to cloak proposed actions in a collectively validated legitimacy. In many of these situations, parochial national or regional interests provided significant motivations for involvement. Self-interested motivations are often substantially greater than that of the general membership of the UN or the Security Council. Where the vital self-interest of the proponent is involved, intervention would occur in any case.

However, where marginally less powerful interests are involved, authorization by the UN can provide a strong presumption in favour of another actor, constraining potential objectors to the intervention while reducing the intervener's potential costs and risks. To the extent that multilateral validation is important to the intervener, the desire for that validation may provide leverage to channel the intervener's actions in normatively more acceptable directions. At the same time, the more essential to the multilateral effort the regional or individual state intervener's capabilities, the more pressure for the multilateral body to authorize intervention regardless of possible self-serving motivations. In a world of global television newscasts, graphic portrayals of human suffering can pressure democratically elected governments to authorize responses by other states motivated by questionable motivations. If the intervener's capabilities are critical for an immediate response, that intervener may dictate the terms of its own authorization even though that authorization is ostensibly provided by the United Nations. Under such circumstances, formal UN grants of authority for action may serve as a none-too-opaque, blue fig leaf covering the ambitions of local or regional actors. This is a subject for the concluding section of this essay.

SERVICE-PROVIDING NGOs

As stated by Leon Gordenker and Thomas G. Weiss in Chapter 2, on a framework for non-governmental organizations, the dynamism and variety of the NGO universe makes generalizations difficult, a point that is clear in light of the four case studies that contain data about $500 million-a-year giants to minuscule grassroots organizations (GROs) and everything in between. On the one hand, an analyst could ask 'so what?' There are also ranges in other types of categories of actors on the international stage – for example, between states like Suriname and Spain, or Chad and China. On the other hand, this very untidiness, ironically, opens up a host of opportunities for UN task-sharing with NGOs. Moreover, if there are key operational problems between the United Nations system and NGOs, a better division of labour should be possible with concerted efforts and incentives by donors and intergovernmental organizations. This is an operational challenge to management, not a structural one to state sovereignty.

To foreshadow arguments in the next section where a comparison of the lessons of 'subcontracting' is the theme, it is worth stating that there is far less doubt about the formal hierarchy, for instance, of relations between the UN and NGOs than between the world organization and regional security arrangements. This applies even to humanitarian relief by NGOs during armed conflicts. This arena provides perhaps the best illustration of the validity of the original hypothesis about privatization as well as an important caveat about moral choices just discussed in relationship to regional security arrangements. Where NGOs are involved, few would entertain serious doubts about the superior authority of both the state with territorial jurisdiction over the region of conflict and the UN acting as either authorizing or formal contracting party. Under any scenario, NGOs must ultimately comply with the directives of either or both of these authorities. As with any organizational structure, practical problems of coordination, logistics and personnel can make operational arrangements differ from formal hierarchical relationships. However, local operational adaptations do not alter the relative authority of the UN and NGOs involved even in humanitarian operations.

Nevertheless, the consequences of NGO humanitarian operations during ongoing armed conflicts raise thorny questions of principle. Rational choice theorists of law and economics have developed the concept of 'moral hazard' to describe the perverse situation in which the provision of assistance to those harmed by an action reduces the negative consequences of the action to such an extent that there is less overall incentive to avoid the initiation of the action in the first place.[10] First utilized to describe the reduced incentives to avoid losses by those who acquired insurance against loss, the moral hazard concept has been found useful elsewhere. In the humanitarian assistance arena, recent examples are familiar. The humanitarian assistance provided to populations displaced by ethnic cleansing in the former Yugoslavia was argued by some observers to ameliorate the horrors of the practice to such an extent that there was less pressure to force the termination of that conduct.[11] Some contend that humanitarian assistance creates a moral hazard by ameliorating the consequences of ethnic cleansing for those of one ethnic group engaged in forced expulsions of individuals of different ethnic groups. Under those circumstances, humanitarian assistance creates a moral hazard.

There is clear evidence that NGOs have provided relief in many circumstances where the UN found itself in difficulties,[12] although the consequences of NGO efforts can be painfully ambiguous.[13] NGOs have found themselves facing lethal coercive pressures that threaten the continued viability of aid efforts in numerous ongoing conflicts, most recently in the Great Lakes region of eastern Africa. In many of these situations, combatants from the victim groups threaten force against NGOs to require payment, either in cash or in kind, for access to civilian populations, resulting in nominally neutral NGOs providing logistical support for active combatants. Humanitarian supplies are regularly confiscated from relief workers by combatants, and medical service providers are coerced to provide preferred treatment to those accompanied by armed relatives. The diversion of humanitarian supplies heightens the dilemma by tainting short-term emergency civilian assistance with forced augmentation of the long-term capacity of combatants to continue the fighting. Some NGO representatives are expressing reservations about continued humanitarian assistance amid continuing conflicts, bearing in mind the need to reduce the risk of involuntarily providing logistical support for combatants as well as the need to lessen the danger to civilian aid workers enduring increasing numbers of casualties in the field. Whatever course is ultimately adopted by NGOs, considerations of international peace and security may cut against providing aid before the termination of hostilities, because humanitarian assistance can be used as a weapon of war.

In spite of these dilemmas and moral hazards, lives are saved by NGOs. By extension, possibilities arise for properly structured cooperation between the UN and NGOs in the delivery of many services. Under the right circumstances then, the original hypothesis about the increasing privatization of world politics was in evidence in war zones and throughout the other cases. NGOs, both as advocates and operators, are increasingly in evidence, usually to the benefit of global governance, by which we mean better responses to problems that go beyond the individual or collective capacities of states. The record also contains examples of major negative externalities – Mark Duffield's possible paradigm of a new political economy of humanitarian efforts is the most controversial. Nonetheless, the benefits of UN task-sharing with NGOs are numerous and valid across enough of the experiences to suggest that the world organization should continue to explore the possibilities for task-sharing with non-governmental organizations while searching for better means to coordinate total inputs and to ensure accountability.

As a result of the in-depth explorations, it is possible now to hazard some tentative responses to the five questions posed in the framework for analysis by Gordenker and Weiss. If the fundamental aim is to foster global governance rather than parochial institutional agendas, the essential assignment is understanding empirical reality in order to identify when it is most appropriate to heat up or cool down enthusiasms about devolving responsibility for the provision of services by non-governmental organizations.

First, 'NGO' is a useful category to examine the phenomenon of contracting for services by the United Nations, in spite of the ongoing and long-standing debate about the appropriateness of this term. In some ways this may have seemed like a rhetorical question – if it were not useful, why would this volume exist? Although there may be 25 other appellations, as Ian Smillie notes, 'non-governmental organization' as a term is specified in Charter Article 71, fits as well as any other and is accepted widely by practitioners even if analysts continue to invent new labels.

There emerge from the cases many unintended consequences of the rise of NGOs and their task-sharing with the United Nations. For instance, all five cases suggest pluses and minuses of the move toward privatization. The same qualification applies to the mixture of multiple funding and market pressures that seem in some cases to have worked against the dominant values of solidarity and social commitment that traditionally have been the strengths of NGOs.

Moreover, and as hinted by Gordenker and Weiss, intergovernmental bodies of the UN system encountered the most problematic relations when seeking help from NGOs whose core functions are advocacy for particular policies or ideologies. These types of activities, whatever the arena, represent only a small percentage (probably 1–2 per cent globally) of total NGO expenditures. Given the controversial and antigovernmental nature of many such efforts (Sheila Jasanoff's treatment of the environment comes immediately to mind, as would human rights, which were not discussed in this volume), it is unrealistic to expect enthusiasm from most governments and the intergovernmental organizations (IGOs) of which they are members regarding NGO activities that are designed to bite some of the hands feeding them. At the same time, the ability of the UN's mechanisms to function even minimally in both the human rights and environmental arenas is precisely because of NGOs. With or without an official contract and financing, NGOs play an essential role in the emerging regimes in these areas. And many states have pro-human rights or pro-environmental stances that logically are fostered specifically by those NGOs combating the contrary orientations of other states.

The size and scope of NGOs no doubt affect their abilities to relate to the United Nations. Coalitions and federations of large organizations may be more convenient partners for the administrators of large international agencies than more atomized forms of non-governmental organizations. Conceptually speaking, it is more judicious to speak of a continuum to reflect such differences and resulting generalizations. But in terms of entering into contracts with the members of the UN system for the delivery of goods and services, coalitions and federations of large organizations are more convenient partners for the administrators of large IGOs than atomized forms of NGOs. This theme was underlying in particular Duffield's depiction of humanitarian relief and Smillie's of development assistance. It also means that the largest private organizations, whose staff and operating cultures many observers suggest are virtually indistinguishable from public intergovernmental or governmental bureaucracies,[14] are increasingly the dominant actors and the basis for policy suggestions here and elsewhere. This lends additional weight to arguments that NGOs should pay careful attention to protecting their distinctness and independence in spite of the seductiveness of new resources. Whether major international NGOs are contributing more to changing world politics and values – as Jasanoff, Smillie and Chand for the most part argue – or to a new paradigm of marginalization and polarization – as Duffield posits – remains to be seen.

Second, there are a number of tasks that NGOs can do better than IGOs. Although there is far from universal agreement on this point, each of the cases contain specific illustrations of the comparative advantages of NGOs. Chand's examination of election monitoring, for instance, provides the most in-depth portrait of a synergistic relationship between non-governmental and intergovernmental action in Mexico in which the non-governmental actors took contentious public stands while the UN maintained its privileged role as a counterpart for the government. What Chand dubs a 'symbiotic' relationship between the UN and international NGOs, on the one hand, and then between these outsiders and local

NGOs, on the other, applies also to Jasanoff's depiction of generating knowledge and changing policy in the environmental arena. She documents a powerful coming together of 'more professionalized multinational NGOs, such as Greenpeace, the Worldwide Fund for Nature and the Friends of the Earth' in a division of labour with 'smaller, community-based NGOs [that] are more likely to stimulate activity at the local level than to initiate sweeping policy change'.

Donor governments should continue considering NGOs as possible conduits for bilateral funds. The analyses here suggest that member states of UN organizations also should consider – on a sector-by-sector or crisis-by-crisis basis – whether NGOs are better equipped than their competitors to deliver humanitarian aid, foster open elections, conduct development co-operation and protect the environment. As Smillie suggests, however, the real challenge is not for the UN to 'mimic what other agencies are doing' but to find a meaningful way 'to create partnerships based on development concerns rather than on perceptions of strategic or organizational advantage'. Full-fledged and equal 'partners' should be the operational label rather than subservient 'contractors'.

Except for the unusual case of humanitarian intervention that has been the object of so much publicity in the post-Cold War era, NGOs hardly can operate completely outside of governmental grasp. Their work, if tactfully done, does not necessarily openly derogate from or erode governmental authority. In fact, NGOs have actually taken over the delivery of many basic social services once thought to be the reserve of governments in the past in many Third World countries. As Chand points out in relationship to the elections in Mexico, the presence of outsiders can actually 'improve the credibility of election results' and 'almost certainly helped reduce the risk of violence'. The provision of social services or the improvement of elections may strengthen rather than undermine governmental authority.

At the same time, sovereign states are not ignorant of those NGOs that have the indisputable capacity to pose prickly issues and ensure especially intense surveillance in places where recipient governmental authority is contested or abusive. This generalization seems to apply equally to raising macro-issues at global conferences or pursuing micro-issues with local and national governments. In this volume, Jasanoff's examination of environmental NGOs best illustrates this more general point, one that would have been clearer had human rights, women's issues or population been examined. At the same time, governments that champion international norms would view these same NGOs not as 'enemies' but as 'partners' who strengthen environmental, human and women's rights or population norms. It also is worth indicating the obvious but often overlooked fact that governments are not monolithic; hence, one ministry or even senior official may be quite pleased to support the work of NGOs that undermines competitors in the same government who are hostile to NGOs.

Third, there are constraints that apply to bringing NGOs into UN programmes. These were broken down in the framework essay by Gordenker and Weiss according to policy-making, autonomy, programme execution and government reactions. For example, financial backers as well as NGOs themselves are proud of their activist 'culture', which creates an almost visceral unwillingness in principle to devote scarce resources to research and reflection. This reluctance raises questions as to the degree that any learning from experience takes place and is transmitted to others in the field or to succeeding generations.[15] Evidence appears in all five cases about the fundraising imperatives of NGOs that impede more rational programming and decision-making. Smillie's detailed analysis of 'rubber accounting methods' and 'shell game economics' provides the most gripping justification for changing the traditional standard operating procedures of NGOs away from reflex toward reflection. Donors as well as staff must begin to learn to live with this reality.

In terms of participation in policy-making, the cases highlight an often-ignored reality that involving NGOs in international policy debates does not automatically eliminate problems of 'democracy'. This term is itself problematic and probably should be abandoned. Here we are not referring to the likelihood or plausibility of choosing 300 to 600 accredited NGOs to form a new 'Assembly of the People' within the United Nations as proposed by the Commission on Global Governance.[16] How can those organizations approved by the UN, now called 'civil society organizations' (CSOs), represent the views of those that have not been accredited?

However, involving almost any group of NGOs makes intergovernmental assemblies more 'representative' or 'pluralistic' in that a wide range of views are introduced. The chimerical notion of constructing the 'perfect' mixture of public and private views is reminiscent of discussions about Security Council reform – and probably is just about as impossible to resolve satisfactorily. The selection of NGOs does not necessarily guarantee an accurate replication of the variety of views on any given subject – surely a Sisyphean task. Whatever the subject matter, however, the five cases suggest that the struggle to include more rather than fewer private voices is worth the effort. Merely in the narrowest of institutional terms, deliberations and decisions by UN organizations have more legitimacy as a result of casting their net wider.

Probably no objective is more important in the philosophy of NGOs than maintaining autonomy. In fact, the use in a definition of 'non', however unacceptable to linguists, is an important indication that NGOs consciously seek in their activities to be alternatives to those of governments. The 'N' in 'NGO' may in fact be the main reason for the term's wide acceptance in spite of numerous other definitional problems. During the Cold War, much heated debate related to disparaging the work of GONGOs (government-organized non-governmental organizations) because their views were indistinguishable from those of the governments in the societies in which they were incorporated. This criticism clearly applied to those NGOs from the socialist bloc mainly because so-called NGOs in them existed only so long as they did not criticize the state or the system that financed them totally. In the West, criticism of GONGOs took the more subtle form of looking askance at NGOs that took too many governmental resources – the logic being that 'calling the piper's tune' was somewhat comparable in East and West.

Here as in so many areas, the end of the Cold War has not ended debate but put the subject back on the agenda, albeit in altered form. The resources channelled to NGOs for both development and humanitarian action are large and growing. As Duffield notes, the enormous increase in '[t]he involvement by NGOs in welfare provision would not have been possible without a growth of aid subcontracting.' Although the nature of relationships to Western governments has changed, the issues before Quangos (quasi-autonomous non-governmental organizations because they receive substantial resources from public instead of private sources) remain unchanged: do their terms of engagement with donors result in an unacceptable loss of autonomy and of flexibility to play catalytic roles? Smillie, Chand and Jasanoff are more sanguine than Duffield, pointing out among other things that frequently there seems to be a double standard for NGOs. Smillie points out that universities or think-tanks are 'independent' even with government grants, and business is 'autonomous' without government contracts.

Perhaps because they are so proud of their activist 'culture', NGOs are often reluctant to spend time and money evaluating their own effectiveness. Smillie, for one, emphasizes that fear of donor retaliation for 'mistakes' often exacerbates already existing financial pressures. But whatever the precise causal explanation, the result is too little critical scrutiny of past operations and too little soul-searching about the increasingly complex contexts in which NGOs operate. Again, there are serious questions about institutional learning and change under such circumstances. Duffield, for instance, would wish for far more self-critical examination by humanitarians to determine whether 'the nature of Western intervention could be further encouraging the political exclusivism and fragmentation that is already underway.'

Evidence appears in all five cases about the fundraising imperatives of NGOs that impede more rational programming and decision-making, that foster moving quickly to the next activity or crisis rather than assessing the value of past activities. Perhaps the most critical perspective comes from Smillie, who analyses 'why NGOs actually avoid evaluation so studiously'. As in other areas, he sees the necessity and possibility, however, of 'changing the mind-set' in order 'to put learning back on the agenda' within an atmosphere in which 'there must be a tolerance for failure' in order to run risks, learn lessons and improve performance. As he notes, a stigma should be attached to a failure only 'when mistakes are repeated or suppressed'.

NGOs may find themselves scrutinized and criticized in new ways when governmental delegations make representations, complain, protest and generally display opposition to the activities of NGOs that have been contracted for work by a particular UN organization. Moreover, this normal quid pro quo for more resources is a subject that will increasingly preoccupy NGO managers who will predictably attempt to protect their autonomy. The visceral and defensive reliance upon non-intervention has an increasingly hollow ring for governments, and the knee-jerk reaction by NGOs that they are somehow above donor scrutiny will be equally unappealing.

Fourth, and growing naturally from the imperatives of resource mobilization, the need to improve NGO accountability is a universal preoccupation in the five case studies. Few would dispute that there is need to enhance accountability to the authority (here, to the United Nations) that decides to share tasks with NGOs. As expected, the debate about ECOSOC rules and regulations (in particular, the modification of Resolution 1296 of 1968 through Resolution 1996/31) is of little concern to most authors. Quite simply, the action is elsewhere, in the programmes that are subcontracted from the UN system with increasing frequency or often simply devolved by states to NGOs. However, the new ECOSOC resolution would have perhaps been more noted had contributors focused on advocacy subjects such as women's or human rights. Under the new resolution, national and regional NGOs, obviously crucial for information about abuses, can now speak with their own voice and in their own name rather than under the auspices of an international NGO in consultative status.

UN oversight and its ability to ensure accountability were central themes, but there was no real consensus about how best to implement measures that would probably be more efficacious through self-regulation rather than outside imposition. Duffield argues that 'NGOs have little accountability either to Western taxpayers or their so-called beneficiaries.' The most controversial counterpoint is made by Smillie, who again points to double standards and wishes to 'decant ritualistic cant', including the notion of accountability. He argues that there really are 'multiple account-abilities' (to boards, members, staff, donors, media and peers), which to-gether 'exert a powerful influence on the behaviour of an NGO'. Duffield does not disagree that there are a multiplicity of such constraints and that NGOs may not be worse than other governmental or intergovernmental purveyors of services. But because of their values, he holds them to higher standards and believes that the sum of existing constraints does not consti-tute meaningful accountability. He marshals evidence that 'the contract culture also acts to decrease accountability', and laments that 'there are no agreed standards of recognized criteria' for international aid workers.

There is no consensus about whether we are moving toward what Gordenker and Weiss characterize as 'a possible new model of coopera-tion with the UN responsible for the formulation of norms, principles and decisional procedures and oversight, on the one hand, and NGOs for the actual conduct of programmes, on the other'. The notion of identifying comparative advantages and working out a new international division of labour is attractive to accountants and theorists, but reality is more ambiguous. Rather than any airtight or mechanistic categories of a divi-sion of labour, the cases point toward a more supple combination of forces for similar tasks but with different emphases.

More particularly, Smillie's partnership in the development arena and Duffield's in the humanitarian one are predicated upon links to local NGOs. This same theme appears in Chand's coming together of various outsiders with local civil society to foster open elections, and in Jasanoff's emphasis on the spread of knowledge and learning in the environmental arena through an effective marriage of international and local NGOs. In comparison with the view first analysed in the 1995 *Third World Quarterly* volume about UN and NGO relationships, the variety of links to local actors is a crucial new perspective that emerges far more clearly in 1997.

This comment provides a segue to the fifth and final query put forward by Gordenker and Weiss. There is a steep learning curve for the ever-evolving relationships among NGOs, IGOs and world civil society. This area clearly is vast and virtually impossible to discern empirically at present. At the same time, the cases provide a host of interesting insights to substantiate the importance of the relationships between 'outsiders' (both intergovernmental and non-governmental) and 'insiders' (national NGOs and grassroots organizations) even if data are and will remain sketchy and suggestive. In the past observers have pointed to the growing importance of NGOs in replacing the state as the primary purveyor of many basic social services. But far less obvious analytical and theoretical insights surface from our cases: Chand's emphasis on the development of local 'social capital' through election assistance, and Jasanoff's call to involve local knowledge in generating scientific knowledge and solutions as well as in learning by institutions. They underscore the vibrancy of local actors, which also permeates the analyses of Duffield and Smillie whose emphasis is more operational but for whom increasing local capacities, institution-building and generally empowering indigenous peoples are no less essential.

It is a formidable task to trace links between the United Nations, international NGOs and healthier local civil societies. The numbers and complexity of intermediaries and their relationships is overwhelming. The presence of millions of grassroots organizations complicates still further any straightforward portrait of UN task-sharing with non-state actors. If the analyses by the authors who examine NGOs for this volume are correct, there is a growing and under-exploited potential for links between local NGOs and all outside actors, be they from the governments, UN system or international non-governmental organizations. Of all the topics that emerge from these cases, this may provide the most substantial and crucial future research agenda.

TOWARD OR AWAY FROM GLOBAL GOVERNANCE?

Evidence from the eight case studies in this volume documents the extent to which the early post-Cold War period has been characterized by 'subcontracting' for military services and some diplomatic functions to regional arrangements and major states, on the one hand, and for the provision of services to international NGOs, on the other. There are a growing number of examples of the UN's devolving military and diplomatic responsibilities, some of which are examined here and some of which are not. Among the latter, for example, the pursuit of the Gulf War and the creation of safe havens for Kurds are clear and successful illustrations of military 'subcontracting'; a more controversial and less successful example is Somalia.

Three Security Council decisions between late June and late July 1994 indicated the growing salience of military intervention by major powers in regions of their traditional interests. These include the Russian scheme to deploy its troops in Georgia to end the three-year-old civil war that is analysed in these pages as well as the French intervention in Rwanda to help stave off genocidal conflict and the US plan to spearhead a military invasion to reverse the military coup in Haiti. Another illustration of this trend involved the decision in Budapest in December 1994 by the Conference (now Organization) on Security and Cooperation in Europe (OSCE) to authorize troops from the CIS and other OSCE member states after a definitive agreement in Nagorno-Karabakh. Earlier efforts by Nigeria and other countries of ECOWAS in Liberia is another example as is NATO's IFOR, both of which are analysed in this volume along with a variety of formal and informal efforts in Central America.

Commentators, military and civilian alike, agree that the results from these arrangements have not been uniformly beneficial to victims or to troop-contributing countries. Contributors to this volume are reluctant to generalize from their cases – and in the former Yugoslavia, even within a case from the two time periods before and after Dayton. The evident gap between the UN's capacities and increasing demands for help could be filled by regional powers, or even hegemons. This clearly is not collective security of the Charter variety.[17] Coalitions of the willing under separate command and control are totally different from the automatic mobilization of soldiers by all member states against an aggressor under the command and control of the UN Secretary-General. In fact, the Security Council is experimenting with a type of great power domination over decision-making and enforcement that the United Nations had originally been founded to end. Such a tactic is increasingly pertinent in light of the inherent difficulties of multilateral mobilization and management of military force.[18] The key, according to evidence from all four cases in this volume, is to temper the necessary devolution of responsibilities in order to ensure greater accountability to international norms and the collective expression of the decisions by the larger community of states. It may also be possible that informal institutional arrangements or *ad hoc* groupings may in some cases be at least as effective as formally constituted institutions.

As Leurdijk argues from the case of NATO in the former Yugoslavia, there was no 'blueprint', nor could there have been because of the continually changing situation on the ground. Moreover, all of the contributors point out that no template could be formulated for such disparate cases. Tacsan prefers to frame the assignment as one of regional institutions and the United Nations 'performing appropriately', by which he means that they 'are able to redefine means and mechanisms when necessary, innovate approaches and foster members' consensus around certain principles, norms and procedures'. Moreover, 'appropriate performers are also good learners', by which he means that adaptation occurs after successes and failures are weighed.

The limited attention span and absorptive capacity of states for crises are factors clearly important in explaining the lack of interest in Liberia's tragedy or in the results of the ECOWAS response. The unwillingness of the Security Council even to authorize financing may have been a flexible response in both Georgia and Liberia. But such adaptability gives pause when it merely rationalizes a blue imprimatur for the pursuit of self-interests by major powers when the Security Council is unwilling to act vigorously itself. The difference between what Michael Barnett elsewhere has called the 'politics of devolution' rather than the 'politics of domination'[19] is the ability to hold subcontractors accountable for actions undertaken on behalf of the United Nations. The danger for domination is present in all the cases but is most dramatic in Liberia and Georgia. MacFarlane, for example, warns that 'reliance on a regional organization may further the hegemonic aspirations of dominant powers.'

Alagappa concludes with a suggestion that the UN's 'moral authority' must be safeguarded by several measures: limited authorizations to ensure reporting; the injection of UN monitors; a joint body to oversee implementation; and an insistence upon respect by subcontractors for international norms. Support for this suggestion comes from evidence in all the cases. Because of the 'messiness' of such operations and the frequent lack of political will and resources, the overwhelming logic of the cases points toward more prevention rather than more reactions, however effective. Although much of the recent policy fascination with prevention as a panacea for the fragmentation of ethnic conflict amounts to wishful thinking,[20] nonetheless earlier actions are clearly preferable to the kind of 'mopping up' exercises, with or without subcontracts, that have been commonplace in the last half decade.

The cases included in this study give an indication of the scope of these problems. Many questions have been raised about the motivations for Nigeria's participation in the Liberian peace operations, for which Adibe's discussions are most informative, and similarly, MacFarlane's portrayal of Russia's involvement in Georgia lays bare multifarious motivations. Although not discussed here, these criticisms resemble those offered by observers to explain the French response to Rwanda.[21] Implicit in Leurdijk's analysis of NATO's involvement in Bosnia after Dayton is criticism of serving particular parochial interests.[22] Many critical observers argued that US involvement in Haiti was designed not for the promotion of Haitian democracy but for the quashing of domestic fears of a deluge of Haitian refugees because of the consequent risks for Florida electoral politics,[23] a theme that joins Tacsan's discussions of the motivations of the Central American presidents in the 1980s.

Where a regional grouping or a local power chooses a course of forceful military or even diplomatic involvement, potential claims of mixed and self-interested motives are unavoidable. It is this conundrum that makes peace operations by either regional arrangements or powerful local states problematic for global governance. To the extent that Security Council mandates are implemented by mechanisms supervised and managed through the UN secretariat, fewer questions are likely about the legitimacy of implementation, although there will be more about their effectiveness.

At the same time, implementation of Security Council mandates may prove more effective if delegated to regional arrangements or to powerful single states. but questions of the legitimacy intrude when that tactic for implementation appears to serve too obviously parochial interests. To the extent that regional institutions along with powerful states are clearly not subordinated in a hierarchy to the UN Security Council, scepticism may taint broad support of such implementation efforts. Conversely, those actions to foster international peace and security that rely only on those capabilities and resources that the UN can bring under its complete supervision and management may prove to be ineffective if the recent historical record is any guide for the future. Striking a balance between legitimacy and effectiveness poses difficult political choices that are often avoided until graphic news reports demonstrate the human costs of the failure to reach decisions. At that point, the pressure to act momentarily overcomes qualms about legitimacy, but then doubts about the legitimacy of the chosen tactics of implementation quickly give way to criticism and recrimination.

Making use of regional security arrangements may disappoint die-hard UN enthusiasts, who emphasize truly universal decisions backed by truly universal means for enforcement, however unrealistic or impractical. But the proverbial bottom-line in these cases is that 'subcontracting' can, under appropriate circumstances, be a sensible step toward improving international peace and security. Major powers inevitably flex their muscles in the pursuit of their perceived interests, but they do not inevitably subject themselves to international law and monitoring. By operating under the scrutiny of a wider community of states, the interveners could be held accountable for their actions.[24] Thus, influencing the behaviour of such would-be 'subcontractors' is a feasible step toward better global governance.

The second element of the subcontracting phenomenon relates to the growing NGO provision of numerous international services – including those discussed in depth here (relief, election monitoring, development assistance and environmental action) as well as those that were not (for example human rights, gender issues, health services). This is part of a larger development, namely the burgeoning of non-governmental organizations in all sectors that have injected new and unexpected voices into international discourse.[25] Over the last two decades, but especially since the end of the Cold War, human rights advocates, gender activists, developmentalists and groups of indigenous peoples have become more vocal and operational in many contexts that were once thought to be the exclusive preserve of governments.[26] As the role of the state dwindles and is reappraised and as analysts and policy-makers alike seek alternatives to help solve problems, NGOs emerge as critical actors – private in form but public in purpose.

Delivery of services is the mainstay of most of their budgets and the basis for enthusiastic support from a wide range of donors. Bilateral and intergovernmental organizations are relying upon NGOs more and more.[27] The last twenty years have witnessed exponential growth, so much so that now the total value of assistance delivered by NGOs outweighs that disbursed by the UN system (excluding the Washington-based financial institutions, the World Bank and the International Monetary Fund). Many NGOs run development programmes, but they have become increasingly active in migration and disaster relief as well as the other efforts discussed in our case studies. Operational NGOs are central to comprehensive international responses. In 1995, at least 13 per cent of total public development aid – some $10 billion and probably much more since neither food aid nor military help figures accurately in statistics – was disbursed by NGOs.

Rather than lamenting, as a World Federalist might, the inability of the UN system to meet human needs across an ever-widening front, it is more pragmatic and sensible to foster multilateralism through a better division of labour, and this inevitably calls for relying upon NGOs for a variety of tasks. One of the challenging analytical tasks is to get a better handle on the complex web of UN, regional and non-governmental institutions of varying sizes, capacities and professionalism that are active on almost every issue and in almost every country.

As a semi-autonomous actor, the United Nations should take maximum advantage of subcontracting possibilities for non-governmental organizations – both international and local. What commends NGOs in this arena and elsewhere is their working relations with community groups. These contacts are further strengthened by their commitment to staying on and their relatively low costs (on average and except for the senior managers of the largest ones, their salary and benefits are considerably less than

those of international civil servants).[28] Non-governmental organizations
have earned a reputation for being more flexible, forthcoming and
responsive than the bilateral and intergovernmental members of the international system. Whether an international NGO is small or large, focused
or far-flung, its activities tend to concentrate on the practical needs of
ordinary people. NGOs endeavour to customize their activities for the
grassroots, which can be legitimately distinguished for the most part from
the 'wholesale' assistance provided by donor governments and the UN
system. These explain why the United Nations, in addition to governmental and individual donors, should continue expanding resources made
available directly to private agencies.

External NGOs also bring weaknesses to their operational field activities, a point that is underlined most dramatically by Duffield and Smillie.
Getting beyond the shibboleth of pristine NGOs is a necessity, not yet
superfluous because many saintly images still permeate much of the hagio-
graphical literature and the views even of informed publics. NGO energy
may lend frenzy and confusion. Careful planning and evaluation are rarer
than they should be. The desire to get on with the next practical activity
contributes to a lack of reflectiveness and an inattention to institutional
learning. Fund-raising imperatives make NGOs as subject as other bureaucracies to concerns about organizational expansion and turf. Well-known
impatience with bureaucratic constraints often reflect naivety about the
highly political contexts in which NGOs increasingly operate, and about
the ramifications of activities. Some NGOs guard their independence so
closely that they miss evident opportunities to expand the impact of their
actions by combining forces with like-minded institutions. How much of
their rising expenditures is due to inefficiencies and increasing administrative costs is, for example, not clear. Having literally hundreds of subcontractors delivering similar goods and services in a disjointed and
competitive marketplace means that part of the dramatic growth must be
driven by NGOs themselves, a phenomenon particularly pronounced in
the humanitarian and development arenas.[29] 'How many angels can dance
on the head of a pin?' has a contemporary counterpart that emerges, for
example, from Chand's case study, 'How many NGOs can be active in
monitoring Mexico's elections?'

After reading the analytical perspectives in these pages, readers could
consider much of the material in this collection a contribution to 'NGO-
bashing', a relative of the 'UN-bashing' that often seems to be the
favourite pastime in Washington, DC. For instance in Duffield's view,
NGOs may be unwittingly contributing to a new paradigm that is better
able 'to contain the effects of poverty and social exclusion' or 'find ways

to work within crises and manage their symptoms' than deal with root causes and the alleviation of poverty.

Unlike the ambiguities and decision-making problems that characterize possible task-sharing between the UN and regional security arrangements, there is no structural reason or consideration of state sovereignty to prevent management decisions about more or better UN subcontracting with NGOs. Stated in another way, the UN system can require more transparency and accountability from NGOs than from regional security arrangements. There thus could and should be a quid pro quo for channelling more resources through NGOs and providing them with better access to decision-making. Donors should insist upon more formal cooperation between NGOs and the United Nations, on the one hand, and more self-regulation among NGOs themselves, on the other.

Perhaps the thorniest decisions for international NGOs will revolve around the need for enhanced coordination, oftentimes under UN auspices. In Duffield's view, 'in practice, the extent of coordination is often minimal' although 'in theory, however, integrated or comprehensive programming operates at several levels'. Andrew Natsios has summarized what may be the best-case scenario within emergencies but with more general applicability: 'The marriage of convenience between NGOs and the UN system in relief responses over time may become comfortable enough that *ad hoc* arrangements will work, even if a passionate love affair never occurs.'[30] He writes elsewhere that 'Organizational autonomy and complexity are enemies of speed and strategic coherence.' One of the explanations, according to Duffield's new paradigm, is that the aid market pushes NGOs to diversify and provide multiple services in order to secure a larger portion of the subcontracting business. This dissipation of energies clearly should be changed, and donors should use their funding leverage to pressure NGOs to emphasize the advantages of collaboration rather than the advantages of independence. This has begun through a variety of formal and informal consortia, within federations and outside of them, within sectors and countries. And it should accelerate.

Greater self-regulation and self-questioning are certainly in order for NGOs, a subject that Duffield argues 'will dominate the scene for the rest of the decade and beyond'. Smillie does well to demythologize debate and call for greater specificity and objectivity, but his own argument suggests the extent to which 'accountability' and 'transparency' have become dominant themes precisely because they are problems that urgently require solutions. If politicians and educators are being asked to meet higher standards of performance and ethics – and certainly states and the UN system are not immune from calls for greater responsiveness[31] – logically

NGOs are next in line. Social workers, school teachers and taxi drivers are normally certified. Why not aid workers, human rights monitors and environmental activists?

NGO managers should regulate themselves and aspire to a new professionalism, or such regulation no doubt will be imposed by others. One possible first step, for example, is to accelerate a certification process signifying professional competence to be active in war zones. This approach could and should be extended to codes of conduct for other arenas, not the ones to govern political activities but rather professional standards. Incentives – essentially more untied resources and greater access to decision-making – should elicit more cooperation than in the past.

An advantage of involving more and more NGOs with the United Nations is that the world organization's legitimacy could be enhanced by its association with what are widely viewed as popular, effective and pluralistic organizations. Making better use of NGOs in tandem with the United Nations could only help build greater public support for the world organization as an independent actor and for multilateralism more generally. This theme permeates the cases – it matters little whether the focus is humanitarian relief, election monitoring, development assistance or environmental action. 'Subcontracting' may be an apt description, but the United Nations and its member states should treat NGOs not as 'contractors' but rather as 'partners'. Smillie summarizes elegantly the view of other contributors: 'This will require a dramatic shift in mind-set … in thinking of NGOs more as a permanent, planned and negotiated part of the landscape, and less as temporary and somewhat troublesome gap-fillers. In this there is a critical role to be played by the UN family.'

As mentioned earlier, recent experience with the devolution of responsibilities from the United Nations to both regional security arrangements and service-providing NGOs contains evidence of both enhanced and diminished global governance. We are in a better position now to understand the factors influencing both the appropriate timing and mixtures for heating and cooling the fervour of proponents and opponents of the UN, regional arrangements and non-governmental organizations. Moving beyond UN task-sharing, or tempering it, is captured by the conclusion to Jasanoff's essay. 'Waiting for a more coherent authority to develop at the supranational level', she writes, 'is not a plausible solution. A more promising avenue is to engage the full range of institutional resources – governmental as well as non-governmental and intergovernmental – to increase the prospects for learning and reduce the potential for inter-organizational conflict.'

The proverbial bottom-line is that the institutions created by human beings can be stronger than the problems facing them. This assumes, however, that there is a commitment to confront problems and stay with them for the long haul. The United Nations, regional security arrangements and service-providing NGOs have made a difference. It is time to move beyond simplistic notions of UN 'subcontracting' in the direction of hard-headed task-sharing and a better international division of labour. This would benefit donors and recipients, institutions and peoples.

NOTES

1. Following the UN Charter's language and the framework spelled out in the first essay of this volume, 'regional arrangements' refers to both formal and informal cooperation at the regional level, and 'institutions' is synonomous. In spite of its prevalence in the literature, the authors avoid the term 'regional organizations' because it was used by NATO to distinguish itself as not falling under the strictures of the Charter and the hierarchy therein stipulated between the world organization and 'regional arrangements and agencies'.
2. See W. Andy Knight, 'Towards a subsidiarity model for peacemaking and preventive diplomacy: making Chapter VIII of the UN Charter operational', *Third World Quarterly*, 17 (1), March 1996, pp. 31–51.
3. As with all simplifications, there are problems with such generalizations because sometimes high and low politics merge. On 12 February 1997, for example, three international NGOs (Oxfam, CARE and Médecins sans Frontières) gave an unprecedented briefing to the Security Council on the Great Lakes region of eastern Africa. This followed upon an earlier procedure in which the International Committee of the Red Cross (ICRC) meets with the president of the Security Council once a month for a briefing on crises around the world.
4. For a discussion, see Thomas G. Weiss, David P. Forsythe and Roger A. Coate, *The United Nations and Changing World Politics* (Boulder, Colo.: Westview Press, 1994), especially pp. 17–59.
5. See Boutros Boutros-Ghali, *Supplement to An Agenda for Peace*, document A/50/60-S/1995/1, reprinted in *An Agenda for Peace 1995* (New York: United Nations, 1995), especially paras 85–8.
6. See Louise Fawcett, 'Regionalism in historical perspective', in Louise Fawcett and Andrew Hurrell (eds), *Regionalism in World Politics: Regional Organizations and World Order* (Oxford: Oxford University Press, 1995), pp. 9–36.
7. Oscar Schachter and Christopher Joyner, *United Nations Legal Order* (Cambridge: Cambridge University Press, 1995), p. 258.
8. Ibid., p. 261.

9. Robert E. Riggs and Jack C. Plano, *The United Nations: International Politics and World Organization*, 2nd edn (Belmont, Calif.: Wadsworth Publishing, 1994), pp. 111–12.

10. See Tom Baker, 'On the genealogy of moral hazard', *Texas Law Review*, 75, 1996, p. 237.

11. See Amir Pasic and Thomas G. Weiss, 'The politics of rescue: Yugoslavia's wars and the humanitarian impulse', *Ethics and International Affairs*, XI, 1997, pp. 105–31.

12. Peter Beinart, 'Aid and abet: The UN's disastrous humanitarianism', *The New Republic*, 30 October 1995, p. 22.

13. See David Reiff, 'The humanitarian trap', *World Policy Journal*, XII (4), Winter 1995–6, pp. 1–12; John Prendergast, *Frontline Diplomacy: Humanitarian Aid and Conflict in Africa* (Boulder, Colo.: Lynne Rienner, 1996); and especially Michael Maren, *The Road To Hell: The Ravaging Effects of Foreign Aid and International Charity* (New York: Free Press, 1997). See also William D. Montalbano, 'Is giving aid worth the risk?' *Los Angeles Times*, 25 January 1997, p. 1.

14. See Peter Uvin, 'Scaling up the grass roots and scaling down the summit: the relations between Third World nongovernmental organizations and the United Nations', *Third World Quarterly* 16 (3), 1995, pp. 495–512.

15. See Ernst B. Haas, *When Knowledge is Power: Three Models of Change in International Organizations* (Berkeley: University of California Press, 1990).

16. The Commission on Global Governance, *Our Global Neighbourhood* (Oxford: Oxford University Press, 1995), pp. 252–7.

17. For discussions, see Leon Gordenker and Thomas G. Weiss, 'The collective security idea and changing world politics', in Thomas G. Weiss (ed.), *Collective Security in a Changing World* (Boulder, Colo.: Lynne Rienner, 1993), pp. 3–18; and George W. Downs (ed.), *Collective Security beyond the Cold War* (Ann Arbor: University of Michigan Press, 1994), especially pp. 11–39.

18. For a clear Realist view on this subject, see John J. Mearsheimer, 'The false promise of international institutions', *International Security*, 19 (3), Winter 1994–5, pp. 5–49.

19. Michael N. Barnett, 'The limits of peacekeeping, spheres of influence, and the future of the United Nations', in Joseph S. Lepgold and Thomas G. Weiss (eds), *Collective Conflict Management and Changing World Politics* (Albany, NY: SUNY Press, forthcoming).

20. Michael S. Lund, *Preventive Diplomacy and American Foreign Policy* (Washington, DC: US Institute of Peace Press, 1994), and *Preventing Violent Conflicts: A Strategy for Preventive Diplomacy* (Washington, DC: US Institute of Peace Press, 1996). See also Stephen John Stedman, 'Alchemy for a new world order: overselling "preventive diplomacy"', *Foreign Affairs*, 74 (3), May–June 1995, pp. 14–20; and Thomas G. Weiss, 'The UN's prevention pipe-dream', *Berkeley Journal of International Law*, 14 (2), March 1997, pp. 501–15.

21. See, for example, Larry Minear and Philippe Guillot, *Soldiers to the Rescue: Humanitarian Lessons from Rwanda* (Paris: OECD, 1996), p. 163; Gérard Prunier, *The Rwanda Crisis: History of a Genocide* (New York: Columbia

University Press, 1995); Joint Evaluation of Emergency Assistance to Rwanda, *The International Response to Conflict and Genocide: Lessons from the Rwandan Experience* (Copenhagen: Joint Evaluation of Emergency Assistance to Rwanda, March 1995), 5 volumes; and Antonio Donini, *The Policies of Mercy: UN Coordination in Afghanistan, Mozambique, and Rwanda* (Providence, RI: Watson Institute, 1995), Occasional Paper No. 22; and United Nations, *The Blue Helmets: A Review of United Nations Peace-keeping* (New York: United Nations, 1996), pp. 339–74.

22.   For instance, Russian officials initially saw NATO's intervention in Bosnia as evidence of the larger designs of NATO for European domination. Steven Erlanger, 'In a new attack against Nato, Yeltsin talks of a 'conflagration of war'', *New York Times*, 9 September 1995, p. 5.

23.   R. W. Apple, 'Showdown in Haiti in perspective: preaching to skeptics', *New York Times*, 15 September 1994, p. 1. See also, Robert Maguire, Edwige Balutansky, Jacques Fomerand, Larry Minear, William O'Neill and Thomas G. Weiss, *Haiti Held Hostage: International Responses to the Quest for Nationhood 1986–1996* (Providence, RI: Watson Institute, 1996), Occasional Paper No. 23; Yves Daudet (ed.), *La crise d'Haïti (1991–1996)* (Paris: Editions Montchrestien, 1996); and Roland I. Perusse, *Haitian Democracy Restored, 1991–1995* (New York: University Press of America for the Inter-American Institute, 1995).

24.   See S. Neil MacFarlane and Thomas G. Weiss, 'Regional organizations and regional security', *Security Studies*, 2 (1), Autumn 1992, pp. 6–37. For an extended argument about a 'partnership' between the UN and regional organizations, see Alan K. Henrikson, 'The growth of regional organiza-tions and the role of the United Nations', in Louise Fawcett and Andrew Hurrell (eds), *Regionalism in World Politics*, pp. 122–68. The discussion about the components of accountability was first made in relationship to Russia by Jarat Chopra and Thomas G. Weiss, 'Prospects for containing conflict in the former Second World', *Security Studies*, 4 (3), Spring 1995, pp. 552–83.

25.   See Bertrand Schneider, *The Barefoot Revolution: A Report to the Club of Rome* (London: IT Publications, 1988); and Lester M. Salamon and Helmut K. Anheier, *The Emerging Sector: An Overview* (Baltimore, Md.: The Johns Hopkins University Institute for Policy Studies, 1994). For a recent set of essays linking this phenomenon to multilateralism, see Thomas G. Weiss and Leon Gordenker (eds), *NGOs, the UN, and Global Governance* (Boulder, Colo.: Lynne Rienner, 1996).

26.   See Paul Wapner, 'Politics beyond the state: environmental activism and world civil politics', *World Politics*, 47 (3), April 1995, pp. 311–39; Peter J. Spiro, 'New global communities: nongovernmental organizations in inter-national decision-making institutions', *Washington Quarterly*, 18 (1), Winter 1995, pp. 45–56; and Weiss and Gordenker (eds), *NGOs*.

27.   For a discussion and statistics, see Ian Smillie, *The Alms Bazaar: Altruism under Fire – Non-Profit Organizations and International Development* (Hartford, Conn.: Kumarian Press, 1995). See also a set of books from Michael Edwards and David Hulme (eds), *Making a Difference: NGOs and Development in a Changing World* (London: Earthscan, 1992); *Beyond the Magic Bullet: NGO Performance and Accountability in the Post-Cold War*

World (West Hartford, Conn.: Kumarian Press, 1996); and *Too Close for Comfort? NGOs, States and Donors* (West Hartford, Conn.: Kumarian Press, forthcoming).

28. For a more critical view, see A. Fowler, *Nongovernmental Organizations in Africa: Achieving Comparative Advantage in Relief and Micro-Development* (University of Sussex Institute of Development Studies, 1988), Discussion Paper 249.

29. See Jon Bennett, *Meeting Needs: NGO Coordination in Practice* (London: Earthscan, 1995).

30. Andrew Natsios, 'NGOs and the UN in complex emergencies', *Third World Quarterly,* 16 (3), September 1995, p. 418, and 'Humanitarian relief interventions in Somalia: the economics of chaos', *International Peacekeeping,* 3 (1), Spring 1996, p. 88.

31. See David Held, *Democracy and the Global Order: From the Modern State to Cosmopolitan Governance* (Palo Alto, Calif.: Stanford University Press, 1995).

Index